Praise for *The Pragma*

"Many authors write about leadership, but few
mands, especially during a crisis—This is what separates Dr. Daniel Monehin's insights from everyone else's."
— Merv Hillier MBA, MSc HR, FCPA, CMC, CDir, DipTh,
Adjunct Professor, York University, and
Managing Director, NuVision Consulting Group Inc.

"I appreciate Dr. Daniel Monehin's emphasis on the productive use of optimism and pessimism—The power of positivity coupled with true commitment and determination can move mountains. A worthwhile read for anyone in a leadership role."
— Mimi Wood, Chief Human Resources Officer, BlueCrest

"I have known Dr. Daniel Monehin as a highly focused and visionary leader. If there is one book you want beside you that can help you navigate a crisis, it is this extensively well-researched one from Dr. Monehin. Go for it!"
— Jayesh Menon, Global Vice President of Human Resources,
Micro Electronics Business & Pall, Asia-Pacific, Danaher Corporation

"Dr. Daniel Monehin has gifted us a must-read piece of genius at such a critical time in the global economy."
— Kola Adesina, Group Managing Director, Sahara Power Group

"This book tells you all you need to know about good and bad leadership during crises."
— Caroline Stockmann, Chief Executive, Association of
Corporate Treasurers, UK, board director, and coach

"Read Dr. Daniel Monehin's *The Pragmatic Optimist* and keep it on your desktop for dealing with your next crisis."
— David Curmi, Executive Chairman, Air Malta PLC"

"Dr. Monehin positions pragmatic optimistic leadership as a state of being, not an act. This is a must-read for all levels of leadership, especially those in healthcare spaces today."
— Francis Garwe, Chief Executive Officer, Carea Community
Health Centers, Durham Region, Ontario, Canada

"Dr. Daniel Monehin's *The Pragmatic Optimist* offers many pieces of advice on how to be a strong anchor for the ship you are sailing on, not just in the harbor but out in stormy waters."
— Edi Schmid, Underwriting Advisor to
Group Executive Committee at Swiss Re Group, Switzerland

"In particular, Dr. Daniel Monehin's strategies of Clarity in Chaos, Conviction to Act, and Conscientious Communication excited my mind."
— Iftikhar Taj, past president of the Institute of Chartered Accountants
of Pakistan and Director of Governance & Strategy at Crowe Pakistan.

"With his vast global leadership experience in the world's top companies and his doctoral research in crisis leadership, Dr. Daniel Monehin offers essential reading for people managing through turbulent times."
— Dr. Johannes Boroh, DBA, Airline Pilot (Captain, B737 Fleet),
Singapore Airlines, and Course Director of B.Sc.
in Aviation Operations, Kingston University, London

"Leaders from the biggest companies to the smallest of start-ups will find great value and useful tools to navigate the rough waters ahead in *The Pragmatic Optimist*."
— Ron Hynes, CEO, Vesta Payment Solutions, Atlanta, Georgia

"Dr. Daniel Monehin's book is an invaluable guide for leaders navigating a crisis. A must-read for leaders seeking to steady themselves and their teams to move successfully through, and beyond, the inevitable crises."
— Heather Conway, Chair of the Board of Directors,
American Express Bank Canada, and
Independent Board Director, Great-West Lifeco

"From just the title *The Pragmatic Optimist*, you know you're in for a ground-breaking perspective on leadership—This book is a must-read for all leaders seeking to navigate through some of the toughest environments."
– Mark Lindley, CAHRI, MCIPD, Human Resources Leader & Influencer, Organizational Transformer & Modernizer, Queensland, Australia

"With this book, Dr. Daniel Monehin shares truths that are precious to your leadership."
– Serguei Ouattara, Chairman,
EU-Africa Chamber of Commerce, Belgium

"Dr. Daniel Monehin has had an outstanding career in business and in this book has translated that experience into practical, reliable, and valuable insights about a subject that has rarely mattered more."
– Dr. Douglas Reid, Ph.D., professor of international business
and strategy, Queen's University, Canada

"Dr. Daniel Monehin explains how challenging times could be taken as a great opportunity to re-evaluate the company's vision. This book is highly recommended."
– Dr. Alexander A. Jurack, DBA, founder and CEO
of the workwear company, Korntex.com, Germany

"As an industry practitioner in global contexts and geographies, I find Dr. Monehin's analogies, approach, and counsel both pragmatic and relevant. It benefits all leaders—experienced and junior."
– Nisar Keshvani, Vice President,
Institute of Public Relations of Singapore

"Hats off to Dr. Monehin! He clearly explains the balance required by today's leaders to keep driving growth and minimizing losses."
– Stephen L Muscat, CFO of Liquigas Malta, and
Chairman of the Malta Institute of Accountants (MIA),
Professional Accountants in Business (PAIB) Committee.

"Dr. Daniel Monehin has gifted the world his extraordinary insight and wisdom through this long-awaited legacy of the leadership book. He crafts out the structure behind chaos, how to create music from noise, and how leaders must have the guts, grit, and vision to face the storm and ride out the eternal waves of challenges and pessimism."

— Binesh Mangar, CEO, AfricaPay International,
and Fintech Capital Chair, Bank of Mauritius

"In this book, Dr. Daniel Monehin provides a timely framework of tips and tools, backed by research and illustrated by examples from his career, essential for anyone striving to be a better leader—before, during, and after a crisis."

— Dr. Sam Sivarajan, DBA, Behavioral Scientist, Senior Financial
Services Leader, and Author of *Making Your Money Work*

"*The Pragmatic Optimist* is a fabulous book. I love how Dr. Monehin illustrates his points with well-known examples and his experience as a global senior executive. A must-read for business leaders, board members, and talent management professionals."

— Peter van Dijk, formerly a senior professional services partner
and senior financial services executive, and
currently an advisor to climate change start-ups

"Invaluable advice on how to deal with a crisis."
— John Bai, CFO and Chief Transformation Officer, City National Bank

"Responding to risk and crisis requires different thinking and strategies, and *The Pragmatic Optimist* provides effective guidance. The book is a great read."

— Dr. Audra Diers-Lawson, Associate Professor Kristiania
University College, Norway, author of *Crisis Communication:
Managing Stakeholder Relationships,* editor for the
Journal of International Crisis and Risk Communication Research

THE PRAGMATIC OPTIMIST

6 Proven Strategies for Leading During a Crisis

Seventy9°
WEST

By

Dr. Daniel Monehin, DBA

Visit the Official Website at: www.resolutconsulting.com

Printed in the United States of America

First Printing: September 2022

Seventy9°
WEST
Seventy9 West Books

eBook: ISBN 978-1-7386529-0-7

Paperback: ISBN 978-1-7386529-1-4

Hardcover: ISBN 978-1-7386529-2-1

Audio: ISBN 978-1-7386529-3-8

Seventy9 West Books' publications may be purchased for educational, business or sales promotional use. Special discounts are available on quantity purchases.

For orders by trade bookstores and wholesalers, please contact Seventy9 West Books via email: books@seventy9west.com.

Disclaimer

While the Author and Publisher have strived to be as accurate and complete as possible in the creation of this book, readers are cautioned to rely on their own judgment about their individual circumstances to act accordingly.

While all attempts have been made to verify information provided in this publication, the author and publisher assumes no responsibility for errors, omissions, or contrary interpretation of the subject matter herein. Any perceived slights of specific persons, peoples, or organizations are unintentional. This book details the author's own personal experiences and opinions.

The author and publisher are providing this information on an "as is" basis and make no representations or warranties of any kind with respect to this book or its contents. The author and publisher disclaim all such representations and warranties including, for example, warranties of merchantability and educational advice for a particular purpose. In addition, the author and publisher do not represent or warrant that the information accessible via this book is accurate, complete or current.

Except as specifically stated in this book, neither the author or publisher, nor any authors, contributors, or other representatives will be liable for damages arising out of, or in connection with, the use of the content in this book. You understand that this book is not intended as a substitute for consultation with a licensed professional. In the event you use any of the information in this book for yourself, which is your constitutional right, the author and publisher assume no responsibility for your actions or outcomes.

To all those who step up during adversity
and lead the way through a storm.

Contents

Foreword

By Dr. Marshall Goldsmith

In the last few years, it has never been more apparent how many great leaders there are in times of prosperity that are utterly unprepared for the skills of leading in crisis.

As an Executive Coach for over 40 years, my mission is to help great leaders get even better. I tell all my clients that if Olympic athletes and top sports professionals in the world need a coach, then so do you. Everyone has the ability to grow and get better, jumping the gap from good to great in their profession and roles. One of the critical things I work on with clients is their agility and responsiveness to a crisis.

Having worked through crises small and large with clients around the world, I'm confident that Dr. Daniel Monehin has written the ultimate guide to address the needs of your company, employees, and management in a crisis of any level. Broken into six succinct leadership strategies, The Pragmatic Optimist equips readers with actionable items to steer through any challenge. Brilliantly blending research, engaging stories, and practical solutions, Dr. Monehin brings the reader on a journey to deeply understand every aspect of a crisis and our responses to it.

One of my favorite clients for many years, and still a great friend, Alan Mulally, was the former CEO of Ford Motor Company. Alan was attributed with a massive turn-around of Ford and brought profits to an all-time high for the modern era. Undaunted by Ford's internal crisis, losing money at an alarming rate each quarter, Alan led with a calm and focused approach that embodies The Pragmatic Optimist. Alan blended passion for the company, its mission, and people with his structured approach to fixing the most critical issues, one at a time. Most importantly, Alan asked for help. He asked for the help of his team and his executives, which fostered a thriving collaboration around issues. For me, Alan became the example I used to help others in overcoming a crisis.

If you want to become the 'example' for leadership to others – in the good times and bad – read *The Pragmatic Optimist* and commit to staying conscious of the mindset and behaviors it puts forward. Dr. Monehin's experience and profound ideas will put you on the path to becoming a more influential leader that thrives in adversity rather than just survives.

Read this book today and watch it change your life.

Life is good.

Dr. Marshall Goldsmith is the *Thinkers50* #1 Executive Coach and New York Times bestselling author of *The Earned Life, Triggers*, and *What Got You Here Won't Get You There*.

Introduction

If you find a book that you really want to read, but it hasn't been written yet, then you must write it.
— **Toni Morrison**, award-winning novelist

Unavoidable and Overwhelming, Yet Unprepared For

"And I remember in that time [of crisis], like it was yesterday, feeling completely panicked, waking up in the middle of the night, panicked. Not being able to sleep. Panic. Looking through my emails. [Wondering] what did I do wrong? How did this go [so horribly]? I mean, complete panic!"

Those were the words of a senior decision-maker overseeing 20+ countries and facing a major crisis that threatened to utterly damage the organization's relationship with its largest client, discredit the brand before governments of several countries that are stakeholders, and inflict irreparable harm to public perception of its operations. With those three significant risks came several uncertainties.

However, two things were certain: (1) the organization would have to suffer billions of dollars in losses as it discontinued operations in all countries in that region, and (2) the leadership team, and many other employees, including the executive recounting the experience to me in an interview, would lose their means of livelihood.

Crises—there is no hiding from them, but we are hardly ever prepared. They are as commonplace in our personal lives as in organizations and governments. From my experience, an overwhelming majority of crises organizations face never make it to the public square; they are either resolved by skilled leaders or, more routinely, swept under the carpet at enormous costs.

While crises impact the organization's financials and reputation, they equally take an enormous toll on the people and every leadership level in the establishment. This book addresses the human toll and people dynamics that are often missed in the commotion of a crisis. The famous Shakespearean aphorism rings true, especially for leaders in crises: "Uneasy lies the head that wears a crown."[1]

Philip Burguieres, one of the youngest to lead a Fortune 500 company, knew this human toll firsthand when he admitted in a PBS interview that the more responsibility one has, the more prone one is to depression. "Depression is chronic and widespread in the executive office because of pressure and isolation…Those at the top are particularly prone."[2, 3] No wonder CEOs experience depression at twice the national average.[4]

Several studies agree that entrepreneurs, whose small and medium-sized enterprises (SMEs) globally account for 90% of businesses and are responsible for 50% of worldwide employment,[5] do not fare better. University of California, Berkeley researchers found that a staggering 72% of entrepreneurs in their sample self-reported mental health concerns,[6] mainly traceable to out-of-control stress usually triggered by crises.[7, 8]

Pressure, stress, and isolation are just some of the hallmarks of a crisis on individuals, and this book unpacks them, providing practical guideposts to navigating them successfully. The darkness of a crisis calls for the light of a leader. Leadership is the towering skill to overcome adversity. Unfortunately, when a crisis comes in through the door, leadership sometimes leaves through the window.

Why I Wrote this Book

When I began my five-year doctoral study in 2014 while working full-time as an executive at an S&P 100 company, I chose the field of crisis leadership as my research focus for three core reasons. First, based on my direct experience running multinational businesses and my proximity to different shades of leaders, I noticed that no event shattered the reality of leaders, generated stress and negative emotions, and brought down organizations like a crisis. The experience knocked the wind out of the best leaders I knew, creating what I call weak-kneed leadership. One such leader told me, "I'd rather handle anything else than face crises." Over the years, I witnessed the high-flying careers of fellow professionals crash and burn due to the mishandling of crises. Those who survived adversity were either left with an indelible trauma or grew and flourished rapidly due to overcoming the predicament. Crisis, it seems, does not leave a person the same way.

Second, for fourteen years before 2014, I had been invited to speak on various leadership topics like visionary leadership, strategic leadership, leading digital transformation, etc. It hit me that no one had ever asked me to talk about crisis leadership, nor did any of the myriads of courses I had attended as a participant tackle the subject. I believe that is because of defective human reasoning called the optimism trap or optimism bias that tends to exaggerate positive outcomes while underestimating negative scenarios.[9, 10, 11] Up to 90% of people do not wish to know about negative events coming down the pike.[12] Thus, organizations are "good-news junkies" that would rather discuss growth and blue skies than prepare to deal with turbulence capable of wiping out decades of success. Yet, when the inevitable occurs, leaders, mostly unprepared, are thrust into the eye of the storm.

Third, when I prepared to speak on crisis leadership (because I had the liberty to choose the topic and felt it was relevant for the audience), I struggled to find published materials on the subject based on empirical research focused on real-world leaders in nonmilitaristic and nonemergency settings. So, I would develop virtually all my speaking materials from my field experience as a corporate leader. However, the enormously positive response from audiences in my crisis leadership sessions made me realize the immense value of the subject. Thus, the words of Pulitzer Prize-winning author Toni Morrison resonated with me: "If you find a book that you really want to read, but it hasn't been written yet, then you must write it."[13]

The Scientific Process Behind This Book

My overarching approach to this book was to base the content on as much empirical research as possible. So, the book's core is based on my doctoral and postdoctoral studies founded on leaders' lived experiences when they faced various crises. Through several scientific tools, theories and methods, I generated an enormous amount of data from in-depth interviews of decision-makers for an average of 75 minutes per participant, analyzed the themes, and extracted practical insights.

Participants were drawn from five continents: North America, South America, Europe, Africa, and Asia. On average, they oversaw their organization's operations across 100 countries and came from twenty-five diverse industries and sectors.

Industry Representation by Study Participants				
Aviation	Education	Industrial	Military	Retail
Banking	Film	Insurance	Non-Profit	Shipping
Construction	Financial Services	Internet	Oil & Gas	Supply Chain
Consulting	Government	Manufacturing	Pharmaceuticals	Technology
Consumer Goods	Healthcare	Media	Real Estate	Telecommunications

Table 0-1: Twenty-five industries and sectors represented by research participants

Although organizational crises formed the launching pad for the study, participants readily drew on personal crisis experiences from their roles as spouses, partners, parents, children, friends, mentors, mentees, or extended family members as we explored the multifaceted nature of crises.

Finally, the book also relied on many research findings from various fields, including business and investing, psychology, organizational behavior, psychiatry, healthcare, military, natural sciences, arts, education, and sports.

Who Is This Book For?

This book was written from the individual's perspective because leadership is more about one's disposition than one's position—formal titles do not bestow leadership because we all know people in positions of authority who lack basic leadership skills. Therefore, mastery of crisis handling in your personal life often predicts how you will respond to crises in your professional life. Character is king in leadership. That is why the fall of organizations is often a result of leadership misbehavior due to derailing personality traits.[14, 15] Since your leadership is primarily driven by who you are, this book seeks to develop you professionally by equipping you personally.

If you consider yourself a leader, regardless of whether you have a formal title or not, this book is for you. If you want to stand tall when the next crisis comes knocking and be a source of hope, assurance, and creativity for others, this book was written for you.

Therefore, if you would like to recalibrate your leadership competency under extreme conditions by taking a fresh look, backed by a combination of long-standing and current research, you will find this book empowering, encouraging, and galvanizing.

Maximizing the Use of This Book

This book is about you, your thoughts, your feelings, and your behaviors when under the enormous stress of a crisis. Please resist the attempt to read this book on behalf of your manager. The more you see yourself in the concepts, examples, research findings, news reports, research participants' stories, and frameworks, the more impactful the book will be for you.

Allow yourself to pause in self-reflection when you need to digest some of the content. Self-reflection is the point where personal change begins. Take a few minutes to complete the reflective activities after every chapter. These activities are designed to connect the chapter's key takeaways with your personal and professional experiences.

The quotations interspersed throughout the book are placed to create a moment of pause. I started curating these quotes daily in 1997, and they have guided my leadership journey, especially during a crisis.

Some readers appreciate author-recommended further reading material to expand their knowledge of the subject matter of a book. This book contains nearly 400 references to articles, news reports, academic publications, and books you can choose from to explore further.

Finally, I recommend you secure the services of an experienced and qualified leadership coach to help you work through the behavioral changes you'd like to tackle. If that is not feasible for whatever reason, the next-best advice is that you coach yourself. Trust me, self-coaching is more complicated than it sounds. However, a book I received as a gift from my manager in 2007 has helped me tremendously during self-coaching and to maximize executive coaching engagements where I was the client. That book is Marshall Goldsmith's *What Got You Here Won't Get You There.* So, you can imagine how excited and fulfilled I felt when Marshall generously agreed to write the foreword to this book.

I invite you to take the journey of becoming a Pragmatic Optimist empowered to shine in the darkest hour of a crisis.

CHAPTER ONE

Crisis: Leading Through Turbulence

Adversity reveals genius, prosperity conceals it.[16]
— **Horace**, Roman poet

What you will learn in this chapter:
- Seeing a crisis in a new light.
- Crisis as the ultimate test of leadership quality.
- Mastery of crisis leads to mastery of leadership.
- Nature and phases of a crisis.
- When crisis meets leadership.
- Six dimensions of crisis impact.
- Top ten ways NOT to respond to a crisis.

Lessons from a Leadership Field Trip

It was a sunny afternoon on Friday, May 23, 2008. It was also the first time in my leadership development experience that I spoke about leading in a time of crisis. The audience was a group of senior management and executive-level professionals, including entrepreneurs from diverse industries and government officials, who had just been as close to the foot of the raging Niagara Falls as possible, onboard the *Maid of the Mist,* North America's oldest tourist attraction. Yes, it was a field trip, and we all got soaked despite donning the boat ride's famous ponchos.

It was Day Five of a six-day leadership development program I organized and titled *Becoming a Multidimensional Leader.* Before that day, five exceptional speakers and I had taught the participants a wide range of subjects like vision development and casting, strategy formulation and execution, leading creativity and innovation, legacy leadership, leaders as builders of culture, and executive presence.

I titled that afternoon's session on crisis leadership *Mastery Over Confusion.* I then used a rhetorical question to introduce the topic and summarize what we spent the rest of the day discussing: "When a crisis comes at you like the roaring waters of the Niagara Falls—you can't hold it back, and you have to lead your team through it—what will you do?"

As participants processed the question with engaging and quizzical looks, I made these emphatic statements that required the audience's response: "There are three groups of people in this meeting room today. Group One, you are presently in the middle of a crisis. You have received several updates about the crisis many times today, and this night will not end without you working to resolve the predicament. Please raise your hand if you are in Group One." About one-third of the class raised their hands.

"Next is Group Two. You have recently come out of a crisis. The harrowing experience is still so fresh in your memory that you can still figuratively smell the scorching fire of the adversity on your body. Please raise your hand if you belong to this category." Half of the audience raised their hands, and some smiled as they figured out my analogy.

"Now, to the final category, Group Three. This is the most dangerous group. All the elements necessary for adversity are coming together along your path, and you are charging toward a crisis, *but you don't know it yet.* I can't ask you to raise your hands because you are unaware that you are on a collision course with the next crisis. Everyone here falls in one of the three groups."

With those questions, I teed up three attributes of a crisis:

1. **Commonality** – Virtually every participant in the program, about 80%, was either going through a crisis or had recently come out of one. Thus, the *prevalence* of crises qualifies it as a critical topic for leaders;

2. **Cruelty** – The brutal, out-of-control nature of crises and the damaging effects crises have are enormous primarily because organizations are built on controls and designed to produce positive results like growth and solutions. Thus, the *price* of crises is too far-reaching for leaders to delegate the response;

3. **Cyclicality** – Crises are not pesky distractions from a well-oiled machine called "normal life." Quite the contrary; crises are a part of ordinary life. We are all in what I call "the vicious cycle of crises" made up of the three parts of my rhetorical questions:
   i.   Presently in a crisis,
   ii. Recently out of a crisis, and
   iii. Unconsciously charging toward the next crisis

Thus, the *periodicity* of crises makes the ability to handle them a must-have skill for leaders.

Mastery of Leadership Requires Mastery of Crisis

No situation reveals the very essence of leadership in its most concentrated, undiluted, and stark form more thoroughly than a crisis event. A crisis tests the mettle of any leader, and it is a revealer of leadership quality. Like the fire heating an assayer's crucible, a crisis burns away the dross in a leader's style, character, attitude, and approach, and leaves behind only the presence—or absence—of pure leadership ore.

If we want to penetrate to the core of leadership, to read its "executive summary," there is no better place to look than at how the leader behaves and performs in a crisis.

A Clearer View of Crisis

"Crisis" is from the Greek word "krisis." The root word "krei-" means "to decide, to sieve."[17] To sieve connotes separating and making sense of the parts. Therefore, a crisis forces a leader to decide and separate the wheat from the chaff. The heart of a crisis is decision-making after a leader has sifted through available data to identify what is perilous, superfluous, and critical.

The classical era physician Hippocrates, and later his protégé Galen, used the term crisis to define the turning point in a disease. When a patient faced a severe illness, the crisis is the turning point where either the patient gets better or worse. It is the phase of a disease's progression where the patient's life or death is determined.

> *"Everybody has a plan until they get punched in the mouth." –*
> *Mike Tyson, heavyweight boxing champion*

More modern definitions take a more generalized and organizational view of crisis beyond medicine as a period of "intense difficulty and danger"[18] or a time of heightened intensity and very high stakes where "uncertainty, confusion, and fear"[19] reign supreme. Organizational leaders often think of a crisis as a threat to the corporate reputation and an unpredictable event that threatens important expectations of stakeholders. Far less talked about is that a crisis often threatens leaders' careers, so they are personally vested in its resolution.

Anything that threatens the expectations of an organization, especially an event that is "sudden, acute, and demands a timely response," is likely to be a crisis. When there is a threat to the continued existence of a company because there is significant doubt regarding the organization's ability to meet its obligations, you have a crisis on your hands.[1]

Participants in my study see crises in two overlapping dimensions—their origin and their manifestation. A crisis may originate externally or internally, and it may happen suddenly or creep up on the organization over an extended period. The 2x2 matrix in Figure 1-1 captures the overlay of these two dimensions and relevant crisis case studies through which research participants lived.

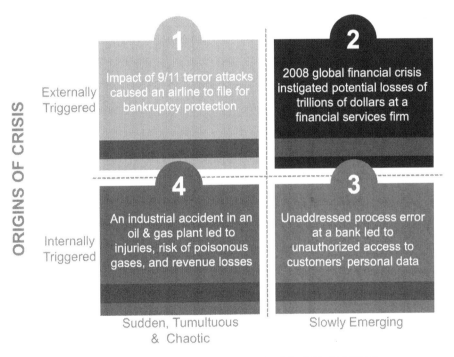

Figure 1-1: Two overlapping dimensions of crisis—origins, and manifestations—and relevant case studies

---

1   The International Financial Reporting Standards (IFRS) recognize the *going concern assumption* or the ability of a company to meet its obligations as the basis for financial statement preparation. Management is required to report "material uncertainties" that raise "significant doubt" about a company's going concern.

In Search of a Leader During a Crisis

My leadership philosophy is that it is not tied to an official title, rank, or status because true leadership is not about one's position but one's disposition. Some individuals with official leadership titles do not actually lead, while some with no official title are de facto leaders. To lead, your mindset is your main asset. I believe that everyone in an organization should see themselves as a leader and develop a leadership mindset.

During noncrisis times, it's essential to have many leaders across all functions and all layers of the organization. Yet, job titles matter when a crisis hits, as people tend to look toward formal authorities for guidance when chaos ensues. All eyes turn to the person in the corner office and the formal leaders of the organization. That is because formal authority is invaluable in a crisis.

If leadership from formal authority had been lacking before the onset of the predicament, the crisis would do an excellent job exposing that leadership vacuum.

The buck stops with the leader with formal authority. That is because, during a crisis, resources (human, technological, financial, etc.) may need to be reallocated, strategic priorities altered, vital plans put on the back burner, or brand-impacting decisions made. Without formal authority, an individual cannot take any of those actions.

Also, every layer of a person's professional competence will be challenged by a crisis:

1. Technical know-how,
2. Management skills, and
3. Leadership capability.

Effective leaders with formal authority are crucial during a calamity as they can transverse all three layers of professional competence to limit the impact of the crisis and chart a path forward.

Buttressing the importance of formal authority during a crisis, a participant in my doctoral study who serves on several boards comes from banking and technology backgrounds and manages global businesses as an executive said, "In a time of crisis, people look up, not down. And I don't know why, but they do ... People look to a leader [with formal authority] in times of great stress and great crisis."

Leaders Step Up When Turbulences RISE-UP

The nature of the effects of a crisis has at least six characteristics from a leader's perspective. I developed the acronym RISE-UP to reflect the complications of the effects of a crisis—risk, impact, stress, (negative) emotions, uncertainty, and pressure—that bear upon the organization and its stakeholders, including the leader. I came up with the RISE-UP model because the human component of a crisis is often neglected. Existing models focus disproportionately on the organization's potential losses expressed in financial and nonfinancial terms while they relegate the human toll.

This section addresses that gap. In my experience, the human effect of a crisis is central to assessing damage, developing solutions, and weathering recovery. Turbulence is personal to individuals who stand to lose in a crisis. "A crisis almost feels like a personal attack on the leader," an executive once told me.

Six Characteristics of a Crisis' Effects (RISE-UP)	
Risk	Danger, high stakes, hazard, and vulnerability
Impact	Specific points of impact, devastating, substantial
Stress	Distressing, demoralizing, disconcerting, painful, anxious
Emotions	Upsetting, sensitive, fearful, irritable, sulky, angry, disappointing
Uncertainty	Loss of control, turmoil, vagueness, disorder
Pressure	Difficulty, complexity, struggle, embarrassment

Table1-1: RISE-UP – Six characteristics of a crisis's effects on the leader

What my clients say they like about the RISE-UP model of characterizing the effects of crises is that it helps them prevent the oversimplification of an inherently complex situation during the crisis assessment phase. Oversimplifying a crisis' impact on self and other internal stakeholders causes a leader to miss two types of opportunities – the first are opportunities for self-care and self-management, and the second are opportunities to demonstrate empathy to colleagues and other internal stakeholders.

"I function better when things are going badly than when they're as smooth as whipped cream. When I'm in a fight I don't worry, but when things are going good, I'm afraid that something's going to crack under me any minute. You may not realize it when it happens, but a kick in the teeth may be the best thing in the world for you." – Walt Disney, The Story of Walt Disney

Understanding the six characteristics of a crisis's effects on people helps you expect a broad spectrum of these conditions as a leader. Such heightened awareness will help you avoid the shock element of a catastrophe. This initial shock magnifies a crisis's impact and may trigger missteps by leaders. Awareness of the human ramifications of a crisis beyond its immediate point of impact will help the organization develop more holistic responses and solutions.

That reminds me of an oft-used Arabic expression I learned when I lived in Dubai, UAE. "Inshallah" translates to "If God wills," and it conveys either hope or resignation, depending on the context. Without a proper evaluation of the human effects of a crisis, one may erroneously embrace *false* hope or inadvisably elect *needless* resignation. Adopt the RISE-UP crisis assessment model, and inshallah, you will better appreciate the task ahead when dealing with adversity.

The Intersection of Leadership and Crisis

It is through difficult situations that a leader's true ability to lead is formed. Leadership is not a skill set that can be learned in school. Instead, it is a mindset that is often honed through the experience of overcoming obstacles and crises that genuine leadership is formed.

It is like the heat of a crucible that forms strong and lasting tools from molten metals. A blacksmith heats metals in a crucible to make them malleable or turn them into a liquid state to create a new shape. The same happens with leaders as they experience crises. They will experience the heat of a crisis and have an opportunity to develop new skill sets that will carry them through the next crises and make them better leaders.

C.S. Lewis, the renowned British author, and philosopher, once stated, "We must stop regarding unpleasant or unexpected things as interruptions of real life. The truth is that interruptions are real life." Indeed, "normal" is merely a preparation period for the next crisis. Normal is always transient.

A Crisis Is the Test of Leadership Quality

Warren G. Bennis, an American scholar, organizational consultant, and author widely regarded as one of the pioneers of the contemporary field of leadership studies, partnered with Robert J. Thomas to investigate a pivotal question: "Why is it that certain people seem to naturally inspire confidence, loyalty, and hard work while others (who may have just as much vision and smarts) stumble, again and again?" As lifelong students of leadership, the scholars wondered whether there is a single characteristic that the best leaders embody that made them much more successful than others.

This is a complex question to tackle since the concept of leadership is multifaceted in nature, and the personalities, backgrounds, cultures, and characters of extraordinary leaders vary widely.

Thankfully, the scholars' research findings published in the *Harvard Business Review* provided the answer:

It's a timeless question, and there's no simple answer. But we have come to believe it has something to do with the **different ways that people deal with adversity**. Indeed, our recent research has led us to conclude that one of the most reliable indicators and predictors of true leadership is an individual's ability to find meaning in negative events and to learn from even the most trying circumstances. Put another way, the skills required to conquer adversity and emerge stronger and more committed than ever are the same ones that make for extraordinary leaders.[20]

So, a sure way to improve one's leadership competency is not to waste the next adversity lurking around the corner and to instead reframe past crises. By doing so, you will move toward the image of a better version of yourself by developing your person. Your leadership sits on your person.

For example, when an individual walks into a meeting room for a job interview, there are, in fact, two people who just entered: the professional and the person. Most interviewers will focus on the *professional*, wanting to know what school the individual attended, their work experience, or their professional accomplishments; the *person* is often neglected. The person represents how the individual thinks, feels, and sees the world; this is dominated by one's mindset.

In leadership matters, the person overshadows the professional. This is especially true during unexpected negative situations. That's why improving your response to adversity is so critical to your leadership development (see Table 1-2).

The Quality of Leadership Revealed in the Time of Crisis	
Ineffective Leaders	**Extraordinary Leaders**
Look back to play the blame game and scapegoat	Look back for root-cause analysis and prevent a recurrence
Dwells on the past; "Coulda, woulda, shoulda"	Driven to create a better future despite the difficulty
Become defensive for fear of being blamed	Become defensive to protect their team from the crisis impact
Miss learning opportunities in crisis	Learn from adversity
Lose the trust of their team	Deepen the trust
Dismissive of opportunities in adversity	Find meaning in difficulties

Table1-2: The quality of ineffective versus effective leadership during a crisis

A Personal Experience with the Unexpected

On December 6, 2019, after a seven-hour overnight flight from Toronto, Canada, to Manchester, England, I arrived at a hotel to check in as I was about to enter the crucial final six hours of my five-year doctoral degree program that would culminate in the defense of my dissertation that afternoon. My plans were simple but critical to my success: check into my room, freshen up, sleep for one hour (since I was up reviewing my thesis and didn't sleep a wink on the red-eye), and study for the last three to four hours before my thesis defense.

To my utter shock, the hotel check-in staff told me that my previously confirmed room was occupied as it had been mistakenly assigned to another guest due to a system malfunction. And, oh, the hotel was fully booked!

My heart raced as several negative thoughts, and unpleasant emotions flooded my mind. This all-important day was unraveling before my eyes and would end badly if I did nothing to change the intended end of the crisis.

So, I started by controlling my breathing, focusing my thoughts, then beaming a broad smile at the apologetic hotel staff and asking for a facility where I could change and freshen up. The hotel manager, who had intervened at this time, led me to a public bathroom on the second floor of the building; the bathroom served all the meeting rooms on that floor. I tucked my luggage into a corner, set my toiletries on the counter, and started brushing my teeth and then shaving. Shortly after, meeting attendees began to enter the bathroom, giving me curious and puzzled looks. I decided to break the ice by striking up a conversation with one of them, Keith.

> *"There are two types of pain; one that hurts you, and one that changes who you are." — Jettie Woodruff, Black Rain*

He was astonished by my experience. "How are you so calm and cheerful after such a disruption to your thesis defense that is less than six hours away?" Keith asked rhetorically. He was aghast. We exchanged contact details before he wished me (better) luck and left.

After freshening up, I found an empty meeting room overlooking a busy street where I set up to do my final review before my dissertation defense. I still needed some rest, so instead of a one-hour uninterrupted sleep on a comfy bed, I laid my head on my folded arms on the desk and had a 20-minute power nap with four interruptions.

Later that evening, I sent Keith an email (and attached a picture we took in the bathroom) letting him know that after 100 grueling minutes of fielding incisive questions from both my external and internal examiners at the thesis defense, I passed! He congratulated me and concluded with a statement that caused me to pause and reflect. Keith said, "I am so glad that you passed your [thesis defense] and wish you every success in the future. *From our brief interaction, I think you will do rather well in <u>everything</u> that you do.*" (Emphasis, mine).

I was grateful for his words of affirmation.

Keith didn't know me beyond the three-minute interaction, but he saw me in a helpless state that was out of my control and how I responded to it. However, Keith knows the world of academia, thesis defense, and the knowledge industry very well. He is Professor Keith Tomlins of the Food and Markets Department at the University of Greenwich, London, UK.[2]

After observing my response to the unexpected, he made far-reaching assumptions and conclusions about me. His suppositions about me are rooted in Warren Bennis' principle that a person's handling of adversity is a predictor of leadership success. Your response to a crisis says more about you than the crisis.

The Nature of Crisis

Have you ever seen media outlets report a catastrophic event as a "black swan event"? For instance, the 2008 global financial crisis was labeled a black swan event. I find such characterization amusing because black swan events are defined as "hard-to-predict and rare events that are beyond the realm of normal expectations in history, science, finance, and technology."[21]

So, are all crises black swan events?

In my view, most organizational crises are not black swan events. Not even the COVID-19 pandemic could be labeled as such.[22]

The term "black swan" comes from Juvenal, a Roman poet who straddled the first and second centuries AD. He described a nonsensical proposition as "a rare bird in the lands and very much like a black swan." Therefore, the phrase was used in response to an outlandish statement or to define something that is not real or will not happen.

At that time, Juvenal and his fellow Europeans only knew of white swans, so the idea of a black swan existing was simply preposterous.

---

2   Prof. Keith Tomlins has since retired but retains a chair at the university as an Emeritus Professor of Food Science, supporting global development and poverty alleviation. He now spends his time producing artworks as an artist. His vivid photo art creations are available via his Instagram handle @KeithTomlins

It was only when sea travel covered long distances that black swans were discovered off the coast of Australia.

Most crises begin as unresolved issues before exploding into a crisis—this is true of the 2008 global financial crisis and the COVID-19 pandemic. So, just like unattended issues that morph into a full-blown crisis, black swans did exist in the time of Juvenal, but he didn't know about them.

"Every organization continues in a state of stagnation, or in uniform motion in a predictable trajectory, unless it is compelled to change that state by forces exerted on it. Leadership is one of those forces, sometimes powered by crises." – Daniel Monehin

"I never thought that this could happen to us" is a common statement that leaders make in response to a crisis. On the contrary, most crisis events are predictable and within reasonable expectations.

More often than not, predictions concerning a crisis predate the crisis but are often ignored by decision-makers. All the warning signs of an impending crisis that occurs in the pre-crisis phase (see Figure 1-2) are often swept underneath the proverbial rug.

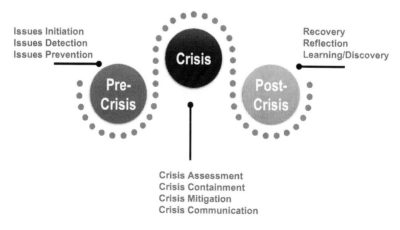

Figure 1-2: The three phases of a crisis

Issues Are Your Geysers—Explore Them

The largest active geyser in the world is the Steamboat Geyser in Yellowstone National Park in the US state of Wyoming, with its eruptions shooting hot water over 300 feet high. Volcano experts study geysers as part of their research to better understand and predict volcanic eruptions. Volcanologist Michael Manga, an earth and planetary science professor at UC Berkeley, explains that "geysers are a model for how volcanoes erupt."

Volcanoes are a lot harder to study than geysers—volcanoes are massive, dangerous, and do not erupt often, while geysers are smaller, less hazardous, and erupt frequently

As harmless geysers are to dangerous volcanoes, so knotty issues are to devastating crises. A better understanding of one leads to a better prediction and effective handling of the other. Issues are an indicator that lets leaders know that a potential crisis is starting to build, enabling the decision-makers to nip problems in the bud. After all, the best-managed crises are the ones that never happened.

Issues Are Like Geysers	Crises Are Like Volcanoes
Small, and easily ignored or missed if not nearby	Large, and problematic to ignore; hard to miss
Straightforward to study	Challenging to study
Its negative impact is limited	Its negative impact is wide-ranging and all-consuming
Can be easily contained	Difficult to contain
The frequency of eruption is high, i.e., issues are many	The frequency of eruption is low, i.e., crises are few
Issues are small-scale crises	Crises are large-scale issues

Table 1-3: As geysers are to volcanoes, so issues are to crises

Leaders shared with me the following productive ways they find and tackle issues:

1. **Remove** organizational roadblocks that may hinder information about detected issues from having a free passage to you, the leader. Ensure that there is a mechanism for issues to be escalated up the hierarchy.

2. **Reach out** beyond your immediate hierarchical layer to consistently do a pulse check of the frontline staff and those in between. Do not rely solely on your direct reports, but engage candidly with colleagues on several levels of the organizational structure.

3. **Rapidly** respond to credible issues. Allowing issues to fester is the cause of most crises.

4. **Reward** and celebrate colleagues who identify and help mitigate potential crises. There is a tendency to label such people as whiners and complainers—instead, welcome complaints as a heads-up about a potential catastrophe.

5. **Retain** a work-in-progress attitude toward your vision, strategy, and execution. That way, you will not dismiss issues that challenge, expose vulnerability or threaten them.

Some leaders miss the clues of a pre-crisis phase until it's too late because they exercise their powers to override facts with their opinions. In a noncrisis period, usually, no harm is done except for some eye rolls by employees close enough to the decision to know that the leader made a suboptimal decision. However, overriding facts during a crisis raises the stakes as the dire consequences of unforced errors are far-reaching.

From one of my childhood heroes, Doctor Who, a relevant, thought-provoking quote comes to mind: *"The very powerful and very stupid have one thing in common. Instead of altering their views to fit the facts, they alter the facts to fit their views."*[23] Authentic leaders will do well to heed the warning of this fictional character.

Case Study of Warning Signs Ignored

Most crises come with specific but easy-to-ignore warnings. The question is, are you listening?

At a 2015 TED Talk titled "The Next Outbreak? We're Not Ready," Bill Gates spoke passionately and convincingly about a clear and present danger of an impending global pandemic. His speech, which garnered millions of views, was based on well-researched data, especially those from the most recent viral pandemic at that time, Ebola. Although Ebola had a high mortality rate of 40%, its spread (infection rate) was limited because its transmission required direct contact with an infected person's body fluids.[24]

Gates warned of a more ominous pandemic if high mortality combined with high infection. In his closing remarks, he stated, "If anything kills over 10 million in the next few decades, it is most likely to be a highly infectious virus. If we start now, we can be ready for the next epidemic. Thank you."[25]

"I never lose— I either win or learn." – Nelson Mandela

Gates's warning fell on deaf ears, as we later discovered at the onset of COVID-19.

In October 2019, two months before COVID-19 was announced, the inaugural Global Health Security Index published a dire warning that "no country is fully prepared" to deal with a pandemic because there was "not enough political will,"[26] a term for leadership inertia.

In the early days of COVID-19 in 2020, Dr. Robert Redfield, the director of the US Center for Disease Control (CDC) stated, "[COVID] is the biggest health crisis in the last one hundred years, and we were unprepared." The same somber assessment emerged from virtually every country around the world. It was a case of large-scale leadership failure.

Crises: Mostly Internal and Generally Avoidable

According to the Institute of Crisis Management, 70% of crises are internally generated.[27] So, while the upheaval of externally generated crises like the 2008 global financial crisis, 9/11, and the COVID-19 pandemic attract significant attention, most organizations face internal and avoidable crises. Therefore, such tragedies are often self-inflicted and traceable to management's laxity since they arose within the organization.

In my experience, well over 70% of crises companies face are triggered internally; most of them just never make media headlines. My estimate is higher because most crisis leadership scholars have an outsider's perspective on organizational crises. They usually know about crises only when they become public. On the contrary, my years of corporate experience and consulting give me an insider's perspective, and I know that most organizational crises, including value-eroding ones, never make it to the evening news.

Illustration by John Cook, a postdoctoral research fellow at the Climate Change Communication Research Hub at Monash University.

https://ncse.ngo/navigating-conversations-climate-change-deniers-read-book

The Six Hats of Crisis Impact—Beyond the Squeaky Wheel

When a crisis appears within an organization, there is usually an initial point of impact (IPOI) on which leaders tend to focus. If it is a crisis that has become public, the IPOI attracts most of the interest. The IPOI gets attention and resources while other areas are neglected. However, what most leaders don't recognize, but often learn the hard way after their crisis response begins to fall apart, is that multiple strategic points of impact (SPOI) also require attention and resources, failing which complications will likely develop.

> "The bravest are surely those who have the clearest vision of what is before them, glory and danger alike, and yet notwithstanding go out to meet it." – Pericles, Greek philosopher and leader

At the point where prevention has failed, and a crisis is inevitable, a leader's understanding of the breadth of the predicament will determine the effectiveness of their leadership response. Misjudging the breadth of a crisis is common, and its repercussion is unforgiving.

In defining the breadth of a crisis, there are two missteps that leaders are prone to make. They either minimize a crisis impact by narrowing their view of its actual breadth or exaggerate the impact by going beyond the true breadth of the fiasco. The former, which is the more common of the two, leads to underestimating the effects and is a recipe for mishandling a crisis; in contrast, the latter leads to overestimating the impact and wasting resources.

Successful leaders demonstrate an astute awareness of the repercussions of a crisis beyond its IPOI to include SPOI. That way, scarce resources are targeted to all impact areas and prevent a situation where only the squeaky wheel gets the grease.

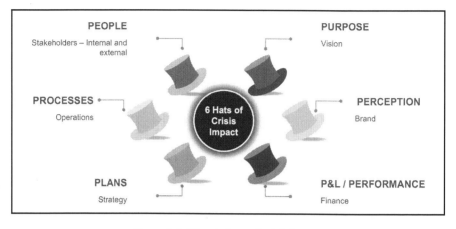

Figure 1-3: The six hats of crisis impact

The imagery that has helped me articulate IPOI and SPOI is that of leaders having to wear multiple hats in a crisis. The "six hats of crisis" (see Figure 1-3) that a leader needs to put on to ensure a comprehensive review of the impact assessment of a crisis are:

1. **Purpose**: the impact on the values, mission, and vision.
2. **Perception**: the impact on the brand or stakeholder view of the organization.
3. **P&L**: the impact on various financial performance metrics.
4. **Plans**: the impact on organizational strategy and objectives.
5. **Processes**: the impact on the operations of the organization.
6. **People**: the impact on internal and external stakeholders.

You cannot manage what you cannot measure. A proper assessment of the breadth of the crisis impact helps you get a handle on the mishap.

"No strategy survives contact with a crisis. A change is inevitable." – Daniel Monehin

The two areas of impact that are often most focused on are *Perception* and the *P&L*. Ignoring the other four areas of impact can be counterproductive. Here is an example of the consequence of unattended damage to *Purpose*: A few years ago, I met up for drinks with Felix, a Fortune 500 company executive committee member in the healthcare industry. We were both formally dressed since it was a weekday. I said, "I have noticed that virtually everyone in your organization, except you, wears the corporate logo-draped lapel pins. Do you just hate the colors?" I asked, half-jokingly.

His response, however, was thoughtful: "In my former job, some crises blew up that flew in the face of what the company said it stood for, its values and vision. In responding to the crisis, the executives did not address the blatant hypocrisy, so most people, including me, lost faith in the leadership. That's why I left. So, I have become cynical—I will only identify with a company's values and vision if the highest level of leaders also subscribes to them. I am still looking for shreds of evidence of such commitment [where I now work]; until then, no corporate lapel pins for me!" Interesting perspectives from a member of a company's exco.

A true crisis will likely impact practically all parts of the six-hat model. Consequently, leaders need to broaden the scope of the organization's assessments by going beyond the IPOI to the SPOI. The squeaky wheel alone shouldn't get the grease while the silent hub is ignored—loudness is not the sole quality of what is important during a crisis. A leader who puts on the six hats of crisis impact will avoid what process improvement authors N.S. Sreenivasan and V. Narayana call the squeaky wheel fallacy.[28]

Top Ten Responses to Avoid in a Crisis

*"It is often the handling of a crisis that leads to
more damage than the crisis itself."*

— Dr. Erika James & Dr. Lynn Wooten

There are at least ten ways NOT to respond to adversity to prevent the crisis from multiplying and potentially becoming worse than when it began.

1. **Deny**: This is the nothing-to-see-here leadership approach to a crisis even when virtually everyone on the team is nervously staring at the elephant in the room. One of the hardest things to watch is a leader who uses their authority, bully pulpit, and other tools at their disposal to deny the existence of an ongoing crisis that is patently obvious to all. It is a live portrayal of Hans Christian Andersen's 1837 Danish fable, *The Emperor's New Clothes*,[29] except some leaders in denial may never be told they have no clothes until it's too late. It would be comical if it weren't so perilous and widespread.

   Generally, such leaders are not victims of swindlers (per the Danish fable); the leaders themselves fall into self-deceit, sometimes caused by a disconnection from the reality of the situation. So, what about unbiased data, analysis, and recommendations of objective subject-matter experts on which management should rely? Leaders who choose to be in denial snub them.

   Sometimes, decision-makers justify being in denial as their way to keep others from panicking. So, they deliberately distort the reality that a crisis has occurred even when the alarms are going off. The leaders get caught in delusions of grandeur by thinking, "If I say that there is no crisis, then there is no crisis." Such assertions mean nothing in reality because a crisis is not a respecter of persons.

   Another reason for denial that I have observed in my proximity to leaders over many years is that some individuals struggle to change their initial (crisis) assessments and decisions, even after more accurate, usually damning, and unfavorable data becomes available that contradicts the earlier position.

   Facts change quickly in a crisis, so decision-makers need not worry about revising earlier decisions. Just do it. When facts change, change your views, assessments, and decisions. Don't believe things simply because you want them to be true.

Unfortunately, the reality is that, according to psychology, it is easy for us humans to deceive ourselves. Self-deception is an easy trap for a leader to fall into and a difficult one to escape.

Finally, Dr. Nassim Nicholas Taleb, the bestselling author of *Black Swan: The Impact of the Highly Improbable*, was the special guest at the Voyage2020 seminar hosted out of India in May 2020. The discussion around the ongoing COVID-19 crisis was facilitated by ET NOW's managing editor, Nikunj Dalmia, who read a quote by Nassim that warned against the risk of self-denial: "People have the problem of denial. This is one of the biggest things I have learned. In Lebanon, everyone who left Beirut when the war started, including my parents, said this will last two weeks. It lasted 17 years. Please do not be in denial mode; learn to live with the reality of that [crisis]."[30]

2. **Delay**: Effective leaders understand that they need to take action at the onset of a crisis, yet some choose to postpone making decisive moves. Inaction in the face of actionable information while handling a crisis will not go unpunished. While some decision-makers fear that taking action will indeed confirm the existence of a crisis, not taking action usually makes already difficult situations get worse.

During the first COVID-19 lockdown in March 2020, Primark, a UK-based fashion retailer, went from grossing $800 million (£650 million) per month in revenue to zero! Why? The large fashion retailer did not have an e-commerce-enabled website. Primark's leaders were sluggish in their response to a slowly emerging crisis in their industry with the deepening of e-commerce and its negative impact on the growth and market share of brick-and-mortar-only merchants like Primark. I can only imagine the presentations made to Primark's management pre-COVID justifying investment in e-commerce. Yet, the company's leaders ignored the proposals to sell online and stubbornly stuck to its 50-plus-year-old go-to-market strategy of physical stores only.

So, when a more complicated and fast-moving crisis arose in COVID-19, Primark's delay in embracing e-commerce and addressing a previous market-based crisis delivered a heavy blow to its revenue and cash flow. Quite the contrary for Primark's competitors like ASOS, which found that the COVID-19 pandemic was wind in its e-commerce sails as it boosted its performance with soaring online sales.

> *"Morality is doing what's right, no matter what you're told. Obedience is doing what you're told, no matter what's right."* - *H.L. Mencken, journalist and essayist*

Staying abreast of current technology will safeguard an organization and help it survive and even flourish in crises. Saying "not now … not yet" to obvious decisions will prevent a company from future-proofing its business and make it susceptible to considerable shocks. Generally speaking, new technologies reduce the impact of crises that affect operations, people, customer delivery, etc. So, be curious about technology and be future-oriented.

3. **Dilly-Dally**: While delay relates to a leader's indecision, often driven by a lack of political will[3] even though the actions to take are clear, to dilly-dally is to never get to the point of decision-making, usually instigated by decision paralysis. The way forward is blurry and unclear because the leader is trapped in a continuous loop of data gathering, assessment, analysis, and generating options without making a decision. Many reasons may cause a leader to get caught up in overanalyzing, overthinking, or overpreparing, which stalls decision-making, but the following two reasons are the most common drivers I have come across:

---

3 Political will is defined as "the extent of committed support among key decision makers for a particular policy solution to a particular problem." (Post et al., 2010, p. 659)

i. Irreversibility of the decision – Leaders ought to take more time to understand and analyze an issue before making irreversible decisions. However, while many decisions in the context of a crisis are important, only a few of them are irreversible, and fewer still are both important and irreversible. The latter category requires thoroughness in analysis, but being thorough does not mean being frozen.

So, identify the interplay between the importance and irreversibility of decisions to know how much time and analysis are required. The matrix in Figure 1-4 has helped me in my leadership career, and my clients confirm its usefulness to their decision-making process.

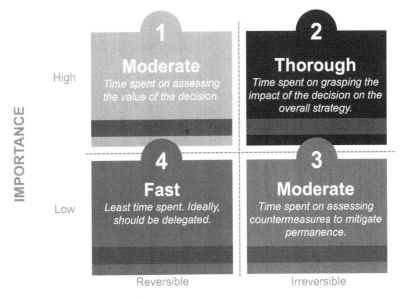

Figure 1-4: Time spent on analysis based on the importance and irreversibility of the decision

ii. Fear of making a mistake – Without a doubt, the stakes are quite high in a crisis; thus, some individuals may hesitate to move away from analysis to decision-making for fear of a misstep. The state of analysis is comfortable because analyzing is an iterative process where corrections can easily be made and mistakes are contained, whereas, the leader is put in the spotlight once a decision is made.

However, since the point of crisis is a point of decision, failure to make decisions due to overanalyzing is a major reason why leaders mishandle crises and why predicaments worsen. Figure 1-4 is also useful to assuage the fear of making mistakes.

4. **Downplay**: Another response to avoid because it leads to dreadful consequences is to minimize a crisis impact by downplaying the severity of the situation or exaggerating the recovery from the crisis. Overly optimistic leaders downplay a crisis when they try to convince stakeholders that the organization is either unscathed or sustained negligible impact when, in reality, as is the case with most crises, the effect is pointedly grave.

My supervisor in my doctoral program at the University of Manchester, Dr. Audra Diers-Lawson, currently an associate professor at Kristiania University College, Norway, partnered with Lorraine Collins to publish a fascinating study in January 2022 titled "Taking off the rose-colored glasses."[31] The scholars found that the higher the income a private-sector employee earned, the less likely they believed their organization was in crisis. Thus, downplaying the impact of an ongoing crisis is one way of projecting that erroneous belief.

Leaders who downplay crises' impact employ any combination of the following tactics:

i. Interference,

ii. Information suppression, and

iii. Intentional production of inaccurate data.

The largest money-laundering scandal in Europe, and perhaps the world, occurred in Danske Bank, a Danish financial institution. In a scathing 2018 report by the Danish Financial Supervisory Authority (DFSA), the director-general of DFSA called out both the management and the board of the bank for downplaying the crisis impact as it emerged.[32] According to DFSA, in April 2014, the leader of the bank's Estonia branch, the epicenter of the scandal, "significantly toned down the [anti-money laundering] issues." The Danish regulator reported that when the bank's board of directors met to discuss a critical report by the Estonian regulator about spurious financial transactions on October 7, 2014, before the crisis grabbed media headlines, the meeting minutes contained a "toned down" version of the proceedings.[33] About a year later, the proverbial stuff hit the fan! The ensuing reputational damage went beyond dealing a blow to the bank to negatively affecting Denmark's financial system

Downplaying a crisis' impact only aggravates the crisis. The cover-up is indeed worse than the crime. Remove the rose-colored glasses. Push back on the bias to downplay bad news. A significant flaw in human nature makes us susceptible to understating bad news and overstating good news, but extraordinary leaders take time to develop sharper and more refined instincts. Above all, they understand that bad news toned down by leaders rarely stays down.

5. **Dysfunction**: This is when the leadership's response to a predicament mirrors key characteristics of the crisis itself: hasty, chaotic, and confusing. We saw this play out during the COVID-19 pandemic around the world. Twelve months into the public health crisis and the government of virtually every major country did not have a coordinated national strategy for responding to the challenges.

Leaders in both public and private sectors are prone to dealing with crisis matters on a transactional, reactive, and whack-a-mole basis instead of putting strategies in place to deal with a crisis as soon as it appears.

Crisis management is not a firefighting exercise but one that demands a deliberate and well-articulated strategy. Unfortunately, some leaders interpret crises as situations where anything goes, processes are jettisoned and strategies are redundant.

"There is no crisis so bad that a leader cannot make it worse." – Daniel Monehin

6. **Distant:** Many leaders dislike crises so excessively that they will avoid their teams and become unsociable during difficult times. Such individuals tend to push others away when things go awry, detach from their teams, and become aloof. They may also become unapproachable and standoffish. Below are some reasons for this unproductive response:

   i. Personality – You have a history of withdrawing into your shell when things go downhill. It is how you have handled disappointments, failures, and crises for as long as you've known yourself. I highly recommend a personality makeover if you fall in this category. An executive coach can help.

   ii. Unskilled – A high-flying manager with a reputation for stellar performance may become uncomfortable in a crisis because they lack the necessary crisis leadership skills to perform at their usual stratospheric level. So, they manifest their discomfort in crisis by being absent.

   iii. Leadership style – Many leaders have practiced "social distancing" with their teams long before COVID-19. Such leaders belong to the "it is lonely at the top" school of thought that is founded on a misunderstanding of leadership: that leaders are supposed to be distant from the people they lead. We will discuss the reasons behind this common but futile leadership approach in Chapter Nine.

Emotions run high and confusion is compounded in an organization when the leader disappears during a crisis. Instead, leaders need to deliberately and consistently engage with their teams as their mere presence is a source of assurance to their colleagues. Also, they are able to create shared realities since a crisis fractures and fragments reality. Everyone in the organization has their viewpoint of the crisis, but a leader who is present has an opportunity to create shared realities for everyone (see Chapter Ten of this book for more discussion about creating shared realities).

7. **Desperate**: This is the "Chicken Little" response where the leader exhibits explosive, raw emotions and overreaction due to the stressful and volatile nature of a crisis. When the leader is frantic, it is a source of major distraction for the team. Frantic leaders inadvertently build toxic work environments, leading to a crisis within a crisis. Emotionally capricious leaders single-handedly create new internal conflicts and "micro-crises" that complicate the primary crisis (see Chapter Six for more discussion about emotions and crisis leadership).

8. **Distracted**: A crisis ranks high on the distraction scale due to the significant risk of damage it poses to the organization's brand, operations, and bottom line. Unfortunately, some leaders become distracted when they succumb to the threats of turbulence—both real and imagined—by becoming overwhelmed by the negativity of chaos. Such decision-makers feel the walls closing in and they respond by veering off important priorities, trying to do too many things at the same time, and dumping values that define the organization. This leadership distraction is a drag on the organization and it sets in motion the destruction of confidence and degradation of enthusiasm to complete the challenging tasks ahead.

Distraction, although common at the start of a predicament, can occur at any stage of the crisis response when the leader

i. loses overall perspective and fixates on the steady stream of bad news,

ii. exhibits frustration from failed attempts at controlling out-of-control elements of the situation, and

iii. adopts a knee-jerk and nonsystematic approach to data gathering and decision-making.

Distracted leaders easily go down the rabbit hole. "Looking back over the course of my career, I can say that my distracted reaction to a crisis was itself a major source of disruption to my team. It is easy [for a leader] to get into a tailspin when what you've worked on for so long is being threatened by major challenges, but the consequences of that response are almost instantaneous: a loss of morale, motivation, and momentum," said Jean-Philippe, my Europe-based client who successfully launched an aerospace contracting startup over 20 years ago.

9. **Discourage**: When some decision-makers do not see an immediate way out of a cataclysm, they inadvertently initiate a discouragement campaign in their organization. It is usually an unconscious response because, from the perpetrator's point of view, they are being frank and matter-of-fact about the dire development. Notwithstanding, there are grave unintended consequences to such a negative approach to a negative situation.

The word "discourage" is etymologically derived from the Old French word *"descoragier,"* which literally means "to take away courage/spirit." The first time I learned that root word and its original meaning, I imagined a hand reaching into another person and ripping out that person's courage and confidence. Since then, that has been the image that my mind conjures up when I witness one person discourage another. When a leader engages in this conduct, it is extremely damaging and toxic in the workplace.

So, from where does a person's confidence come in the first place? An understanding of the making of confidence will help us appreciate how it may be damaged. As we will discuss in greater detail later in this book (Chapter 5), self-confidence, a major and essential belief that is necessary to overcome adversity, is derived from the social concept of verbal affirmation. Put another way, what people who matter say to us and about us directly influences our confidence. By "people who matter," I mean those with considerable influence over us, like our parents, spouses/partners, managers, and teachers.

Thus, discouraged leaders discourage their team. They also achieve this through a verbal process of put-downs and disaffirmation. They unintentionally strip their organization of the courage, confidence, and creativity needed to rise up to the challenges of a crisis.

10. **Despair**: This is to respond to a crisis with hopelessness. A leader is then overtaken by crisis and the feeling of being despondent. Putting things into perspective, I admit that it is a normal human reaction to feel downcast when we hear bad news. But leading from a state of dejection is a choice that is powered by a pessimistic mindset.

I recall attending a senior leadership meeting off the back of a hugely successful earnings call with analysts and investors. Things were looking up and prospects couldn't be brighter. During the first coffee break, the meeting room was buzzing with energy and filled with plenty of bright and hopeful faces. Suddenly, I felt the energy slowly get sucked out of the room as people's demeanor began to change to bewilderment and concern. Small groups started to form to discuss a new negative development of immense impact on the brand and future of the company.

The most senior executive at the event summoned a group of subject-matter experts (I was one of them) and asked us a series of thoughtful questions to get to the root of the issue and discuss options for resolution. When the meeting resumed, she took the stage, interrupting the agenda, to acknowledge the crisis, delineate the root causes, identify impacted internal and external stakeholders, and proffer preliminary indications of how decision-makers would resolve the fiasco. She spent the final 25% of her impromptu remarks in a hopeful state, expressing her confidence and infusing assurances in the leaders gathered there while encouraging them to rally their business units as the organization worked through the crisis.

The energy in the room returned as dejection gave way to determination.

As with many crises, it wasn't a quick fix. It took six months to resolve the complications but the impact on the brand and finances was significantly dampened and negligible. In fact, the handling of the debacle opened up new growth opportunities for the organization. And, oh, as serious as the crisis was, it never made the news. Conversely, I have also witnessed firsthand the utter mishandling of crises when the decision-maker leads from a state of despair and hopelessness. Some of the results were fear, chaos, disorganization, finger-pointing, wasted resources, brand damage, and, in virtually every case, enormous (avoidable) losses.

Figure 1-5: Top ten crisis responses every leader should avoid

These ten leadership responses to avoid during a crisis (summarized in Figure 1-5) are by no means an exhaustive list. They represent the most common botched responses I found in my research, corporate leadership experience, and consulting practice.

I have also found that these ten injudicious responses are based on faulty mindsets, so they rarely occur individually. For example, people who tend to *downplay* a crisis are also inclined to respond with *dysfunction*. Similarly, individuals who tend to *delay* taking action on adversity are likely to be distant, while those who are susceptible to discouraging others will *dilly-dally* and are easily *distracted*, and leaders who *deny* the existence of full-blown crises are predisposed to being *desperate*.

The more of these ill-conceived responses individuals exhibit, the more new disasters they create while working to solve the initial predicament. If there is ever a poster child for a problem masquerading as a solution, it is leaders who respond to incredibly difficult times in the ways described in this subsection.

In the next chapter, we will dive deeper into the flawed mindsets that could trigger these responses.

Up Close and Personal

Think of the last time that you and your organization experienced a crisis. What was the crisis and how did you initially react?

_____

_____

_____

_____

What was the consequence of your initial reaction?

_____

_____

_____

_____

How would you have liked to react to this crisis, and how do you plan to react differently in the future?

_____

_____

_____

_____

What "geysers" can you identify or build in the organization that will lead you to discover potential crises before they occur?

_____

_____

_____

_____

Which of the "Six Hats of Crisis Impact" are you prone to neglect in the heat of the moment?

_____

_____

_____

_____

What assessments and strategies can you implement now to identify and act on issues before they morph into a crisis?

_____

_____

_____

_____

Using the 2x2 matrix in Figure 1-1 (the two overlapping dimensions of crisis) as a guide, populate the four quadrants with crises you have lived through.

_____

_____

_____

_____

CHAPTER TWO

Optimism Mindset: Leading from the Inside Out

Forces beyond your control can take away everything you possess except one thing: your freedom to choose how you will respond to the situation.
— **Victor Frankl**, neurologist & psychiatrist, and Holocaust survivor

What you will learn in this chapter:
- Why successful leaders have an optimistic mindset.
- The science behind human behavior.
- Effective leadership as an antithesis of a crisis.
- How optimism and pessimism impact everyday decisions.
- Four types of unrestrained optimism to avoid.

When I ask leaders if they have an optimistic mindset, they mostly shy away from saying "yes." But when I ask them to describe their model for leadership and business success, nearly one hundred percent of the time, they narrate their version of an optimistic mindset. Why do most leaders avoid identifying as optimists? Because of a widespread misunderstanding about optimism. This chapter equips leaders to appreciate, embrace, and optimize their optimistic mindset.

Optimism is like an operating system humming in the background, while business and personal activities are like apps. Making positive or hopeful predictions is the outcome of optimism. So, forecasting revenue and projecting earnings for the next quarter require some optimism. Optimism relates to what is happening in your mind, how you process information and see the future, and allows you to take advantage of many situations, including crises.

The Science Behind Behavior

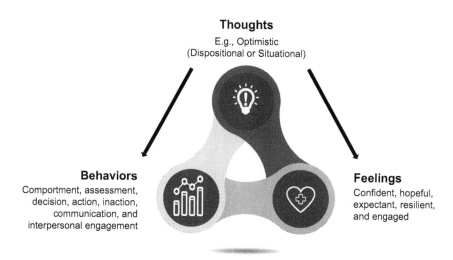

Figure 2-1: The Cognitive Behavioral Model[34, 35, 36]

The cognitive behavioral model is popular in psychology, developed in 1964 by psychiatrist Dr. Aaron Beck, and has been used in therapy for several decades (see Figure 2-1). The model says that your thoughts or cognition or mindset or perception of events is the primary driver of your emotions and behaviors. Your thoughts and beliefs reflect your mindset. Optimism is an example of a mindset, and it may produce feelings of confidence, hope, expectancy, and resilience, as well as behaviors that align with the mindset and feelings. Therefore, gaining a better understanding of the huge impact your mindset has on your emotions and behaviors will help you leverage your mindset to create the outcome that you desire.

Unraveling this knowledge was the basis for my doctoral dissertation, where I wanted to explore and highlight the behaviors of effective leaders during a crisis. The six leadership behaviors that I discovered are covered in Chapters Four to Nine. What

"The eye sees only what the mind is prepared to comprehend." – Robertson Davies, in The Wordsworth Dictionary of Quotes

I learned as a whole is that the behaviors of leaders are greatly dependent on their physiological and emotional health.

During leadership development workshops, I love asking, "Is optimism important to leaders? Why or why not?" That is the overarching question as you realize how important your mindset is during a crisis. Here is a hint: Your view of the future influences your view of virtually everything else, and optimism/pessimism is the lens through which you view the future.

Be A Thermostat

If you look up a list of qualities of an effective leader, chances are that you will find visionary, strategic, organized, measured, focused, and thoughtful. However, a crisis is the antithesis of these leadership qualities as it creates a sense of hopelessness, chaos, short-term thinking, disorganization, and value destruction. When a crisis hits, I find that many good leaders begin to replicate the qualities of the crisis they face. They become negative about the future, flustered, disorganized, chaotic, and destroyers of value.

A crisis says, "There is no future." But an effective leader should say, "There is still hope."

Optimism is a mindset because it reflects *your* beliefs. It is a state of the mind and *not* a state of your affairs. We tend to react to our environment based on what is going on. But a leader should be a thermostat, not a thermometer. A thermometer goes up and down based on the temperature in the environment. A thermostat, on the other hand, relies on its internal settings to control the environment, bringing it in line with the desired temperature. True leaders regulate their environments instead of merely reacting to them. That is what the right mindset can do for you if you handle it intentionally.

True Leadership Is the Opposite of a Crisis

Optimism is activated from the inside out and not from the outside in. Our behaviors are determined by our mindsets and not by external factors in our environment. The inside-out attitude is the thermostat approach, while the outside-in philosophy is the thermometer approach. Leaders should be the opposite of a crisis to manage it successfully.

Since helplessness is a learned trait, it follows that optimism can also be learned and improved. One of the main points that Wineland made during her TED Talk is this: "You can have a painful life, you can suffer ... and yet you can make a life for yourself that you're very, very proud of." That is because no matter the crisis you face, you can choose the outcome you want to experience by cultivating an optimistic mindset.

One way to hone your optimistic mindset is to contrast your beliefs with the nature of a crisis.

A Leader Stands in Contrast to Crises

When a crisis says...	An effective leader believes...
"Doom and gloom."	"Hope and resolve."
"This is the end of the road."	"This is a necessary detour in our journey to greatness."
"There is no future."	"We will create a better future from here."
"Cut and run."	"Push forward."
"It's time to panic."	"It's time to rally."

Table 2-1: Contrasting a crisis and an effective leader

Optimism Makes the World Go Round

Virtually every human endeavor, from the mundane to the extraordinary, runs on optimism.

A financial system like the stock exchange that is numerically and analytically dependent is heavily influenced by human emotions. Benjamin Graham, generally regarded as the "Father of Value Investing" and former mentor of Warren Buffett (arguably the greatest investor of our generation), stated that even though stock prices are meticulously analyzed and computed, at the end of the day, they are still affected by human mindset and emotions.[37] He argued that investors' optimism and pessimism greatly influence stock prices. Graham wrote in his book, *Security Analysis,*

> Hence the prices of common stocks are not carefully thought-out computations, but the resultants of a welter of human reactions. The stock market is a voting machine rather than a weighing machine. It responds to factual data not directly, but only as they affect the decisions of buyers and sellers.

In other words, optimism about a company will drive up its popularity, which will drive up its stock price; the converse is true for pessimism. Even institutional investors with access to cutting-edge analytical technology are influenced by human emotions when making investment decisions. The driving force behind the 2020 Meme Stocks Revolution was coordinated optimism using social media.

Here is another illustration of the pervasiveness of optimism. When an entrepreneur comes up with an idea for a business venture, it is a journey in optimism. For example, Angela developed a solution that could solve municipalities' congestion and road repair problems using cameras, digital technology, and her proprietary artificial intelligence solution. She emptied her 401K (retirement savings account) to develop a minimum viable product. She raised funds from family and friends (aka "Love Money") for sales and marketing to secure her first client. Angela then approached a group of angel investors who saw the prospects of her solution and provided the funding needed to scale.

Every part of Angela's entrepreneurial experience required optimism. She poured her retirement savings into the business because she was optimistic that her solution would work. She was confident that municipalities would buy in. She sold that optimism first to her family and friends and later to angel investors. Your view of the future influences your perception of virtually everything else.

I am a member of the world's largest angel investment group, Keiretsu Forum. Every month, I see entrepreneurs like Angela from various industries give their ten-minute pitches about the basis of their optimism. Their pitches are successful when they instill optimism into enough investors to meet their funding round goal. The optimistic entrepreneur is usually energetic, committed, and involved.

Optimism Is Inescapable

When a hiring manager employs a new staff member, that is one of the most consistent acts of optimism in an organization. The hiring manager usually does not know the candidate, but reviews their resume, interviews them, and (sometimes) checks out their references. The hiring manager can't be sure how the new employee will perform until they start working, but hopes they are a great hire. That is an act of optimism by the hiring manager.

The same is true of the employee who left the known (past employment) for the unknown (new employment).

While there is no universal definition of a strategy, a common thread in all definitions is that it is future-based and documents specific actions that will deliver success for the business. In other words, a strategy is a path to achieving future positive expectations. That makes a strategy a document of hope. The underlying mindset of a strategy is optimism. Thus, while hope is not a strategy, there is no strategy without hope. Hope does not give you a strategy—hope powers your strategy.

On a macroeconomic level, when you consider the Consumer Confidence Index (CCI), it is a measure of consumers' optimism and pessimism against a benchmark about their projected financial condition and the economy. If CCI is down, meaning consumers are pessimistic, several economic indicators may decline, e.g., consumer spending, capital expenditure, corporate revenues, and employment rate. Conversely, when CCI is up, meaning consumers are optimistic, the economic indicators go up.

The United States has the largest external debt in the world. It attracts funding because the lenders are optimistic that the United States will continue to prosper. That is optimism in action.

When confidence is negatively impacted and lenders become pessimistic about a country, they will recall their loans. Hypothetically, if enough lenders recall their loans, a country's economy will face a swift collapse, thanks to pessimism.

Similarly, the value of a country's currency reflects a collective optimism about the country's economic prospects. A strong currency reflects high optimism in the economy, and a weak currency indicates high pessimism of economic prospects. The Russian ruble crumbled by almost 40% in just over two weeks between February 22 and March 11, 2022. The currency collapse was primarily because of pessimism surrounding the Russian economy due to unprecedented sanctions by the West and its allies over Russia's February 24 invasion of Ukraine. Likewise, Sberbank, Russia's biggest bank, lost about 95% of its value over the same period for a similar reason. Russia's central bank suspended the sale of foreign currencies and shut down the Moscow Exchange at the onset of the war and sanctions to forestall a crash. Horrendous things happen when optimism leaves the building.

How Optimism Impacts Leaders

Optimism is personal and relates to who you are as a leader. To understand how leaders lead in general, we need to understand the two parts of a leader's competence: managerial and leadership.

The managerial part represents executing strategies and performance assessments, managing operations, planning, organizing, controlling, and information flow while overseeing human and organizational resources. These are the elements that make an organization function. Managerial is the "how" of an organization.

The leadership part is where your vision and strategy formulation sits; it is where you exhibit self-knowledge, self-evaluation, and the physical and mental conditioning that you bring to the table. Leadership is an organization's "who" and the "why."

Being in a leadership position is different from holding managerial responsibilities. Nothing you do as a leader is a cut-and-paste of what you or others did before. It is an application of who you are much more than what you know or what you do. Leadership is where your personality and character come in. Your character will overshadow your certificates and what you've learned in the past.

Your mindset is more pertinent than your managerial knowledge in a leadership role. Your mindset will lead the way for your skill set.

Napoleon Bonaparte famously said, "A leader is a dealer in hope." He learned that he could conscript people into the army, but he needed to convince them to fight bravely. The will to fight is driven by a hope of a better tomorrow or optimism. Leaders will lack genuine followers without offering hope. Influential leaders are a reservoir of optimism in times of crisis. Under challenging times, the team turns to their leader to draw from their storage of optimism.

The Doctor as a Prescription

Dr. Michael Balint, a psychoanalyst and a renowned name in general practice, stated, "The doctor herself/himself is the most frequently prescribed medication." In other words, the physical interaction between the doctor and the patient is as important as the medication that is being prescribed.

The prescription itself is analogous to managerial competence, while the doctor's interaction with the patient is comparable to leadership competence. That is why study after study shows that a placebo works. When a doctor confidently tells a patient that the prescribed medication will help them get better, that conversation prepares the patient's mind to begin the healing process. The doctor's words have been proven more potent than the sugar pill with no active drug ingredient used in a *placebo* experiment.

The opposite is also true with the *nocebo* effect. When the doctor says to expect pain in a specific part of the body, say the forearm, scientific experiments have shown that the patient will likely begin to feel pain in that area even though a harmless treatment is being administered.

Both placebo and nocebo are about programming the patient's mindset to expect a positive and negative outcome, respectively. That is because what you expect in the future influences what you experience in the present.

While technical and managerial competencies rely on what you know, leadership competence is based on who you are. Thus, leaders should exercise care not to put out negative vibes in the organization because it could become a self-fulfilling prophecy. Unfortunately, due to the immense stress and pressure of a crisis, leaders are prone to falling into the nocebo trap if they are not mindful of their mindset.

Defining Optimism vs Pessimism

How do you define optimism? In what way would you describe it to someone else? The definition I'm presenting to you goes beyond just having positive thoughts. Optimism is having *positive expectations* about a future outcome. While many leaders try to avoid defining themselves as optimistic due to a general misrepresentation of the term to mean "wishful thinking," this book clarifies that true leaders regularly make optimistic projections about the future of their organization and align energy and resources to accomplish them.

One of the most quoted takeaways from Stephen Covey's *The 7 Habits of Highly Effective People* is, "Begin with the end in mind." For a visionary leader, there is no beginning without articulating an end, usually a positive one. What you do today (including the when, how, and with whom) is primarily a function of what you expect tomorrow. In other words, your expectation determines your preparation. Optimism is about your expectation of tomorrow.

Optimists believe that *what* they do can positively impact the future. They don't just believe that the future can be better, they believe that they can do something about it. That is why you get out of bed in the morning, because you're ready to do something about your future today. As the Roman poet Tibullus stated, "Credulous hope supports our life, and always says that tomorrow will be better."

Pessimism, on the other hand, is having negative expectations about future outcomes. Pessimists believe that no matter what they do, it will not hinder the future results from being negative. The American Psychological Association defines pessimism as "the attitude that things will go wrong and that people's wishes or aims are unlikely to be fulfilled."[38] A person with a pessimistic personality tends toward a more negative—or some might argue, realistic—view of life.

Pessimists usually expect negative outcomes and are suspicious when things seem to be going well. Pessimism is not a trait to which most people aspire. It's often associated with a "glass half-empty" attitude. A healthy dose of negative thinking isn't necessarily all bad either. In fact, sometimes, a little pessimism might actually be a good thing—we will get into that later.

Pessimists focus on what can go wrong in a situation. They often think that the risks almost always outweigh the benefits. They assume that all good things will eventually come to an end. And they find it easier to live with the status quo than change things for the better.

A Case for Pessimism

One of the perspectives I find interesting about a pessimism-led approach to crisis is University of Houston professor emeritus Robert Heath's work that argues pessimism should not be dismissed outright.[39] He and other experts argue that leaders' pessimism is good for a crisis and recommends that managers take a pessimistic view during turbulent times.

Heath explains that pessimists effectively curtail crisis damages because they can better pursue abandonment activities, like cutting sunk costs. Because pessimists tend to concentrate on worst-case scenarios, they avoid a dangerous de-emphasizing of and underplaying the risks of a crisis event. In other words, they do not ignore the risks to which optimists are prone.

While delivering a keynote titled "Leading with Resilience" to a large group of Canada-based healthcare professionals a year into the COVID-19 pandemic, I asked the audience the following question in a poll:

When I heard about Canada's first COVID-19 case reported on January 25, 2020, I thought the pandemic will last for:

A: 0 – 3 months

B: 3 – 6 months

C: 6 – 12 months

D: 12 – 24 months

E: Over 24 months

The result was telling. A significant majority of this group of highly trained, superbly qualified, and exceptionally experienced healthcare professionals believed, at the onset of COVID-19, that the pandemic would be over within six months! That substantial optimistic underestimation of the duration of the pandemic aggravated the crisis for frontline professionals in many ways, not the least of which was burnout. A pessimistic view would have anticipated a much longer pandemic and would have been mentally prepared.

I have witnessed many examples of gross underestimation of risks or crisis impact in several sectors where leaders greatly underrated the negative effects of what was happening. This optimism-fueled lapse in judgment will cause a leader to fall down a rabbit hole. Those with a pessimistic view, since they expect the future to get worse, can avoid that trap.

On the downside, Heath and other experts admit that pessimists are vulnerable to catastrophizing, a distorted cognitive view that makes an individual believe that unfavorable situations will get worse.[40] This deteriorating view of a crisis can be crippling to the organization as the leader may become either frozen into inaction or triggered into overreaction.

Dispositional and Situational Optimism

Dispositional optimism is having a positive outlook about life in general. It is your normal-state optimism and is generally stable or consistent.[41, 42] It forms part of your worldview about every aspect of life, including personal affairs and organizational leadership.

How you *view* your life completely reflects on how you *live* your life.

Situational optimism, on the other hand, is having a positive outlook on a specific event or situation. Hence, your situational optimism is a subset of your dispositional optimism but could vary or change.

While one's dispositional optimism influences one's situational optimism, studies have shown that it is possible to be dispositionally optimistic, yet situationally pessimistic about an event.[43, 44]

This distinction is critical to improving your self-awareness as a leader. In noncrisis times, the differences between these two forms of optimism may be negligible, and even when they vary, the impact may be minimal. However, while facing a predicament, a leader's situational optimism may take such a significant hit that it notably diverges from their dispositional optimism, creating perplexity and contradicting behaviors. But recognizing it is OK to feel less optimistic about a situation but remain more optimistic about life in general, will help you restrain the negative effects of a crisis from bleeding into other parts of your life.

While reflecting on his experience with this divergence of dispositional versus situational optimism after learning about it for the first time, Diego, a client of mine and a seasoned executive in the South American construction industry, said

> My response to crises has always baffled me. Normally, I have a rah-rah, nothing-can-stop-me attitude those oozes with optimism. Everyone knows that about me. However, when [my organization] hits a crisis, my optimism dips and I start thinking doom-and-gloom. I'd start behaving in a way that is inconsistent with my established pattern. Now, I know that's my situational [optimism] kicking in and my dispositional optimism is just fine. That knowledge has greatly improved my self-management.

Diego then learned how to optimize his situational optimism.

Most of this book is dedicated to equipping you to optimize your situational optimism when it is needed most—in the face of turbulence. But in the words of management consulting pioneer Peter Drucker, "If you can't measure it, you can't manage it." So, first, let's talk about measuring optimism.

How Does Your Optimism Measure Up?

As of the time of writing this book, I am not aware of a test to measure situational optimism. However, the Life Orientation Test, Revised (LOT-R) tool is widely used to measure an individual's level of dispositional optimism.[45] This is a useful measure of your general optimism that will improve your awareness of your situational optimism.

Ranging on a scale from 0 to 24, the LOT-R does not have prescribed scores for optimism or pessimism. Instead, the tool's developers use the scale "as a continuous dimension of variability." I will share how I interpret the LOT-R in my practice. Based on an extensive use of the tool with over 750 senior professionals in the past two years alone, I have found the interpretations of the scores from the tool, as shown in Table 2-2, to be useful:

Score Range	Interpretation
0 to 11	Low Optimism or High Pessimism
12 to 16	Moderate Optimism
17 to 24	High Optimism or Low Pessimism

Table 2-2: Interpretation of LOT-R scores

It is fascinating but not surprising to me that 73% of the executives who participated in my doctoral study scored 17 or higher on the scale, making them high optimists. The remaining 27% scored between 12 and 16, making them moderate optimists. None of them scored in the Low Optimism range. Also, among the over 750 senior professionals to whom I administered the tool, about 75% of them scored in the high optimist range.

Why am I not surprised? Because leaders are believers.

You Can Control Your Response

You can control and influence your situational optimism much more than you thought. Your dispositional optimism is usually the starting point of your situational optimism. The latter can change—lower or higher—depending on your outlook on a specific event. You can affect your situational optimism by becoming more aware of how you respond to a certain scenario.

When situations go out of control or deteriorate in ways for which we did not bargain, it is normal for us to try to explain these adverse events, first to ourselves and later to others. Pay attention to your pattern of self-explanation as it could either render you feeling defeated, demoralized, and depressed (a pessimistic pattern of self-explanation) or resourceful, result-oriented, and resilient (an optimistic pattern of self-explanation).

Martin Seligman, a distinguished professor of psychology and former head of the American Psychological Association (APA), has extensively studied optimism and pessimism. His three dimensions below capture the patterns of self-explanations adopted by individuals facing unfavorable and favorable situations:[46]

1. Stable vs. unstable – This relates to an individual's view of the **permanence** of a situation. A pessimistic self-explanation sees a setback as fixed and irreversible (stable or high permanence), while an optimistic self-explanation interprets it as temporary and changeable (unstable or low permanence).

   - The reverse self-explanation occurs when the event is positive. A pessimistic self-explanation treats it as fleeting and capricious (unstable or low permanence). Meanwhile, an optimistic self-explanation sees it as enduring and predictable (stable or high permanence).

2. Global vs. specific – This relates to an individual's view of the **pervasiveness** of an event. A pessimistic self-explanation sees a misfortune as a reflection of their life as a whole (global or high pervasiveness), while an optimistic self-explanation views it as a distinct and separate part of their life (specific or low pervasiveness).

- The reverse self-explanation occurs when the event is positive. A pessimistic self-explanation views it as narrow and segregated (specific or low pervasiveness). Conversely, an optimistic self-explanation addresses it as a definition of their life as a whole (global or high pervasiveness).

3. Internal vs. external – This relates to an individual's view of the *personalization* of a situation. A pessimistic self-explanation views a negative event as attributable to one's characteristics (internal or high on personalization), while an optimistic self-explanation interprets it as attributable to environmental forces (external or low personalization).

   - The reverse self-explanation occurs when the event is positive. A pessimistic self-explanation sees it as outside their control (external or low personalization). In contrast, an optimistic self-explanation treats it as attributable to their personal characteristics and within their control (internal or high personalization).

Based on my personal experience and the experiences of clients with whom I have worked, it is abundantly clear that you can tweak your self-explanation to influence your optimism in any direction you wish.[47]

Your self-explanation pattern is critical because your explanation of the present reflects how you will prepare for the future. So, take control of it.

Optimism Is Not All Roses

Most of the business executives I interviewed for my doctoral studies and those I have met during my career hesitated to label themselves as optimists. This is because of the prevailing (but erroneous) understanding of who an optimist is. Many people consider an optimist to be an unrealistic person with their head in the clouds who should not be taken seriously.[48, 49, 50]

However, when I ask the same leaders to describe their outlook on life and business, almost all of them invariably depict themselves as optimists without using the word. Frankly, if the wrongly held view of an optimist is true, I wouldn't want to be identified as one, either. But it's not.

Having said that, there are legitimate proven concerns and downsides to optimism.

Too Much of a Good Thing

Optimism can be overdone, which is why the "inverted-U" theory applies to the concept. The inverted-U theory, proposed in the domain of sports performance, states that increased arousal (defined as activity and alertness of an athlete) will result in increased sporting performance until the latter peaks at the point of optimal arousal. Beyond this point of optimal arousal, performance will begin to decline with additional arousal. [51, 52]

Similarly, studies have shown that optimism generates constructive behaviors in individuals that lead to improved performance until an optimal point is reached and performance peaks. Additional optimism after the optimal point produces destructive and unwholesome behaviors that deteriorate performance, as illustrated in Figure 2-2.

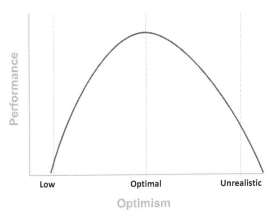

Figure 2-2: Optimism Overload: Peak and Plummet Performance[53]

The generally accepted caricature of the starry-eyed, impractical, and unrealistic optimist as the representation of optimism is why many professionals don't think of themselves as optimistic when, in fact, most of them are. However, by misclassifying their mindset, they miss opportunities to maximize the upsides of optimal optimism and minimize the inherent risks of unrestrained optimism.

Thus, understanding how optimism can go wrong and avoiding it is pivotal. Unrestrained optimism is optimism gone awry.

Four Types of Unrestrained Optimism

Applying the inverted-U theory shows that for optimism to produce peak results, it should build up to an optimal point, after which it should be curbed or restrained. What is the nature of unrestrained optimism? How can it be identified and restrained? Below are the four types of unrestrained optimism I have found along my professional journey and research studies.

Excessive Optimism

This form of unrestrained optimism has caught the most attention among experts, so most studies focus on it. The #1 culprit for the bad reputation optimism receives is **excessive optimism**. Individuals with this mindset will push the envelope on what is originally plausible to the realm of absurdity. This approach takes optimism that is rooted in reality into exaggeration that is rooted in fantasy. This is where optimism becomes "too much of a good thing." One of the best descriptions of excessive optimism comes from journalist Chris Hedges, who said,

> Optimism becomes a kind of disease. It's what created the [2008] financial meltdown where you have this kind of cheerful optimism in the face of utter catastrophe, and you plow forward based on an optimism that is no longer rooted in reality.

If hope becomes something that you express through illusion, then it's not hope; it's fantasy.[54]

Excessive optimism relates to prognosticating with exaggeration and irrational exuberance. A leader with this mindset will go beyond aiming for what is possible based on logic to boldly pursue what they wish for based entirely on their desire. This is the meaning behind Aesop's caution, "We can easily represent things as we *wish* them to be."

In 1999, James Glassman and Kevin Hassett predicted that the Dow Jones Industrial Average (the Dow) would hit the 36,000 milestone between 2002 and 2004. So certain were these Ivy League-educated authors about their forecast that they titled their book *Dow 36,000*, published by a subsidiary of Penguin Random House. To put this excessive optimism-fueled projection into perspective, the Dow index was introduced in 1896 and closed at 10,273 points on October 1, 1999, the day of the book's publication.[55] This means that the authors were convinced and tried to persuade everybody else that what took the index 103 years to achieve would be tripled in a mere three to five years.[56]

What happened in reality? The Dow did hit the 36,000-mark, but not until November 1, 2021! Glassman and Hassett's forecast was off by a whopping 17-19 years. While the hyperbolized projection, infamously called "perhaps the most spectacularly wrong investing book ever," may pave the way for high-profile political appointments (Glassman became a US undersecretary of state in 2008, and Hassett was appointed as a chief economic adviser to the US president in 2017), it is usually a kiss of death for a leader's career in the business world. Such a leader would not be taken seriously.

Therefore, it is little wonder that responsible leaders cringe at the thought of being perceived as overly optimistic. But there is a better way to deploy a restrained optimist's mindset and we will discuss that in the next chapter.

Speculative Optimism

More observable and widely reported in asset trading and investing, speculative behavior is spurred by unrestrained optimism. These fields strongly lend themselves to optimism or pessimism because they are primarily about future expectations. To fundamentalists in asset trading and investing, "speculation occurs when an asset is bought for its short-term expected gain, at a price higher than the expected discounted value of dividends."[57] The behavior will destabilize the market if widespread, e.g., during the meme stock revolution in 2020.

Generally, **speculative optimism** is the mindset behind gambling. A 2016 study that analyzed a massive data set of New York City lottery gambling found that a person's tendency to gamble increased significantly when positive mood-inducing but completely circumstantial and unrelated events occurred, e.g., a sunny day or a win by a local sports team.[58] So, it is a conjecture-fueled optimism.

Speculative optimism pays little to no attention to critical, dispassionate, and objective assessments about the future because it is more rooted in the emotions of the decision-maker. This flawed mindset associates one's current positive mood with a future positive outcome. When a leader's assertion "I have a good feeling about it" is the primary basis for a decision with future outcomes—and I have seen quite a few of these in my experience—that is speculative optimism.

Back to investing. A 2020 report based on a fifteen-year study found that nearly 90% of actively managed funds failed to beat the market.[59] These underperforming actively managed portfolios are typically handled by highly educated and full-time professionals with sophisticated analytical tools at their disposal and access to extensive research; their sole objective is to outperform the market. But they mostly fail. Despite this high failure rate among professional investors, many amateur individual investors, fueled by speculative optimism, firmly believe they can pick stocks that will outperform the market. However, the outcomes show that nonprofessional investors also fail to beat the market at a greater rate than professionals, yet persist in speculative behavior. Speculative optimism is as stubborn as it is spurious.

Speculative optimism is more commonly practiced in everyday business than acknowledged. The mindset causes us to think that we will be outliers for positive outcomes only. That failure happens to others, but not to us. We exempt ourselves from the population with no basis for the exemption other than unfounded reasons.

In a 1985 interview, Sylvester Stallone described his optimistic mindset and worldview: "I believe any success in life is made by going into an area with ... furious optimism,"[60] and so should you. But do not equate furious passion with spurious conjecture—speculative optimism belongs in the latter category.

Naïve Optimism

In 1913, Eleanor Porter authored a novel named after its main character, Pollyanna, a young girl who played the "glad game."[61] The game involves seeing something to be glad about in every occurrence. Thus, the *Pollyanna principle* has been adopted by psychologists and social scientists to describe a human propensity to recall past events in a more favorable light than reality.[62]

Similarly, the *Pollyanna hypothesis* denotes a generic human predisposition to communicate using more positive words than negative.[63] Organizational leaders in general and corporate communications professionals in particular routinely demonstrate this bias for upbeat words and good news, primarily because that is what the market rewards.[64] Conversely, this preconception also causes management to withhold or delay bad news to the board and/or investors.

The Pollyanna influence on human memory and language is all well and good until it seeps into our thoughts and conditions our view of the future. That conditioning to view future events in an unsophisticated manner is what I call **naïve optimism**.

What naïve optimism lacks in malicious intent, it more than makes up for in inexperience and imprudence. Leaders are most susceptible to this flawed optimism when they step into a new terrain like launching a new solution, entering a new geography, competing in a new vertical market, or executing mergers and acquisitions (M&A). Of course, professionals in organizations sharpen their pencils and conduct deep-dive reviews and analyses—like analysis of synergies, the basis of consideration offered/received, assessment of goodwill, etc.—before embarking on such high-stakes new ventures.

However, having participated in and led several of these strategic initiatives in various organizations, I can confirm that the prevailing optimism mindset of the most influential decision-makers overshadows the most comprehensive analyses. The excitement of a potential win makes an individual susceptible to naïve optimism.

Let's take a closer look at M&As. These are critical components of the growth strategy of several companies. M&As are high-visibility transactions of a multimillion or billion-dollar nature that normally bring together the best brains in the organization to package and execute. According to McKinsey & Company, in the second half of 2021 alone, large deals (exceeding $25 million per transaction) totaled a staggering $5.9 trillion.[65] It is therefore alarming to note that 80% to 90% of M&As flop![66, 67]

Several researchers have examined why most M&As do not meet their objectives. The most common reasons for their spectacular failure—culture clash, integration issues, and inadequate leadership involvement—point to a faulty mindset: naïve optimism. If decision-makers knew better, they would have done better. The naïveté of memory, language, and thought combine to lead to blissful ignorance where leaders are not keen to hear about potential problems. They just want to get the deals done.

Naïve optimism would rather not confront emerging problems, causing momentous failures in organizations. This mindset can be destructive during a crisis. But as Thomas Paine aptly stated,

The harder the conflict, the more glorious the triumph. What we obtain too cheaply, we esteem too lightly; it is dearness (or costliness) only that gives everything its value. I love the man that can smile in trouble, that can gather strength from distress and grow.

Deceptive Optimism

In military parlance, a smokescreen is a cloud of smoke created to shroud the position and activity of military personnel and equipment. It is a deceptive strategy that aims to give an advantage to the user. The same thing can happen when a person subscribes to the mindset of **deceptive optimism**. This rampant but less-talked-about form of mindset uses optimism as smoke and mirrors, from job interviews to multimillion-dollar fundraising.

In my mind, the case of Theranos, a now-defunct biomedical company, is a poster child for deceptive optimism. Despite its public display of exuberant confidence, the company's leadership knew right off the bat that its claims of a revolutionary breakthrough in blood testing, clinical data, laboratory reports generated for customers, and rosy financial projections were baseless.

With just a single pinprick of blood, Theranos claimed it could conduct a never-seen-before number of lab tests, as many as 240. CEO Elizabeth Holmes, oozing confidence and gracing the covers of major publications, convinced some of the world's most successful businesspeople to invest as much as $700 million in the company. In January 2022, she was found guilty of defrauding investors.

People who employ deceptive optimism use the promise of a highly favorable but illusionary future to win the confidence of their victims before executing their scam. The word "con man" (and its derivative "con-artist") has its roots in an 1849 *New York Herald* article that described swindler Samuel Thompson as the "Confidence Man." That is the model for deceptive optimism, a con based on effusive confidence.

In a crisis where confidence in the brand and/or management is usually shaky or lost, it is awfully tempting for the leadership to default to a deceptive optimistic mindset, to say what people want to hear in order to put a lid on the predicament. In reality, a crisis addressed this way rarely stays down. I remember when I asked a leader after a business meeting why they had published false information regarding an ongoing business. Their answer was, "I would have lost the business if the public knew the truth." Well, six months later, the truth came out, and the company went out of business—not because of the crisis the CEO was trying to keep down, but because of the misleading press statement.

Optimism vs Pessimism: Is There a Third Option?

Traditionally, psychology splits people into two groups regarding their future expectations: Those who expect their future to be bright, and those who always see a storm on the horizon. Either see the sunshine through the clouds or say, "Give it five minutes. It's going to get cloudy again." Therefore, many traditional psychologists have a unidimensional view of optimism and pessimism where they are mutually exclusive. They view them as bipolar—two ends of the extreme. The LOT-R tool is based on this traditional view.

However, is there another view besides the opposite view of optimism and pessimism? What about "realists"—could they be a viable alternative to optimism and pessimism?

We will discuss a more productive mindset in the next chapter.

Up Close and Personal

Activity: Life Orientation Test, Revised

Take the time to visit this link and see for yourself where you stand on the LOT-R scale: click here for the survey (www.psytoolkit. org/cgi-bin/3.4.0/survey?s=aga3a).

Use this test to determine your dispositional optimism on a scale of 0-24.

Use Table 2-2 in this chapter to locate your score in the score ranges and match it with the corresponding interpretation. The table is in the section titled "How Does Your Optimism Measure Up?"

In what ways has your level of optimism or pessimism influenced your leadership?

_____

_____

_____

_____

CHAPTER THREE

The Pragmatic Optimist

The optimist[s] can be, if it's unjustified optimism, disconnected with the struggle and the suffering of people [impacted by the crisis] and of the organization and stakeholders. If it's pessimism, then they can be demoralizing to the team. And it can actually limit the creativity of communication and action.

– **Research participant**, heads a multinational consulting firm
in North America

What you will learn in this chapter:
- The reality about being realistic.
- The best of both worlds: The pragmatic optimism mindset.
- Pessimistic and optimistic traits to avoid and exhibit.
- Benefits of pragmatic optimism.
- Day-to-day living as a pragmatic optimist.

As shown in Chapter Two, there are many advantages and disadvantages to both an optimistic and pessimistic approach to leadership. On the one hand, pessimists often take actions that could aggravate a crisis, decrease organizational morale, diminish communication, and weaken crisis management. Still, they are also capable of seeing the entire scope of a predicament before or when it happens.[68] On the other hand, an optimist might underestimate a crisis due to overconfidence, risk-taking, or a failure to prepare for diverse outcomes—but may also have the endurance to weather the storm and the perseverance to keep pushing toward a lasting solution.[69]

Another point driven home in the last chapter is that while leaders realize that it is counterproductive for them to be viewed as pessimistic, they mostly shy away from being labeled as optimistic due to their misconception about the mindset.

Enter the realist to resolve this dilemma.

With plenty of downsides between the optimistic and pessimistic mindsets, it is no wonder that some individuals avoid either label and opt for being "a realist." But how real is realism?

Getting Real About Realism

Epistemology defines realism as the possibility to obtain knowledge about an object that exists independently of your mind;[70] while in psychology, realism focuses on the existence of an object regardless of the presence of an observer.[71]

So, when leaders describe themselves as realists, they are considering the psychological definition of realism that is appropriate for subject matters that have occurred. However, claiming to be a realist fails when the subject matter is about prognosticating because the future does not yet exist. Instead, realists simply express their desire to be viewed as unbiased and objective.

A Desire to Be Unbiased

Leaders who choose to be labeled as realists set a bar for themselves to be seen as professional, rational, and thoughtful. In practice, however, the bar for being truly realistic is, well, quite unrealistic. Besides being required to be devoid of future expectations (because they are not real), as previously noted, being realistic also connotes being utterly unbiased in one's judgment.

Yet, science says that cognitive biases are "design features" of the brain.[72] The brain cannot function any other way. The key to success is recognizing and understanding one's biases and embracing counteracting processes that limit the adverse effects of those biases. A person cannot be devoid of biases. Being completely objective is virtually impossible because leadership decisions are subjective by nature.

Several subjective decisions that differ significantly can emanate from the same objective data set. You can present the same objective data to fifty leaders, and each may come up with their own subjective decisions that differ from their colleagues' decisions. Inherent in decision-making is the notion of subjectivity. I have found that people who are most vehement about being objective and realistic decision-makers tend to be as subjective as everyone else, if not more. So, embrace subjectivity as a leader.

A Desire to Be Respected

The previous chapter on optimism showcased how pessimism and optimism are often misrepresented. For example, to avoid sticking out like a sore thumb and being viewed as a carrier of negative energy (a conventional but misconstrued view of pessimism) or not to be considered as a naïve, happy-go-lucky leader with one's head in the clouds (the prevalent but erroneous view of optimist), some leaders may choose to identify as a "realist." Decision-makers, understandably, recoil from such negative descriptions.

These leaders see themselves as more dignified, professional, and balanced as they focus on the desire to be taken seriously. In truth, most leaders who label themselves as a realist during a planning, problem-solving, or decision-making scenario (all critical to addressing a crisis) tend to make pessimistic arguments that poke holes in what they perceive as imprudent positive expectations. Such leaders are more likely to elevate negative expectations as unavoidable, which is similar to making a pessimistic argument. Rarely do so-called realists argue for more optimistic positions.

A Desire to Be Certain in an Uncertain Future

As human beings, we are curious about the future and often make projections. That is why more than 2.5 billion devices query the services of The Weather Company (a subsidiary of IBM) 40 billion times a day for weather updates.[73] The high frequency of weather checks relates to the fluidity of our perception of the future. We just don't know the future for sure.

"Face reality as it is, not as it was or as you wish it to be." – Jack Welch, business executive

When making plans or decisions about the future, which are necessary activities when responding to a crisis, some leaders identify as realists to make prognosticating appear more practical and grounded. Yet, how can anyone be a realist about the future that is not yet real?

Reality means a certainty, while crises (and most noncrisis in the enterprise) are inherently uncertain. As long as the future is the backdrop of any subject matter, like a crisis, it triggers future expectations or conjectures instead of certainties. It is unnatural and arguably impossible to be completely neutral when future expectations are involved. Even inaction is based on the leader's view of the future, whether positive or negative; it is a byproduct of their optimistic or pessimistic mindset.

Finally, being realistic is similar to the motivation for being pessimistic because, according to Thomas Hardy, it is "… playing the sure game. You cannot lose at it; you may gain. It is the only view of life in which you can never be disappointed."[74]

There Is a Better Way: Pragmatic Optimism

Since realism is not a better construct than optimism and pessimism, I believe that what I call *pragmatic optimism* is superior to either mindset. Pragmatic optimism is a hybrid mindset developed by an individual by combining what they view as the productive traits of optimism and pessimism while discarding what is considered unproductive attributes of both optimism and pessimism. Pragmatic optimism selects the best of each nature and merges them for optimal outcomes while consciously sidestepping the landmines inherent in optimism and pessimism mindsets.

The presence and utility of the pragmatic optimistic mindset were the most unexpected and the most significant findings in my research study for three reasons:

1. Throughout my comprehensive review of previous research on optimism and pessimism, I found that scholars viewed those two common mindsets on a unidimensional scale where they are opposites. In other words, possessing one mindset meant relinquishing the other. For example, as individuals demonstrate the attributes of a pessimistic perspective, they are not expected to exhibit optimistic traits.

   However, from the first executive I interviewed for the study through to the final one, using a rigorous interviewing method with open-ended questions and follow-ups, I discovered that the chasm between optimism and pessimism has connecting bridges in certain parts built by the individuals, that formed a more sophisticated mindset that I call pragmatic optimism. I later found contemporary studies that support the likelihood of the described practice of merging two seemingly incompatible perspectives into one.

2. While a rigorous analysis of the interview data confirmed that practically all the senior decision-makers in my study demonstrated

varying levels of pragmatic optimism, only 13% of them did so on purpose. Let's call them the *Intentional Pragmatic Optimists*. The remaining 87% of the executives in my sample—the *Unintentional Pragmatic Optimists*—practiced pragmatic optimism subconsciously.

The intentional pragmatic optimists were alert to the drawbacks of a leader espousing either optimism or pessimism because of their personal experiences and their keen observations of colleagues in the workplace. According to them, these drawbacks quickly escalate to severe adverse effects during a crisis. As a result, they intentionally practiced pragmatic optimism as a more progressive yet balanced mindset.

Unintentional pragmatic optimists take a more iterative approach to adopt the hybrid mindset. Their style was more situational, where they varied and tweaked their optimism based on the circumstances by downplaying certain optimistic traits they felt would backfire while displaying openness to some pessimistic traits that they found helpful to resolving the crisis and advancing the objectives of the organization.

Intentional Pragmatic Optimists	Unintentional Pragmatic Optimists
Conscious – done with full awareness	**Unconscious** – done mainly subconsciously
Calculated – an intentional practice	**Unstructured** – resourceful & opportunistic
Consistent – predictable & refined	**Unique** – varied by situation & unarticulated

Table 3-1: Intentional vs Unintentional Pragmatic Optimists

3. Pragmatic optimism is an evolved mindset that grew out of the extensive and profound experiences of my study participants as they recounted the inadequacies of either optimism or pessimism

during a high-stakes and high-risk situation like a crisis. Often reflecting on several mishandled crises over their careers (either when they were the decision-makers or supported the executive in charge), the study participants recounted scenarios where they realized that two mindsets are better than one.

The executives in my study did not try to dampen their optimism or deny their pessimism; they combined them. The resultant pragmatic optimistic mindset became the foundation for their leadership behaviors during a crisis, which most of them also carried into noncrisis. They simply saw pragmatic optimism as the ideal mindset for leaders in all situations.

The Science Behind Pragmatic Optimism

As discussed above, traditional psychology researchers who study people's views about future life expectancies treat optimism and pessimism mindsets as polar opposites. To those who hold this conventional interpretation, the two worldviews of optimism and pessimism exist as extremes on a unidimensional scale that makes it impossible for an individual to subscribe to both worldviews simultaneously.[75, 76] To them, one is either an optimist or a pessimist.

But participants in my research thought otherwise. Owing to the inadequacies of optimism and pessimism and relying on their several years of managerial experience (my sample's average number of years of leadership experience was twenty-six years), these senior decision-makers have evolved a third mindset that I call **pragmatic optimism**. This evolved mindset, mainly operating subconsciously, treats optimism and pessimism as two separate constructs that can be purposefully combined to create a more superior worldview that brings together the best of both worlds.

This finding was surprising and exciting because it turned the traditional understanding of the subject on its head. I also found it curious that some contemporary studies that employed various statistical tools (a different approach from my interview-based data collection and analysis) concluded that optimism and pessimism are two separate psychological constructs with a weak correlation.[77,78] Yes, you read that right: the two constructs are not mutually exclusive but dissimilar.

In fact, a team of German researchers examined the results of a representative sample of over 46,000 individuals between the ages of 18-103 who took an optimism-pessimism test (LOT-R) and concluded that the two mindsets are separate constructs that exist on two different dimensions.[79] This German study also found that both worldviews became more distinct and independent as the ages of participants increased. That may explain why my sample of seasoned executives with an average age of 50 had developed the ability to treat the two mindsets as distinct and therefore combinable.

I did not find existing research showing that individuals actively combined both worldviews. My study is the first to demonstrate that approach among organizational leaders, especially when responding to a crisis.

One executive from my doctoral research said, "I think excessive optimism or pessimism both have risks because both have to be constrained." Similarly, but more pointedly, another participant stated, "I would say when you're in the middle of a crisis, you've got to have a balance of pessimism and optimism." The bottom line is that an effective leader, especially one responding to a crisis, cannot afford to be one or the other. They must be able to balance both mindsets. The following section explains how to do so.

The Pragmatic Optimism Traits Model

The Conflict and Its Resolution

When an individual simultaneously holds two contradictory views or beliefs, e.g., expecting the worst possible outcome from a crisis (a pessimistic trait) and focusing on solutions that will resolve the crisis favorably (an optimistic attribute), tension, anxiety, and stress may arise. This is symptomatic of a mental conflict called cognitive dissonance, and its effect increases in proportion to the magnitude of negative consequences of the contradictory views.[80, 81] Inherent in an experience of cognitive dissonance is a motivation to resolve the conflict.

So, how does a leader solve the mental contradictions that may emerge from developing a hybrid mindset of pragmatic optimism that concurrently holds both traits of pessimism and optimism? Experts agree that there are at least three ways to resolve cognitive dissonance:

1. Alter one of the worldviews, attitudes, beliefs, or behaviors to align with the other;
2. Abase the significance of one of the beliefs through justification; or
3. Acquire new information that overshadows the conflicting beliefs.

In my work with leaders to adopt the pragmatic optimistic mindset, #3 has proven to be the most effective. Applying this approach to the example given above, the new information about pragmatic optimism interprets expecting the worst possible outcome from a crisis as a necessary productive trait that will help the individual accomplish their other belief of focusing on solutions that will resolve the crisis favorably. Thus, both views become consonant; cognitive dissonance is fixed, and pragmatic optimism is operational.

Let's explore how to use this new information—the pragmatic optimistic model—to deepen the quality of your leadership.

The Model and Its Use

The model in Figure 3-1 illustrates how participants in my study, while responding to a crisis, rejected certain aspects of pessimism and optimism and combined specific properties of both mindsets. The model presents four components: pessimistic and optimistic traits avoided, pessimistic and optimistic qualities exhibited, and examples of each.

The Pragmatic Optimism Traits Model

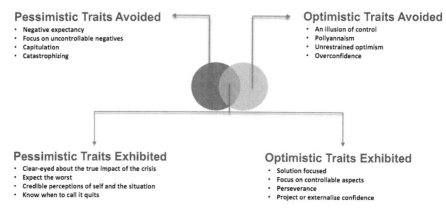

Pessimistic Traits Avoided
- Negative expectancy
- Focus on uncontrollable negatives
- Capitulation
- Catastrophizing

Optimistic Traits Avoided
- An illusion of control
- Pollyannaism
- Unrestrained optimism
- Overconfidence

Pessimistic Traits Exhibited
- Clear-eyed about the true impact of the crisis
- Expect the worst
- Credible perceptions of self and the situation
- Know when to call it quits

Optimistic Traits Exhibited
- Solution focused
- Focus on controllable aspects
- Perseverance
- Project or externalize confidence

Figure 3-1: The pragmatic optimistic model

Let's look at each component of the model, along with an explanation of each example listed, and a relevant quote from a research participant.

Pessimistic Traits to Avoid

1. **Negative expectancy** – This is a tendency to expect negative outcomes from difficult situations despite any intervention to resolve the issue.[82, 83] It is an attribute that believes that unpleasant conditions will *always* worsen regardless of an individual's actions to

correct them. Instead of working on resolving the crisis, people with this mindset often expend energy on gathering evidence with which to blame others, discourage the team, or protect themselves/ their careers.

- *"If you feel as if you're going to fail no matter what you do, then you're going to become defeatist and not push that extra inch that would have [delivered the] victory, and then you're going to fail. Everybody [on your team] is going to say, 'We knew we were going to fail anyway because the manager already said this or did that,' or whatever. And [negative expectancy becomes a] self-fulfilling prophecy."*

2. **Focus on uncontrollable negatives** – Leaders who reflect this trait focus a disproportionate amount of energy on occurrences outside their locus of control. They become overwhelmed with adverse developments they cannot do anything about and cannot separate uncontainable elements from manageable ones.

- *"I think those things you can't control, I just think you can't worry as much about. But I think a lot of people do worry about that, and so that drags them down."*

3. **Capitulation** – This is giving up and abandoning hope in difficult times, a hallmark of pessimistic individuals who lack the endurance to withstand shocks and are devoid of the perseverance to pull through challenging times.[84] They might not give up on day one, but they will be looking for an off-ramp and a way to shirk responsibility for the failure or future criticism (also known by the euphemistic acronym "CYA").

- *"Certainly, for the early part of the crisis, you don't want to give up on the goals... You don't say... 'Okay. I'm not going to hit it.' Even though things may look [difficult]... you sort of figure out what could be done."*

4. **Catastrophizing** – This is a form of cognitive distortion, defined as an erroneous or ineffective way of processing information that

involves jumping to the worst form of conclusions about emerging circumstances regardless of how implausible they are.[85, 86]

- *"[In] a time of crisis...things have very negative consequences; it's never tea and biscuits. So, if you have [a decision-maker on your team] that is extremely excitable and all the feedback you get [from them about the crisis] is over the top, that person is good for a different thing in your life, but maybe not [a] crisis."*

Optimistic Traits to Avoid

1. **An illusion of control** – This is the propensity to believe that one has more control than one truly does.[87] This is a potentially dangerous view because a crisis, by its nature, contains major elements that are entirely outside the control of a leader. This illusion should be avoided because it gives the leader and their organization a false sense of security.

   Without a doubt, crisis leadership aims to bring a predicament under management's control. However, the debacle usually starts as an out-of-control situation, and an optimist's critical mind may be lulled with false assurance.

   - *"So I think the best way to describe [a crisis] is an out-of-control situation. That's the way I would look at it. And obviously for it to be out of control, [it means it] probably wasn't foreseen."*

2. **Pollyannaism** – This is a strong propensity to focus exclusively on the positive aspects of any situation.[88] A crisis is generally a perplexing and damaging situation. Therefore, when optimistic leaders adopt a nothing-to-see-here approach to a crisis by dwelling solely on the benefits while avoiding and ignoring the apparent challenges, they lose their credibility. Pollyannaism is a potentially perilous trait for a leader facing adversity because it delays

or halts the deployment of countervailing measures to tackle the crisis.

- *"Interesting that a person [like me] with a very positive disposition generally, immediately upon crisis, starts thinking of the end of days, right? But that mechanism enables almost a process orientation to managing those doomsday scenarios— to put risk mitigation plans in place."*

3. **Unrestrained optimism** – As mentioned in Chapter Two, unrestrained optimism sometimes manifests as a belief that a negative event (a crisis) will not occur or if it occurs, to underestimate it.[89] Having a mindset that a crisis only happens to other organizations, or that fails to appreciate the full ramifications, is a recipe for mishandling a catastrophe. Such a distorted view will hamper crisis prevention or incapacitate a crisis response.

- *"But it's almost like a fireman goes to work in the morning knowing [full] well that there might be a fire... expecting a call to crisis... that is how I've lived [as an executive]. And it makes [crisis] easier to handle."*

4. **Overconfidence** – This is basically an error of judgment that is one of the most prevalent psychological biases known to plague humans.[90] So, if the general population, due to their optimistic bias, is overconfident by nature, how much more confidence does one need to possess to become a successful leader? Answer: A lot![91] Research has linked CEOs' overconfidence to better firm performance during noncrisis years.

While overconfidence can be an advantageous trait that distinguishes highfliers, it is the root cause of many leadership debacles during crises (e.g., organizational, national, and global financial crises).[92] Overconfidence is such an easy trap for leaders to fall into since it is usually their towering strength. However, leadership overconfidence torpedoes the crisis management process and it rarely goes unpunished.

- *"We need to combat the psychology of overconfidence or of excessive optimism."*

As you reflect on the pessimism and optimism traits that a pragmatic optimist avoids, I'd like you to take a look at the cover of this book. In the process of developing the concept for the cover design, I came up with the idea of illustrating the avoided traits of pessimism and optimism as blurry and out-of-focus in contrast with the pragmatic optimist's view that is sharp and in-focus. The faded words and phrases on the book cover that are not discussed above are as follows: *fearful, careless, castle-in-the-sky, naïve, withdrawn, casual, isolated, la-la land, doubtful, inattentive, starry-eyed, despondent, doomster, presumptuous, nervous, cocky, ruffled, loss of control, unrealistic, Chicken Little, helpless, gullible, demoralized, reckless, rattled, laissez-faire, half-baked, and overconfident.*

Pessimistic Traits to Exhibit

1. **Clear-eyed about the true impact of the crisis** – This is the gravitation toward the facts, figures, and other empirical data of the crisis, no matter how gory. A willingness to be grounded on the issues by understanding the distressing situation's depth, magnitude, and ramifications. Leaders who demonstrate this trait are perceived as authentic and grounded.
   - *"Get the facts. Get the facts. Immediately, get the facts, because the truth is the first victim of war, and the truth is the first victim of a crisis as well. So, first of all, get the facts before offering the facts."*
2. **Expect the worst** – Leaders with this trait expect the worst in a crisis but not in a defeatist, negative expectancy way. They understand that circumstances change quickly during a crisis, and by believing that things may change for the worse, they are better prepared to counter it. Such individuals appear to be several steps

ahead of the crisis instead of being caught flat-footed. Having a risk management view seeks the worst-case scenarios and continues to look for them with a plan in mind to protect the organization.

- *"Cataloging the risks and working through the worst-case scenarios, etc. It's essentially what we do as managers; to mitigate any potential worst-case scenario. There's an innate positivity [and] confidence that we're going to get through this because you trust the system that you've created for yourself. It's essentially a protection mechanism because you want to be able to put a stamp down that says, 'I've done all that I could.'"*

3. **Credible perceptions of self and the situation** – Understanding your own and the organization's true strengths in light of your inadequacies concerning the difficulty will influence you to call for reinforcements when needed, and avoid the traps of overconfidence.[93] However, optimistic leaders tend to overestimate their strengths and trivialize their limitations, thus increasing the risk of mishandling certain aspects of a multifrontal fiasco. A credible perception of self and the troubling situation helps leaders know when to raise their hand and call for help.

- *"It would be arrogant for anyone to say, 'Oh, this [crisis] is going to end great.' You have to assess the situation critically—be honest with yourself."*

4. **Know when to call it quits** – While perseverance is a necessary trait for success in general and especially during the heightened pressure and uncertainty of a crisis, pragmatic optimists are comfortable with knowing when to pull the plug after exhausting all alternatives. At the right time, and as a well-thought-out trade-off, successful leaders know how to give up strategically. They know it is OK to lose a battle in order to win the war.

- *"[Crisis leadership] is that sort of thing [where] you win some things and you lose some things. 'Yeah, we're going to lose this deal.' And if you dwell on that, you can't move forward."*

Optimistic Traits to Exhibit

1. **Solution-focused** – Reasoning our way out of tricky and highly complex situations is how our species has evolved, hence, a significant percentage of the brain is dedicated to problem-solving.[94, 95] This quality empowers an individual to direct their attention, mind power, and energy into a creative process that develops possible solutions to resolve the predicament at hand. This trait also prepares the individual to anticipate and prepare for failures. If one proposal fails, they have other options lined up.
   - *"When a crisis comes, it's about concentration. It's about focusing on the solution."*

2. **Focus on controllable aspects** – Leaders who take time to decipher which part of the crisis they can control are able to deploy and maximize resources effectively. As they reallocate their time, energy, and resources to the controllable portion, more often than not the parts of the crisis that were once uncontrollable become manageable. This is how true leaders gain ground in a crisis and build morale for the team.

   Resolving a crisis may be likened to solving an algebraic problem or expression. The universally accepted approach to doing so is inherent in the name of that branch of mathematics, derived from the Arabic "al-jabr," meaning "reunion of broken parts."[96, 97] Algebra involves breaking up a problem into component parts, solving from the known elements to the unknown portions, and, finally, bringing the parts together for the solution.[98] Thus, by focusing on the controllable aspects of a crisis, the leader finds that previously uncontrollable portions begin to get clearer.

- *"So [I focus on] those things I can control... and over time, I've become more confident in putting the balance of my energy in the things that I can control, and not putting my energy in the things I can't."*

3. **Perseverance** – On February 18, 2021, NASA landed an unmanned rover named Perseverance on Mars that is equipped with nineteen cameras and two microphones. In his winning essay that topped more than 28,000 entries for naming the robot, seventh-grader Alexander Mather from Virginia wrote, "But, if [names of] rovers are to be the qualities of us as a race, we missed the most important thing. Perseverance."[99] Interestingly, NASA also made a twin of Perseverance and called it OPTIMISM.[100]

   A recurring theme in decades-old experimental studies of human behavior is that optimists do not give up easily. These words by John Lennon sum up the life of the unrelenting: "Everything will be okay in the end. If it's not okay, it's not the end." Pragmatic optimists dig deep to find the resolve to keep pushing ahead to find a solution despite severe conditions because they believe they will be successful eventually.

   - *"I push myself and I push the team even in the event of things not looking so well. I'm the [kind of] person that will keep pushing at that door to make sure that I've exhausted all options because my intention is to get a favorable outcome."*

4. **Project or externalize confidence** – A mindset of perseverance, being solution-focused, and managing controllable situations of a crisis, lays a foundation of self-confidence in the leader. Beyond that, I found that pragmatic optimists intentionally display or externalize their confidence to their teams. They recognize that their teams feed off the leaders' confidence, especially during times of immense uncertainty. They recognize that their self-confidence is a critical input into their team's morale.

- *"I find very little advantage of showing that I am really concerned and worried [to the whole team] because I find that [negativiy] spreads very easily."*

In summary, while pragmatic optimism is a blend of both pessimism and optimism, it is wrapped around a progressive kind of optimism that says, "The future can be brighter, and I can do something about it." This hybrid mindset allows a leader to press toward the positive side of a situation without losing sight of the associated negative aspects of the current crisis. Pragmatic optimism embraces productive pessimism and leverages objective optimism to create a positive outcome.

"Both optimists and pessimists contribute to our society. The optimist invents the airplane and the pessimist the parachute."
– Gil Stern, humorist, Chicago Tribune

Pragmatic optimists prepare for what could go wrong and are passionate about what could go right. These leaders view a crisis through the lens of their optimism instead of viewing their optimism through the lens of the crisis. They have learned to shine in their darkest hour. Pragmatic optimism combines hope with strategy. Hope says, "Tomorrow will be better," while strategy says, "Let me show you how tomorrow will be better."

An Illustration of Pragmatic Optimism

In 1999, biology major Doug Lindsey was struck by a mysterious illness that left him so weak that he could not continue his college education and was bedridden for 11 years. After getting sick with the family "curse," a condition that would later be termed *bilateral adrenal medullary hyperplasia,* he set out on a journey to understand his ailment, recruit help from scientists, and convince a surgeon to perform an unproven and risky procedure on him to save his life. After years of research, Doug invented the surgery that would cure him. Let us break down how a pragmatic optimistic mindset powered Doug on this life-changing journey.

Pessimistic Traits Exhibited

Doug was clear-eyed about the negative situation because he'd grown up watching his mother suffer from the same condition. The symptoms to which he suddenly fell prey were not unfamiliar, just unexplained and unexpected. He did not shy away from the negativity of the disease; quite the contrary, he learned as much as he could about it.

In the beginning months of his condition, Doug knew to expect the worst. He was not under any illusion. He knew that if left unchecked, the health crisis that made him incapacitated for 22 hours a day would not improve and could be fatal. After researching the history of the disease in his family that went beyond his mother, and affected his aunt, he expected the worst to prepare for the best-case scenario.

Negative visualization (NV) is a practice that can help in a crisis. In ancient Rome, NV was called *futurorum malorum praemeditatio*, which in Latin literally means "pre-studying a terrible future."[101] Doug took stock of the debilitating progress of the disease and learned what could go wrong with his health in the future. In a crisis, NV asks, "How bad can things *really* get?"[102] A sincere answer to that question enables a leader to build a defense to limit negative impacts and develop an offense to create positive outcomes. On the contrary, an optimistic mindset truncates the process of NV, leaving the organization ill-prepared against downturns, since the optimistic leader's preferred state of mind is to visualize positivity.

Doug gained a credible perception of himself and the situation at hand. He demonstrated this by recognizing his limitations in medical science and seeking the help of

"Nothing happens to the wise man contrary to his expectations…Above all, he reckoned that something could block his plans." – Seneca

several medical professionals, one of whom was Dr. H. Cecil Coghlan of the University of Alabama-Birmingham. Dr. Coghlan is a medical professor and scientist in nervous system disorders with one distinguishing quality: inquisitiveness. Doug's connection to Dr. Coghlan made the difference after several other scientists from reputable medical research organizations had turned him down.

Thinking he'd found a solution by discovering a drug that had shown the ability to lower adrenal production, Doug was willing to try it but soon discovered that it only helped him stand for a few short hours and he had to be on a drip line around the clock. Mission failed. This is when Doug knew he needed to give up on the idea of discovering a medication to help with his illness without giving up on finding a solution.

Doug focused on the controllable aspects of his condition. Though he was powerless to stop his body's process of shutting down (a significant part of his life that was beyond his control), he focused on what he could control: staying alive as long as possible to find a solution.

Positive visualization (PV) is well known in positive psychology. It engages the power of one's imagination to envision the desired outcome that may also be vocalized through mantras.[103] When I practice PV, I make sure to picture positive outcomes for controllable aspects distinctly from the uncontrollable parts. That way, I focus my resources on executing the former while recognizing that the latter is out of my hands.

Optimistic Traits Exhibited

Doug was solution-focused by being deliberate, thoughtful, attentive, and single-minded in his desire to resolve his health crisis. He did not waver from his pursuit of a solution, even though no precedent existed for the solution. He did not allow discouraging feedback from scientists like, "This has never been done before" to hold him back.

His primary healthcare physician was so concerned about Doug's laser focus on finding a solution that he referred him to a psychiatrist.

One adjective that perfectly describes Doug kept ringing in my mind as I read his story and watched him narrate his experience: tenacious. He had every reason to give up hope. Medical doctors from Ivy League universities, elite academic medical centers, and the country's top medical research agency (the National Institutes of Health) said, "It is impossible!" But through perseverance, he found every reason to press on. His fears did not go away, but they were paired up with unwavering hope.

For a leader to preserve through turbulence, the crisis resolution plans cannot be rigid or conclusive but must be fluid and adaptable — allowing for false starts, failures, and course correction. The majority of crises are uncertain and unique. No matter how familiar the variables are, crises are full of surprises and your plans must be malleable enough to adapt.

Suffering is compatible with a crisis. Through the RISE-UP and Six Hats models discussed in Chapter One, both the organization and its people suffer during a predicament. Thus, in practical terms, perseverance means knowing how to suffer. Author and martial artist Deng Ming-Dao puts it this way: "Those who don't know how to suffer are the worst off. There are times when the only correct thing we can do is to bear out troubles until a better day."[104]

Doug was very systematic in his approach, which was intertwined with his perseverance. He began his research by studying endocrinology textbooks and then started digging deeper into cases

"There will always be suffering. But we must not suffer over the suffering." – Alan Watts, British philosopher & writer

similar to his condition that hadn't been fully diagnosed or termed. It wasn't until he labeled his condition that he found similar surgeries performed on animals that would lead to his surgery on his adrenal glands. Other manifestations of his optimism were overcoming several roadblocks, dead ends, and hopeless moments.

In the early 2000s, my team and I faced a major crisis while implementing a multimillion-dollar ERP project involving the trifecta of IT issues colloquially known as "PPT": people, process, and technology. It was our ninth backup plan, or Plan "J," that eventually cracked the problem. Leaders must always have a backup plan but realize that even a fallback is also prone to failure. So, if your Plan "B" fails, remember that there are twenty-four other letters after that in the English alphabet.

> *"Whatever you are looking for is also looking for you... Be available and ready when it shows up."*
> *– Sahndra Fon Dufe, Cameroonian screenwriter & actress*

It is safe to assume that Doug's level of optimism was not constantly at the highest level throughout the extended period of his illness. Such is the ebb and flow of optimism. However, he learned to adapt his optimism and pressed on. The element of adaptability is an essential component of pragmatic optimism.

If optimism is adaptable, then it is learnable and improvable.[105] Crisis does not come with a how-to guide. Most times, responding to a crisis requires a new path in mindset, mission, and methods, just as Doug demonstrated. He was result oriented and could rally himself.

At the end of this chapter, you'll be able to dive deeper into Doug's story to understand the parts of pessimism and optimism that he was able to avoid.

The Nature of Pragmatic Optimism

Pragmatic optimism is rooted in the reality of the current crisis but is not restrained by it. Pragmatic optimism is seeing current reality as it is and seeing the future as what it could be. You cannot implement the desired change in a crisis if you do not accept the reality of that crisis.

A leader who stops questioning has stopped leading. So, to get a grasp of and navigate through a crisis, effective leaders tend to ask questions like:

1. Who and what was impacted?
2. Where are we?
3. How did we get here?
4. Where are we going?
5. What are the implications of this proposed action?
6. How has this crisis changed us?
7. What are the opportunities in this conundrum?

Quite often a leadership mindset that balances pessimism and optimism is needed to get to the root of these questions as some of the answers may be superficially contradictory but are highly effective when combined.

Combining Seemingly Opposing Personality Attributes Is Not New

I was about eight years old when I first heard the terms extroverts and introverts. It was also when I found out I belong to the latter group.

I am a reserved and quiet person who does a lot more thinking than talking. I also spoke with a stutter well into my high school years, and yes, I detested speaking in public settings with

> *"I'm a pessimist because of intelligence, but an optimist because of will."*
> *– Antonio Gramsci (Letters from Prison)*

every fiber of my being. I'd flop any school assessment that involved a presentation. I was happy and fulfilled living in my own space in a world that is generally biased against introverts.[106, 107]

As I joined the workforce and rose to middle management, I learned to be a successful introvert in a world designed for extroverts by excelling at achieving my objectives while avoiding tasks outside my comfort zone. All that changed in 1998, seven years after

I graduated college, when I was thrust (kicking and screaming) into a high-profile four-hour speaking assignment. I had never felt that much stress in my life.

I spent four to five hours every day over the following twenty-one days I had to prepare for the event by studying online about public presentations. This was a few months before Google launched, so I had to rely on far less efficient search engines while using a dial-up internet connection. The speaking engagement was a resounding success and it launched me into the world of public speaking, my gateway into extroversion. Here are a few things I learned from that experience:

1. Effective public speaking and other extroversion-leaning skills are learnable.
2. I did not stop being an introvert; I only learned to be an extrovert as well.
3. Combining introversion and extroversion traits delivers better results.

Nowadays, when I tell an audience that I am an introvert by nature, they often laugh, thinking it's a punchline.

Another example comes to mind. In January 2005, the entire MBA class in which I enrolled at Queen's University, Ontario, Canada, took a psychometric test as part of the introduction to the program. The results showed that only two or three of the over sixty students could be described as combining optimism and pessimism worldviews. I was in that minority group.

Throughout my career, my acquired extroversion skills put me in the spotlight of public-facing roles and tasks. I have spoken to audiences ranging from fifty to two thousand people, and at global events and venues like the World Economic Forum, the United Nations, the European Union, and Money2020 as a spokesperson for an S&P 500 company. My innate introversion skills have kept me grounded.

People like me who combine introversion and extroversion are called **ambiverts**, a term created by psychologist Edmund Conklin in

1923.[108, 109, 110] Therefore, combining personality traits is not a new phenomenon.

In his 2013 study titled "The Ambivert advantage," Adam Grant, professor of psychology at the University of Pennsylvania, challenged the notion that extroverts are more successful in sales environments. He discovered that the highest-ranking salespeople are ambiverts who fall in the middle of the extroversion scale.

"Because they naturally engage in a flexible pattern of talking and listening, ambiverts are likely to express sufficient assertiveness and enthusiasm to persuade and close a sale," [111] Grant writes in the publication's abstract. In addition, ambiverts were found to be "more inclined to listen to customers' interests and less vulnerable to appearing too excited or overconfident." Thus, combining seemingly opposing personality attributes delivers better results, even in settings that are traditionally viewed as the domain of extroverts.

In the same way, pragmatic optimism combines mindsets that are traditionally seen as contradictory and mutually exclusive into an adaptive worldview that maximizes the strengths of both worldviews and tones down the weaknesses of both traits to deliver superior results when the organization is in a dire need of true leadership.

A Harmonized Conflict

The pragmatic optimism model harmonizes conflict. This model recognizes that conflicts may arise when combining both mindsets. That is where the synthesis skills of the leader come into play. An individual's ability to reflect on and harmonize differing viewpoints, a hallmark of true leadership, is paramount.

A renowned epidemiologist on the front lines fighting the spread of infectious diseases worldwide said in the heat of the COVID-19 pandemic: "I stay optimistic but not unrealistically optimistic. The one thing I try very hard, and I think I succeed… I act optimistic. I give the appearance of being optimistic. But deep down, I just do everything I possibly can assuming the worst will happen and I've got to stop the worst from happening. So, you know, it's a little bit of a conflict there."[112]

If you've ever felt that kind of conflict, that is pragmatic optimism. That is when you realize that you are putting the two mindsets together.

It is a harmonized conflict because attributes of both optimism and pessimism are delicately balanced to produce the most effective leadership behaviors. This interplay between both mindsets was well captured by an eminent money manager, Sir John Templeton, who stated, "Bull markets are born on pessimism, grow on skepticism, mature on optimism, and die on euphoria."

Like any new habit, you will get better as you practice it until it becomes second nature.

An Antidote to Toxic Positivity

An earlier section of this chapter referenced a memorable activity at the start of my MBA program at Queen's. Another unforgettable incident happened at the end of the program. It was the final class of a technical accounting course led by a distinguished professor whose personality can best be described as even-tempered and formal. So, you can imagine everyone's astonishment when as he ended the class, he pulled out a costume, cued a music recording, and sang and danced to Monty Python's "Always Look on the Bright Side of Life"

It was hilarious. Some of us joined in while others were too captivated to react.

The song is popular as it encourages positivity that feeds into our optimistic bias as humans. The blockbuster song is so well-liked that it was played at the closing ceremony of the London 2012 Summer Olympics.[113] That is because positivity has several advantages; but when it is coerced, especially by someone in a leadership role, it may backfire.

Here are three questions on which to reflect:

1. Have you ever felt pressured by a leader to "suck it up," cheer up, and go with the flow?

2. Have you ever felt compelled to disregard your misgivings and negative emotions about a development in the workplace so as not to irritate your manager, even when you know that your concerns are legitimate yet unaddressed?

3. Have you ever been exposed to a work culture of 'bright-siding'[114] or "Prozac Leadership"[115] where employees are encouraged to be hopeful and discussing obvious and pressing challenges is frowned upon?

If you answer yes to any of these questions, then you have experienced what is known as **toxic positivity**.[116]

Tabitha Kirkland, psychologist and associate teaching professor at the University of Washington, said, "Toxic positivity is a way of responding to your own or someone else's suffering that comes across as a lack of empathy. It dismisses emotions instead of affirming them and could come from a place of discomfort."[117] More often than not, the toxic part of positivity is an unintended consequence of not knowing how to respond to difficult and uncomfortable situations.

A leader with a pragmatic optimistic mindset is open, honest, clear-eyed about ongoing challenges, and motivated to rally resources to address them.

"Research shows pessimists see the world more accurately, but optimists get more good things done!" – John Hume, Director, Michigan Economic Center

Instead of being dismissive of the negative emotions of team members, a pragmatic optimistic leader listens to, appreciates, and validates the negative emotions with a view to supporting affected colleagues to find solutions.

Pragmatic Optimism as Consensus Building

The best leaders encourage counter viewpoints that can sometimes be polar opposites but enable an environment of cooperation and collaboration. The viewpoints are analyzed, giving a leader the opportunity to synthesize them. The best leaders know how to build a bridge across differing ideas to create synergy.

Leaders can successfully create this enabling environment through consensus building in decision-making. In reality, the best practice for consensus is not about aiming for unanimity, conformity, or even majority votes to agree on a decision; it is about leadership's response to dissenting perspectives. True leadership is not democratic in nature, but neither is it autocratic. In enabling workplace cultures, leaders respect, request, and record dissenting viewpoints. By contrast, managers who create toxic work environments revile, repress, and ridicule differing opinions. (see Table 3-2)

Toxic Culture	Enabling Culture
Revile – condescending and censuring	**Respect** – appreciative and attentive
Repress – stifling and discouraging	**Request** – open and encouraging
Ridicule – derisive and belittling	**Record** – valued and noteworthy

Table 3-2: Reaching an agreement in two workplace cultures – toxic vs. enabling.

Since most organizational decisions are forward-looking, the decision-makers' future orientation or mindset, that is, whether they are optimistic or pessimistic, is a determining factor. Thus, a consensus-building leader requires a pragmatic optimistic mindset to be:

(1) open to both optimism-based inputs and pessimism-based ideas,

(2) appreciative of and able to analyze each contrasting contribution into its parts,

(3) able to combine the different worldviews through synthesis and form the most optimal decision for the organization.

The act of synthesizing traditionally opposing worldviews of optimism and pessimism, whether in a team environment or within oneself, is pragmatic optimism. A leader's approach to dissenting viewpoints is easily assessed by the people with whom they work.

In a crisis, virtually every fact pushes you down toward pessimism—only your will can pull you up in the direction of optimism. Pragmatic optimism lets you maximize the best of both worlds, as depicted in Figure 3-2.

The Pragmatic Optimist Is Able To...

Visualize positivity, yet envision negativity

Persevere, yet give up strategically; lose to win

Prepare for the best, yet expect the worst

Focus on success, yet driven by loss avoidance

Focus on the solution, yet concentrate on the problem

Display hopefulness, yet admit the difficulty

Externalize confidence, yet know limitations

Seek to restore control, yet avoid uncontrollable elements

Figure 3-2: Pairings of optimism with pessimism traits to form the pragmatic optimism mindset

Up Close and Personal

Take the time to read more about Doug Lindsay's story to gain a deeper understanding of his pragmatic optimistic approach to his medical crisis and later the surgery that saved his life. You can follow the link here, or Google *This college dropout was bedridden for 11 years. Then he invented a surgery and cured himself, by Ryan Prior.*

After reading more about Doug, what pessimistic and optimistic traits do you think Doug avoided?

_____

_____

_____

_____

What pessimistic and optimistic traits (other than those already discussed in this chapter) did he exhibit?

_____

_____

_____

_____

Which of the blurry words or phrases on the book cover are you susceptible to when a crisis hits and how do you plan to avoid them in the future? Here is the list: *fearful, careless, castle-in-the-sky, naïve, withdrawn, casual, isolated, la-la land, doubtful, inattentive, starry-eyed, despondent, doomster, presumptuous, nervous, cocky, ruffled, loss of control, unrealistic, Chicken Little, helpless, gullible, demoralized, reckless, rattled, laissez-faire, half-baked, and overconfident.*

_____

_____

_____

_____

CHAPTER FOUR

Clarity in Chaos

Left unchecked, history will seek to repeat itself—it is the vision of leaders that changes the course of history.

What you will learn in this chapter:
- The value of vision in a crisis.
- Seeing through the fog of crisis.
- Crisis: a brutal test of your vision.
- The infectious nature of vision.
- How a purpose recreates a path and a plan through a crisis.
- A vision as the antithesis of a crisis.
- How your vision sustains you in a crisis.

A Leader's Vision in a Crisis

The previous chapter presented pragmatic optimism as the optimal mindset for a leader at all times, especially during a crisis. Yet, what does that translate to concerning behaviors? The cognitive behavioral model in Chapter Two displays how a person's mindset generates thoughts that lead to feelings and behaviors. But what are those particular behaviors reflected in a leader with a pragmatic optimistic mindset? This and the following five chapters are about *the six behaviors of pragmatic optimistic leaders*.

A significant characteristic of a crisis is that it puts organization-al goals in jeopardy, and one of the leader's most important roles is to respond to the predicament, resolve the catastrophe, and put the organization back on track.[118, 119] If a development does not assail your vision and cast doubt over it, it is likely not a crisis. Studies show that optimists have a higher chance of achieving success and accomplishing their goals despite a crisis.[120] Thus, *clarity in chaos* is a vision-driven determination of a pragmatic optimist to achieve their objectives despite difficulties and obstacles created by a crisis. For pragmatic optimists, it is not about the proverbial light at the end of the tunnel; it is about perceiving their vision as the light that guides them through the tunnel of tribulation. This is the first of six strategies for leading during a crisis based on the pragmatic optimism mindset.

Some time ago, I stumbled on an article produced by one of the Ivy League business school publications that essentially said, "Vision does not matter during a crisis! Because there are many urgent matters to attend to, vision must take a back seat." Nothing could be farther from best practice. Based on my hands-on experience, exposure to leaders of every stripe, and empirical research findings, the paraphrased statement is not only false; the opposite is the truth. Vision matters the most during a crisis.

"My interest is in the future because I am going to spend the rest of my life there." - Charles Kettering, social philosopher

A vision is an outward expression of an optimistic mindset because it positively depicts a future-based expectancy. I have yet to see a leader who succeeds with a pessimistic vision. In fact, the words "pessimistic" and "vision" do not belong in the same sentence. Having said that, many visions have gloom and doom as a backdrop—but, at the same time, the contrasting proposition of the vision, that ideal expressed in the mission, vision, and values that the organization strives for and bends its energies toward, is almost always positive. Otherwise, what is the point?

A Crisis Kicks the Tires on Your Vision

How can we determine the quality of a vision? In the long run, the enduring and sustainable growth of the organization relative to its peers is an output of the quality of the leader's vision.[121] That is the thesis of Jim Collins' bestseller *Good to Great*. Making that determination takes many years of painstakingly documenting and rigorously analyzing the performance of the subject firm and its peers.

There is another way to test the quality of a vision that is faster to produce, easier to assess, narrower to analyze, but more brutal in its operation. Crises are a more frequent test of the quality of a vision. According to our research-backed arguments in Chapter One, nothing reveals a leader's true substance better than a crisis. Therefore, since a vision is an integral element of leadership, it is no surprise that a crisis reveals a vision's true essence, strengths, and weaknesses.

What I like about this approach is that you do not need an army of analysts to verify whether your vision has passed the crisis test. It is a vision quality test that can be self-administered, and you can make changes on the go.

There are at least three areas of a vision on which a crisis will kick the tires. Adversity will reveal whether a vision:

1. **Was ever *conceived*:** Does a true vision *really* exist? It may surprise you that many organizations do not have a true vision. While many establishments have written vision statements, in reality, the words have never leaped off the pages. It could be that the vision was never operationalized or only comes alive when convenient or active in a haphazard way. So, the firm that does not live its vision has no advantage over a firm that does not have a vision. When a crisis hits and the vision takes a back seat, it confirms that a true vision was never conceived in the first place. Finally, more

evidence of a nonexistent or ill-conceived vision is persistent confusion and a lack of clear direction when the enterprise is thrown into adversity.

2. **Has your** *commitment*: What became clear to me at an early stage as I managed senior leaders, partnered with fellow executives, reported to top decision-makers, and now teach leaders, is that it is easy for leaders to have a perfunctory or noncommittal relationship with vision. This is the trap into which many professional managers fall.

   Many leaders inherited their vision and never took the time to develop a commitment to it. When a leader's desire to resolve a crisis rises above their commitment to their vision, that leader's vision has failed a crisis-administered quality assurance test. How far will a crisis have to push you before you scrap your vision? It is not surprising that several internally-originated crises that involve the leader usually result from a lack of leadership commitment to the vision. Typically, it may be hard to differentiate committed from noncommitted leaders, but not during a crisis. Adversity lays bare the quality of an individual's commitment to the vision they purport to champion.

3. **Has a broad** *connection*: A well-conceived vision that is operationalized and backed by a strong commitment from leadership may still fail a crisis-induced quality assurance assessment if it does not connect with the hearts and heads of the team. You may believe in the vision, but does your team believe in it, too? Interestingly, my research data empirically links a team's belief in a vision to the team's belief in the leader. In other words, if your team does not believe in you, they will *not* believe in your vision. The leader is inextricably interwoven with their vision.

   It may be challenging for leaders to validate their team's connection to the vision. The leader may miss the uncomplimentary whispers, eye rolls, and cynical remarks, signs of a disconnected team in noncrisis times. But watch out for the team's connection to your organizational aspirations during turbulence, and you will notice what has been hiding in plain sight.

Vision is Contagious

An English translation of the original German quote by Fredrich Nietzsche states: "He who has a WHY to live can bear with almost any HOW."[122] If you have a why—a purpose, or a vision that is based on your values—if you understand what is driving you, you can endure virtually all difficulties that come your way.

Gordon Allport is regarded as the father of personality psychology since he was the first to concentrate on the study of personality. Allport, in the preface he wrote for Viktor Frankl's *Man's Search for Meaning*, a book that has sold over 10 million copies and has been translated into 24 languages, positioned having a purpose in life (PIL) as fundamental to the human experience in general and periods of crisis in particular.

> "If there is a [PIL] at all, there must be a purpose in suffering and in dying. But no man can tell another what this purpose is. Each must find out for himself, and must accept the responsibility that his answer prescribes. If he succeeds, he will continue to grow in spite of all indignities."[123]

Frankl was a vocal poster child for the central role of purpose in life in general and during adversity in particular.

"Be like a postage stamp. Stick to it until you get there." – Anonymous

He frequently quoted Nietzsche's epigram, "He who has a why..." and credited it for the extraordinary resilience and perseverance that saw him through three years in Nazi concentration camps and the murder of his parents, brothers, and wife.

As crucial as PIL is to the individual, so is a vision to the organization. Your organizational vision is the WHY of your existence.

A study conducted on Nietzsche's epigram tested whether having a why, a vision, is a source of resilience when facing difficulties like a crisis. The study concluded that "... in the times of adversities, high levels of PIL can engender the ability to bounce back... Overall, therefore, our findings draw attention to the interconnections among PIL, resilience, and life goal attainment." [124]

Millions of people around the world are inspired by Frankl's optimism-fueled vision because of the contagious nature of vision.[125] Pragmatic optimistic leaders recognize that when they act on their vision with optimism, their stakeholders are more likely than not to respond with optimism. For example, when insiders at a publicly traded company, such as senior executives and other key decision-makers, buy the company's shares, the stock price tends to increase. Why? Because such an expression of optimism by insiders creates a bullish investor sentiment (the stock market's phrase for optimism) that leads investors to buy more of that company's shares. Consequently, stock prices go up because leaders are seen expressing their commitment to the organization's vision.

A leader's vision is also contagious during a crisis. When a leader takes action and creates a clear vision of optimism, stakeholders around them will take note of their confidence-expressing behavior. Such stakeholders will become motivated by the leader's optimistic outlook on the situation and adopt similar forward-looking behaviors. Subsequently, they will go out of their way to influence others and garner support for the leader's vision.

Vision: The Distinguishing Quality of a Leader

It follows, therefore, that if one competence qualifies an individual to be called a leader, it is the ability to take a group of people from where they are to where they can be. Here is my view on leadership and vision. The verb "lead" and the noun "leader" assume the presence of three essential elements:

1. A purpose
2. A path, and
3. A plan.

I have found this three-prong approach to articulating a complex subject like vision to be simple to grasp and streamlined for execution. Based on the purpose, path, and plan (3Ps), a leader will determine the overall goal for the team and delegate actionable objects[126] based on each team member's specialty.[127] The team as a whole determines the overall level of success of a goal.

A participant in my study recalled how a seasoned health and safety executive said to a multidisciplinary crisis response team in the wake of a fatal industrial accident in an oil and gas operating facility, "Your job is X—go and get X done. Your job is Y—go get Y done… if we do all what [we are] supposed to do, the outcome [will be] good." The crisis was successfully brought under control in record time, operations came back online sixty percent sooner, and millions of dollars of daily production value were saved. Such is the power of cohesive activities aligned with the organization's 3Ps.

Purpose — To borrow Nietzsche's usage, this is the WHY of an organization. Here, I bundle three separate but interconnected elements together—mission, vision, and values (MVV)—to form an organizational purpose. Let's define them.

A mission is critical. Your answer to the question "What does the organization exist for?" is your mision.

On the other hand, a vision is the *future-focused* summary of goals and aspirations that can be explained in one

"There were three additional rules of Einstein's work that stand out for use in our science, our problems, and our times. First, out of clutter find simplicity. Second, from discord make harmony. Third, in the middle of difficulty lies opportunity."
— John Archibald Wheeler (1979), US theoretical physicist

sentence or phrase. A vision asks, "Who would you like to be when you grow up?" It is future-oriented. Visions are prospective, constructive, and optimistic by nature. Vision sets the direction for everyone in the organization in the broadest possible terms.

Your vision should stretch you without breaking you. It should dominate your waking thoughts without keeping you awake all night.

Research has shown that leaders who are committed to their vision are more likely to pursue those goals and achieve them than those who may be equally optimistic but don't value their vision.[128] As you reflect on your leadership, what is your mission? What do you exist for? What are your values? What do you stand for?

Path — This is HOW your organization will accomplish its purpose.

This is more commonly known as the strategy: the comprehensive map that charts the path for moving an organization from where it is to where it desires to be, as articulated by its purpose. The path is one level below MVV in terms of details.[129] Strategy narrows the broad direction established by MVV. It transforms purpose into significant objectives, competitive positioning, resources required, partners needed, major activities, what success looks like, and performance metrics that must be monitored to achieve the vision over a multiyear time horizon. A crisis tests multiple components of a strategy.

As stated in Chapter One, no strategy survives contact with a crisis. A strategy is usually so significantly impacted by a crisis that it should be revised as part of a post-crisis review. However, many leaders miss this salient point, resulting in mortally wounded strategies that have lost their effectiveness.

The best strategies are translated into roadmaps, a visual aid that captures complex strategies on a page. This roadmap shows everyone in the organization the path that should be taken to achieve the strategy's overall aim.

The shelf life of a strategy varies by organization, competition, industry, consumer taste, and regulatory environment. Notwithstanding, the consensus among management experts is the days are gone when a strategy can last fifteen-plus years. Today, strategies need to be revised every three to five years or in the aftermath of a crisis. The depth of revision following a predicament depends on the severity of the crisis.

Plan — This is the WHAT that identifies specific tactics.

The plan operationalizes the path. Therefore, tactics contain far greater details than the strategy and reflect a shorter time horizon. A plan converts the components of the path into activities, decisions, and actions that need to be taken hourly, daily, weekly, monthly, quarterly, and yearly to accomplish the strategy.

A plan is far nimbler and more amenable to change. It can change as often as necessary to achieve the strategy. Among the 3Ps, the plan is the most exposed to a crisis and where leadership success or failure begins to occur when faced with adversity. Therefore, let us drill down deeper into what should happen when goals encounter a crisis.

Focused, Yet Flexible — Avoid DUMB Goals

A common weakness I've observed among leaders is an unwillingness to adjust pre-crisis plans to crisis realities. This flaw is widespread among individuals with unrestrained optimism. Such leaders have an illusion of control in an out-of-control situation, thus appearing to be out of touch and lacking credibility by insisting on pursuing unrealistic goals.

Crisis, by its nature, significantly undermines the assumptions underlying some strategic objectives and plans. When leaders treat these pre-crisis goals as sacrosanct

> *"Start where you are. Use what you have. Do what you can."*
> *– Arthur Ashe, tennis player*

and unchangeable, they set up their organization to flounder through adversity. A pragmatic optimist walks the fine line between being determined and being obstinate.

A failure to adjust organizational objectives to reflect crisis realities could turn SMART goals into DUMB goals. How do you recognize a DUMB goal? It is:

D- Destructive in its aim. A crisis naturally stirs up desperation; if left unchecked, desperate people do desperate things during desperate times. Refusing to realign your goals in the light of crisis-induced developments by failing to revise assumptions may cause a leader to desperately look for quick fixes that complicate an already complex situation.

U- Unrealistic in its form. A significant purpose of a well-executed crisis assessment is recognizing and defining new realities. This is because a crisis is a reality-altering event, business as usual becomes business unusual, and leaders will do well to acknowledge its impact on specific objectives. Ignoring this truth leads to chasing the wind and aggravating the frustrations of one's team because what used to be a rallying plan has become a discouraging myth. Speaking at Yale University in 1962, US President John F. Kennedy said, "For the great enemy of truth is very often not the lie—deliberate, contrived and dishonest—but the myth—persistent, persuasive, and unrealistic."

M- Machiavellian in its execution. Wielding the power of their office, leaders can force the continued implementation of goals that a crisis has viciously damaged. Forcing the execution of unrealistic goals may derail the organization from its publicized values. Denial of a crisis impact's reality usually leads to deceit and trickery during implementation.

B- Baseless in its purpose. Continuing to work on the goals that are no longer reasonable disconnects you from the three components of your purpose: MVV. Consequently, the goals become baseless during a crisis, since they only make sense when connected to the path (strategy) linked to the purpose.

The 2018-2019 Boeing 737 MAX airplane crashes offer a relevant case study illustrating how SMART goals morph into DUMB goals.

In a television documentary investigating the two airplane crashes that resulted in the deaths of 346 people, US Congressman and Chair of the House Committee on Transportation and Infrastructure Peter DeFazio lamented, "'Hurry it up! Hurry it up!' described the culture of Boeing."[130] This work environment encouraged frontline employees to push product design and development beyond its limits, which led to the cascading of multiple crises.

As the company was developing the Maneuvering Characteristics Augmentation System (MCAS) technology, new software for the 737 MAX designed to make the aircraft safer, Boeing ran into an emerging crisis. Safety concerns about the MCAS created the potential failure of missing the deadline to release the upgraded aircraft into the market.

Boeing discovered significant safety issues with the MCAS two years before any fatal crashes occurred. Internal documents later showed that the company's chief technical pilot, Mark Forkner, sent an alarming message to a colleague saying that the MCAS was "running rampant in the [simulation]" and described the experience as "egregious" or horrifying.[131] That was the initial crisis, the consequences of which included a negative impact on revenue, earnings, market share, stock price, and executive compensation.

Instead of adjusting their objectives, deadlines, and external commitments to focus on resolving the software issues, Boeing's leadership simply pushed ahead. This meet-the-objectives-by-all-means-necessary approach created a crisis that transformed Boeing's otherwise SMART goals into DUMB goals because they were destructive, unrealistic, Machiavellian, and baseless. The ill-advised approach triggered a culture of concealment, denial, lack of integrity, and inauthenticity because it violated two central values of the company on how it operates and acts: "Start with engineering excellence" and "Lead on safety, quality, integrity, and sustainability." [132, 133]

The avoidable crisis directly cost Boeing a staggering $20.7 billion due to the grounding of the 737 MAX, and when all was said and done, the indirect cost stands at an astounding $60 billion.[134, 135] With that, the combined cost to Boeing has claimed the inglorious title of the most expensive corporate crisis in history, surpassing BP's mishandling of the 2010 Deepwater Horizon crisis (which cost a total of $68 billion).

"Your goal should be out of reach, but not out of sight." – Anita DeFrantz, captain of the American rowing team at the 1976 summer Olympics.

Without a doubt, a crisis will threaten to derail organizational goals articulated by the leader. However, a pragmatic optimist is more likely to succeed at their goals despite a crisis because they will adjust them to current realities. A pessimist, on the other hand, is more likely to disengage when faced with difficulties, while an optimist tends to be overconfident.[136, 137] The conscious process of pragmatic optimism that combines pessimistic and optimistic mindsets helps create a decision-making framework that avoids DUMB goals.

A Crisis Reduces the Visibility of Vision

On a clear and sunny day, you can see the picturesque city skyline of Toronto, Canada, from Lake Ontario opposite the metropolis. But on some days, usually in the early morning when the air on the land's surface becomes saturated due to the influence of the lake, thick fog engulfs the city, and visibility becomes poor. The fog appears like a low-level cloud and just sits there, obstructing the view—that is an analogy for how a crisis engulfs an organization and risks obscuring its 3Ps.

In fact, a crisis is the antithesis of the 3Ps. The primary value of the 3Ps is to create clarity and confidence by providing direction, while a crisis aims to create ambiguity and doubt by casting a fog of uncertainty over an organization.

A crisis stands between an organization and its 3Ps, making it appear as though they are unattainable. The fog of war, in military terms, is a situation that is filled with confusion and chaos.[138] That is the unfortunate perception that internal and external stakeholders have of an organization reeling in a crisis. When poorly handled due to the wrong leadership mindset,

> *"If your faith doesn't remove the mountain... get to climbing."*
> — *Johnnie Dent Jr., author*

the fog of a crisis could result in the mission being mistaken, vision being vulnerable, values being violated, the strategy being stranded, and plans being perplexing.

True leaders know that the present, no matter how desirable or disastrous, does not define the future; that is why they create a vision and develop the 3Ps. In a crisis, the present attempts to erode the gains and goodwill of the past while it seems to consume the prospects and plans for the future—all you see is the upheaval. However, a pragmatic optimistic leader sees through the fog of a crisis by reinforcing it. Many crises are not bleak—an individual's perception of them usually may be bleak. Having clarity amid chaos is the value of a pragmatic optimism mindset.

Vision is the Antithesis of Crisis

Here are at least four ways a vision is the converse of a crisis: focus, future, formation, and feeling. These distinctions are crucial to help an individual develop an effective pragmatic optimistic mindset by recognizing the appropriate traits of pessimism and optimism to combine or cast off.

First, a leader's vision **focuses** the mind on opportunities and possibilities, while a crisis forces the mind to emphasize threats and uncertainties. A vision's focus is squarely on growth maximization, while a crisis's focus is on the introduction of risk, ambiguity, and damages. Thus, in response, a pragmatic optimist will seek to keep driving growth while minimizing losses from the crisis.

Second, vision says, "There is a **future** full of success and fulfillment if we do A, B, and C." That future is worth spending resources on to achieve that vision. A vision points the organization toward a fruitful future. On the contrary, a crisis says, "The future is at risk, and your survival depends on what you do in the here and now." Turmoil considerably constricts the time horizon to the immediate and discourages forward-looking actions. But a pragmatic optimist attends to the immediacy of a crisis to mitigate the risks and lower uncertainties without losing sight of the long-range vision. Your belief and conviction in your vision have to supersede the doubt that comes from a crisis.

Third, the **formations** of a vision and a crisis are vastly different. A vision is a product of thoughtfulness, creativity, and intentionality. Leaders imagine their vision, work on it, dream of it, constantly think about it, articulate it, pitch it to others, and enlist others to adopt it. On the other hand, a crisis is unintended, unplanned, and unexpected. Yet, because a crisis is as certain in our world as there will be a tomorrow, a pragmatic optimistic mindset enables you always to consider downside risks as much as you focus on upside opportunities.

Fourth, a vision is defined by a hope that stirs up **feelings** of confidence and optimism expressed through the 3Ps. A strategy is a document of hope; according to Napoleon Bonaparte, the leader is a dealer in hope. A vision creates feelings of positive expectations, while a crisis causes feelings of hopelessness and helplessness. A crisis threatens the going concern assumption of an enterprise. This is why pragmatic optimists exert themselves during a crisis to continue pursuing their 3Ps and infuse hope into an otherwise hopeless crisis.[139, 140]

Your "WHY" in Your "Why Me?" Moment

A ship has two anchors. One fits the popular image of an anchor and is used in a harbor to stay in position. This conventional anchor is dropped to keep the ship from drifting away from the shoreline. The other, far less known anchor, is used when a ship is in the middle of the sea and caught in a storm. This other device is called a sea anchor or parachute anchor. When deployed, its parachute-like form stabilizes the ship as the storm rages.

The "why me?" moment is a crisis phase where uncertainties and doubts replace certainties and confidence. Like a sea anchor, a leader's WHY will steady them in their "why me?" moment and stabilize them through the disorder in these four ways: rallying point, relevance, reward, and resilience (4Rs).

First, your WHY creates a vision-based clarity within the confusion of a crisis that becomes the **rallying point** for your team. Effective leaders remind their team of the purpose of the organization, as well as the path and plan. They ensure that the mission is top of mind and dig deeper into the organizational values. A silo mentality and interdepartmental turf wars severely damage an organization during turbulence. Beginning with the WHY and reinforcing it throughout the ordeal will rally the team behind a common cause and temper divisions that a crisis tends to exploit.

Second, a clear vision creates **relevance** that connects a team to the 3Ps, the organization and the leader. Relevance means that a vision gives meaning to work and makes team members feel that they are a part of something greater than themselves. Conversely, a crisis diminishes the meaning of work and casts doubt on the once esteemed purpose. To counter that erosion of confidence, true leaders use their vision to remind their team of the relevance of their work and to give meaning to all they do. When a leader does not lose sight of the vision but continues to connect it to team/individual goals and objectives, the team members will regain a sense of relevance and resolve.

Many years ago, during an interview for a senior management position, I asked my interviewer, an executive in the company, "Ten years is a long time to be with an organization. Why have you spent that long with the company?"

I hoped for a genuine response but readied myself for corporate-speak that I would need to poke at with follow-up questions before extracting useful content. But I didn't need any follow-up questions. The executive was forthright right off the bat: "It's because I see the decisions that I make in my office come to life on the streets and influence people's lives," he said as he turned toward the window and pointed to the busy street below.

> *"Be bold and be right. If you're not bold, you're not going to do much of anything. If you're not right, you're not going to be here."*
> *— Steve Ballmer to Satya Nadella, incoming CEO of Microsoft*

That was an important lesson for me. From then on, I'd take the time to understand my role's relevance in the vision's context. It made my job more meaningful and steadied me like a sea anchor through difficult times. That is the power of relevance.

Third, a leader's WHY is the source of their **reward**. People in public-facing positions in a company are often easily rewarded for their vision, like the executive in the interview story above, because they see the value of their output in the marketplace. But I believe that even people in back-office roles who do not engage with the public, such as medical researchers, can also develop a reward system connected to the WHY of their organization. Yes, they have to be more creative to see the connection between what they do and the reward that comes from seeing its impact, but it is doable.

Here is a story that illustrates what I mean. In January 2017, Tomas Dahl faced a dire health crisis when he was diagnosed with tonsil cancer. All conventional treatments—radiation, chemotherapy, and surgery—failed, leaving him only "a few months to live."[141] However, in 2018, after undergoing a breakthrough cancer therapy newly developed by Dr. James Allison[4] and Dr. Tasuku Honjo, Dahl became cancer-free!

When the two immunologists were being awarded the 2018 Nobel Prize for Medicine, Dahl got a chance to meet the medicine laureates and expressed his profound gratitude: "Thank you for saving my life!" Overwhelmed with a sense of relevance, Dr. Allison said this about meeting Dahl: "Meeting the people who have benefitted from our research is the real prize for me." To Dr. Allison, feeling a sense of relevance is at least as important as the exceptional prize he received.

Unfortunately, the higher you go up the corporate ladder, the more disconnected you could be from the frontlines where your purpose and relevance reside. Dare to build a bridge across the moat and step out of your walled castle for regular doses of relevance.

Lastly, your WHY generates your **resilience**. Diligence, powered by resilience, beats intelligence. Dr. Angela Lee Duckworth, professor of psychology at the University of Pennsylvania, demonstrated in her research that grit is the strongest predictor of success.[142] She defines grit as the ability to pursue one's goals despite setbacks and crises.[143]

Your WHY is the key to your grit. It allows you to keep moving even when you're facing a ferocious headwind.

One of the vital lessons I learned in my doctoral journey is that attaining the highest level of academics is not determined by intelligence but by resilience, driven by one's WHY, rooted in endurance, and powered by perseverance. Sounds counterintuitive, I know. The saying is true: "The fastest runner doesn't always win the race, and the strongest warrior doesn't always win the battle."

---

4   As of the writing of this book, Dr. Allison is the chair of immunology at the M.D. Anderson Cancer Center, University of Texas, while Dr. Honjo is a professor of immunology at Kyoto University.

You may be fast or strong, but if you don't add grit to your portfolio, you'll lose the race or the battle when a crisis ups the ante. Astonishingly, according to the Council of Graduate Schools, nearly half of doctoral candidates—despite their impressive academic pedigree—do NOT graduate in a ten-year window.[144] It won't be an exaggeration to assume that the incompletion rate could be higher than 50% if one considers the standard program duration of three or five years (depending on the program).

Such a poor success rate by arguably some of the most intelligent people (at least from an academic perspective) is a telling sign of the power of resilience.

Willingness to Fight

There is a principle in military history and literature that refers to a military force's willingness to fight, and several studies have examined soldiers' will (or lack thereof) to engage enemy combatants in dire circumstances.[145, 146, 147]

Reflecting on the 2014-15 collapse of the Iraqi Army, US Secretary of Defense Ashton Carter said, "What apparently happened is the Iraqi forces just showed no will to fight… We can give them training, we can give them equipment—we obviously can't give them the will to fight."[148]

The proverb "You can lead a horse to water, but you can't make it drink" rings true in this context. Soldiers who have the most sophisticated weapons, equipment, and supplies but who lack the will to fight will lose to an ill-equipped and underfunded but highly determined opposing force with such a will.

While willingness to fight can be outwardly influenced, it can only be internally produced. One's will is deeply personal and powered by intrinsic values like honor, national identity, determination, responsibility, resolve, national pride, doggedness, and courage.[5]

Your WHY creates that will to fight because it gives you and your organization the reasons to engage. Your will to fight must shine through if your organization is to stand a chance against and excel in a crisis. That is what it means to have clarity in chaos.

Having the resources to fight means little without reasons to fight.

The image below represents the best of both worlds that the pragmatic optimistic mindset enables you to have in relation to clarity in chaos.

To Achieve Clarity In Chaos, The Pragmatic Optimist Is Able To...

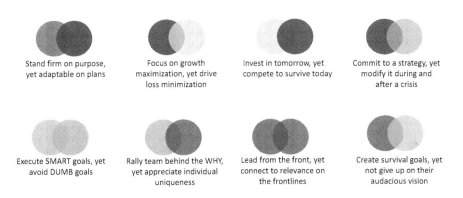

Stand firm on purpose, yet adaptable on plans

Focus on growth maximization, yet drive loss minimization

Invest in tomorrow, yet compete to survive today

Commit to a strategy, yet modify it during and after a crisis

Execute SMART goals, yet avoid DUMB goals

Rally team behind the WHY, yet appreciate individual uniqueness

Lead from the front, yet connect to relevance on the frontlines

Create survival goals, yet not give up on their audacious vision

Figure 4-1: Pairings of optimism with pessimism traits to form the pragmatic optimism mindset for achieving clarity in chaos

---

5   Lacking the willingness to fight is not the same as retreating from battle to fight another day, which is a strategic move.

Up Close and Personal

To have clarity in chaos, a leader needs to have a vision. They must understand their mission and values. These characteristics describe the leader and can be easily observed by all the team members. Take the time to understand where you are now as a leader, and where you see yourself in the future based on your vision.

What is your mission? ("What do you exist for?")

_____
_____
_____
_____

What is your vision? ("Who would you like to be when you grow up?")

_____
_____
_____
_____

What are your values? ("What do you stand for?")

_____
_____
_____
_____

CHAPTER FIVE

Control Under Fire

If you [the leader] are scared, terrified, hungry, and cold, they will be scared, terrified, hungry, and cold.

— **General Colin Powell**, former US Secretary of State

What you will learn in this chapter:
- Your feelings influence your leading.
- The myth of a "tough leader."
- From self-regulation to group regulation.
- The power of a leader's calm in a crisis.
- How a crisis transforms you into a different person.
- Three conditions for group regulation.
- The positives of negative emotions.

How You Feel Directs How You Lead

In 2011, US White House Fellow Amy Wilkinson asked General Colin Powell during a Q&A session about the main characteristic of effective leadership. She wanted him to boil down the extensive field of leadership into a single quality that the best leaders demonstrate.

The first word out of General Powell's mouth was "trust," which is an emotional state of the brain.[149, 150] The retired military officer strongly linked emotions and leadership in his response. In Chapter

Two, I stated that what you know in a profession's body of knowledge drives your technical skills, but who you are as a person drives your leadership skills. Thus, leadership competency is heavily influenced by an individual's emotional state, which influences and determines the team's emotional well-being in any situation.

General Powell stated that great leaders consciously create an environment that engenders trust. He then proceeded to home in on the role of emotions and self-regulation by recalling his military training at the US Army Infantry School, Fort Benning, Georgia:

> They would teach us at the Infantry School. 'No matter how cold it is, Lieutenant, you must never look cold. No matter how hungry you all are, you must never appear hungry. No matter how terrified you are, Lieutenant, you must never look terrified. Because if you are scared, terrified, hungry and cold, [the soldiers you lead] will be scared, terrified, hungry and cold.

It is noteworthy that the scenario Powell chose to situate leaders in, where their quality can be assessed, is a crisis condition defined by risk, impact, stress, emotions, uncertainty, and pressure (RISE-UP). This view aligns with the justifications presented in Chapter One to the effect that nothing reveals the quality of a leader better than a crisis.

Why do emotions play such a critical role in your leadership? It is because emotions have a three-prong influence on:

1. You, the leader – **Personal engagement**. A leader brings their complete self to their leadership role. Personality. Feelings. Behaviors. Memories. Your whole self.
2. Your relationship with your team – **Social engagement**. In an interpersonal engagement with the world, a leader becomes aware of the emotional state of their team and is driven to become more aware of those around them.

3. Your team productivity – **Organizational impact and leadership outcome**. A leader is focused on the output of their team.

This chapter examines the elephant in the room when crisis leadership is discussed: the importance of understanding and managing the emotions of the leader and their team when their world is turned upside down.

You Cannot Regulate What You Do Not Recognize

The import of emotional influence is lost on many leaders because they disavow emotions (sometimes vehemently) and are generally oblivious of their impact. Here is how I have seen it develop: As leaders progress professionally and become more immersed in their careers, they tend to believe that they are more rational than emotional. A common way of thinking for them is, "I do not make emotional decisions because of all the knowledge I've acquired about the business and industry. I am fully rational in what I do."

Nothing could be farther from the truth because, as Carl Jung asserts, "Emotion is the chief source of consciousness."[151] If you are conscious, you are emotional; deal with it. Yet, many leaders embrace the common myth of an entirely rational image of themselves.

The reality is closer to the configuration of a digital device. Your professional body of knowledge is like an app; it solves problems and executes commands. Your emotions are like your operating system (iOS, Android, etc.); you cannot engage as a human being, including professionally, without emotions, just as an app cannot function without an operating system.

Generally, most people don't pay attention to their operating systems until it is unavoidable, like when it's time for an upgrade. Unfortunately, many leaders allow their emotions free rein to process inputs unconsciously in the background without their discernment. However, when emotions become a potential problem (e.g., a source of career derailment), some leaders start to recognize their importance and "update" them.

Whether you recognize them or not, emotions power your self-reflections, social engagements, productivity, and decision-making. They act as your interface to the world. Ignoring them makes them a potential tripwire instead of an ally. That is because "the psychological rule says that when an inner situation is not made conscious, it happens outside as fate."[152] The first step in managing anything is acquiring information about it; you cannot regulate what you do not recognize. Leaders, as humans, are emotional beings who are grounded in sentiments, and emotional awareness is a powerful capability, especially during a crisis.[153, 154, 155, 156, 157]

Stone-Cold: The Tough Leader Myth

Let's examine one of the most common leadership myths regarding emotions, which is the "Tough Leader" myth. The first part of General Powell's description of an effective leader, which describes the ideal behaviors of leaders when under intense pressure, is one of the most misunderstood leadership principles worldwide. *"No matter how cold it is, Lieutenant, you must never look cold. No matter how hungry you all are, you must never appear hungry. No matter how terrified you are, Lieutenant, you must never look terrified"* is often misinterpreted to mean that a leader must show toughness by being:

1. **Expressionless** – This reflects how the "tough leader" interacts with the world: deadpan, inexpressive, and inscrutable.[158] I have seen leaders take pride in being poker-faced because they believe the people won't know what they are thinking.

2. **Affectionless** – This is how the leader interacts with themselves; ruthless, unfeeling, and unemotional.[159]

3. **Humorless** – This is an effort to appear severe and a wish to be taken seriously. Such individuals are grim, stern, and unsmiling.[160] Some humorless leaders don't bother acknowledging greetings;

they grunt in response as they continue on a critical mission to save the world (insert sarcasm here).

4. **Aloofness** – This is being distant, disengaged, and unapproachable.[161, 162] Some leaders believe that they will be disrespected if they show up often. Even when an organization has an "open-door policy," team members can see the barricade of aloofness around such leaders.

5. **Blameless** – This is the "tough" leader who puts up a persona of being inerrant, faultless, and perfect. The inability to make a mistake is crucial to a "tough" leader's image; many of them demonstrate this trait. They misuse their formal authority to create an image of perfection. Such individuals typically struggle in leadership contexts where formal authority is absent, and they have to rely on "soft power" and relationship-building to earn the trust and commitment of the team.[163]

6. **Heartless** – This is a cold-hearted, unfeeling, uncaring, and non-responsive leadership that results in low employee engagement and morale levels.[164] Such individuals see it as a strength to be unmoved and insensitive, even during a crisis. When being unflappable (which can be a strength) is taken to the extreme or overused, the leader may be seen as heartless.

7. **Fearless** – This is leadership that projects being unafraid, dauntless, and intrepid. This mythical leadership persona equates strength with being fearless and appearing ready to lose everything. In reality, fear is a call to action, a sign that something valuable is at risk and needs to be preserved. A fearless individual can be a dangerous leader because that person is susceptible to taking egregious risks. Being fearless is not being courageous. When leaders are courageous, they acknowledge the presence of fear but still press forward to lessen the impact of fear. They can be successful despite being fearful.

I have always found these common misinterpretations of leadership to be quite striking and somewhat dramatic. Unfortunately, it is the root of several leadership challenges.

During my career, I have participated in and chaired several Talent Review Committees where promotions of employees are determined. So, I have witnessed the transitions of several professionals from individual contributor roles to frontline management and all the way to the C-suite. As individual contributors, many candidates are warm, kind, friendly, sociable, accountable, compassionate, and courageous. But the moment they become managers and begin to go higher on the corporate ladder, some of them reveal their deep-seated belief in the prevalent "tough leader" myth and become less expressive, less affectionate, less humorous, more aloof, more blameless, more heartless, and more fearless.

For some individuals, their approach to leadership is the outcome of a national culture entrenched in this "tough leader" doctrine.

Contrary to this unreasonable expectation of leadership, I believe leaders should embrace the fact that they are subject to emotions and see that mental state as an ally that can be leveraged to produce *control* under fire.

What Is Control Under Fire?

Most of the executives who participated in my doctoral research and postdoctoral study demonstrate what I call *control under fire* by combining the principles of self-regulation with the doctrines of group regulation in a crisis context. The former is deeply researched, while the latter, though equally critical, is not yet well studied.

To define control under fire, let's use an analogy in the science of sound waves. The amplitude is the amount of energy a wave carries. Waves with high and low amplitudes carry large and small amounts of energy respectively. Amplitude is represented as up-and-down waves above and below a baseline. Thus, the amplitude of a wave is the measure of the peak swings (up or down) versus the baseline (see Figure 5-1).

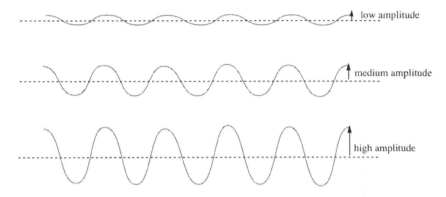

Figure 5-1: The amplitudes of sound waves

In the same way, emotions are like waves. Hence, when they come thick and fast, you might describe the feeling as having "a wave of emotions." Even when you don't sense these emotions, their ebb and flow continue subconsciously. Therefore, self-regulation is a conscious attempt to either reduce and increase the amplitude of your emotions through "self-generated thoughts, feelings, and actions that are planned and cyclically adapted to the attainment of personal goals."[165, 166] It is cyclical because self-regulation is an iterative process where the output from previous actions is evaluated, tweaked, and adapted as an input into an ongoing scenario that requires control under fire.

Self-regulation is not advocating for a denial of emotions—quite the opposite.[167] Self-regulation requires a recognition, understanding, and embrace of one's emotions before one can deliberately apply one's beliefs and motives to lessen or intensify the amplitude of one's emotions depending on one's objectives. So, instead of being thrown around like a rag doll on a roller coaster of emotions, self-regulation puts you in the driver's seat.

The key to self-regulation is its variability, which is driven mostly by one's aims. On the one hand, a leader presenting to an audience of investors who wants to use excitement to amplify a salient point may increase the amplitude of emotions. On the other hand, a leader responding to a predicament may find it more helpful to temper their amplitude.

Seasoned managers who lead effectively find a way to reduce their emotional swings above or below a baseline—they are rarely over the top and hardly down in the dumps.[168] Self-regulation is the ability to create calm within you when you cannot calm the storm around you. This behavioral quality, a hallmark of pragmatic optimists, is challenging to achieve. Still, group regulation is even harder to accomplish because of the complexity of dealing with multiple personalities.[169]

Control under fire is about getting hold of your emotional amplitude—managing your emotional amplitude first, then your stakeholders'. The dynamic regulation of the emotions of others is group regulation. If you struggle to control your emotions, the chances are slim that you can positively influence the feelings of others.

The Science of Emotions

To understand self-regulation and group regulation, we must first understand the assortment of emotions leaders and their teams feel in general and during turbulent times.

Attempts at categorizing the plethora of human emotions date back a millennium with *The Book of Rites,* where Chinese philosopher and politician Confucius documented the seven "feelings of men" as anger, joy, fear, sadness, love, disliking, and liking.[170, 171] Since then, several Western scholars, from emotional theory pioneer William James to more recent contributors like Paul Ekman[172] and Robert Plutchik,[173] have authored different but comparable versions of the basic human emotions. While there are hundreds of emotions, I will concentrate on the most basic human emotions.

For our deep-dive discussion, I relied on a more contemporary basic emotions model, the Emotion Wheel, developed by the Juno Institute: fear, anger, sadness, surprise, joy, and love.[174] My attraction to this model stems from its comprehensive arrangement of numerous nuanced emotions derived from the six basic emotions.

Similar to how the Pragmatic Optimistic Traits Model discussed in Chapter Three empowers you to become more self-aware by being able to name and manage the optimism/pessimism-based traits you are experiencing, the Emotion Wheel (see Figure 5-2) accomplishes the same for the naming and management of emotions. As discussed earlier in this chapter, recognizing and naming emotions is a critical step toward reflecting on and regulating them, a core behavior of pragmatic optimists.

Deepening your competence to be emotionally literate enough to recognize, reflect on, and regulate emotions will make you outstanding in tumultuous situations like a crisis when most people quickly lose the ability to self-monitor and become prone to alexithymia, Greek for "no words for emotions."[175, 176] Statistically, one out of ten people is believed to experience alexithymia.[177] That is a significant number of people struggling with emotional illiteracy. However, stressful conditions like a crisis short-circuit the self-monitoring process, making it challenging for most people to recognize and regulate their emotions.

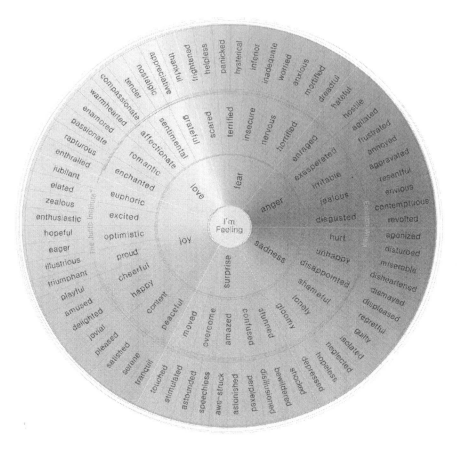

Figure 5-2: The Emotion Wheel by Juno Institute

The model contains 102 second- and third-layer emotions,[178] allowing you to view the interconnectivity of emotions from the outside in or the inside out. The Emotion Wheel is helpful to unpack, put words to, and situate your basic emotions and their offshoots for a comprehensive understanding of your feelings or those of your stakeholders.

Here is an example of an outside-in approach to using the Emotion Wheel. Let's assume you are feeling frustrated. The Emotion Wheel will let you see the possible connection of that emotion to the feeling of exasperation, which you can then explore and reflect on. After that, you will notice that exasperation is rooted in anger over a situation or toward a person, a feeling you might not have recognized initially when all you could articulate about your emotion was frustration. Thus, understanding that your feeling of frustration is rooted in anger can help you manage the emotion better.

Let's look at another example, this time working in the opposite direction. If you want to better understand a basic emotion you are feeling, you can start from the inside of the wheel and work your way out. So, if you are feeling sad, you can look at the secondary level of emotions to determine whether you are hurt, unhappy, or disappointed. Once you can name the second-order emotion, let's say "disappointed," you can then move to see whether it is due to being dismayed or displeased. Now, you have a better grasp of the original emotion and its other layers that can help you regulate them with your self-directed thoughts and reflections.

Under the traumatic conditions of a crisis, emotions cut across all six basic emotions. Few situations in life elicit such an array of reactions—some contradictory. Table 5-1 shows twenty-nine words that executives in my study used to describe their emotions during a crisis. Using the Emotion Wheel, I classified the emotions under each of the six basic emotions.

Fear	Anger	Sadness	Surprise	Joy	Love
"Anxious"	"Disgusted"	"Agonized"	"Bewildered"	"Hopeful"	"Grateful"
"Helpless"	"Exasperated"	"Disappointed"	"Confused"	"Optimistic"	
"Inadequate"	"Frustrated"	"Gloomy"	"Disillusioned"		
"Insecure"	"Irritable"	"Guilty"	"Overwhelmed"		
"Nervous"		"Regretful"	"Perplexed"		
"Panicked"		"Shameful"	"Shocked"		
"Scared"			"Speechless"		
"Worried"			"Stunned"		

Table 5-1: Quotes from research participants depicting emotions experienced during a crisis and categorized into the six basic emotions

Table 5-1 shows that most of the twenty-nine unique emotions I extracted from my interview data fall under *fear* and *surprise*—representing over 55% of the total. This is not unexpected because those basic emotions relate to people's reactions to unwelcomed, threatening, and jarring situations like a crisis.

What I found interesting about this data is that the words used to describe emotions by my research participants almost match the Emotion Wheel. Over time, they learned to be emotionally literate, since most of them confirmed that they struggled with managing emotions during a crisis in the early years of their careers. Their growth in emotional fluency confirms that self-regulation, one of the six behavioral components of the pragmatic optimism mindset, is a learnable skill.

A Crisis Brings Out Your Dark Side

A different, more disruptive, and unflattering side of you shows up when you are in stressful situations, negatively affecting colleagues and increasing your chances of failure. You become a changed person in high-risk, turbulent, and uncertain events like a crisis. This is one of the significant research findings on which the Hogan Assessments (Hogan) are founded.[179]

Developed over 30 years ago, Hogan is one of the world's oldest and most trusted workplace-based psychometric tests. Hogan is used by organizations of various sizes, including seventy-five percent of Fortune 500 companies. Relying on data from over 180 countries, Hogan is a science-based personality assessment for the work environment with a strong predictive validity.[180]

Only one of the three main Hogan reports is most relevant for this book, but briefly defining the trio is helpful to gain a holistic view of the assessments:[181]

1. **The Inside:** This report's formal name is the Motives, Values, Preferences Inventory (MVPI). It uncovers an individual's core values. It identifies a person's innermost motives and ideals which

may end up being misaligned from what the person actually does in a situation. MVPI reveals cultural and organizational fit.

2. **The Bright Side:** This report's formal name is the Hogan Personality Inventory (HPI); it captures a person's bright-side personality and uncovers how they behave at their best. HPI is a person's day-to-day or normal personality, and it helps to reveal their strengths, weaknesses, and how successful they can be in the organization.

3. **The Dark Side:** This report's formal name is the Hogan Development Survey (HDS). It is the most relevant for our discussion in this book. HDS measures and unveils dark-side personality triggered mainly by overused strengths, creating significant problems. Dark-side behaviors are also known as derailers because of their ability to cause setbacks, disrupt relationships, and undermine organizational goals.

The dark-side personality results are usually a moment of profound insights, exceptional clarity, and thoughtful discovery for leaders when I debrief them on their HDS results. While all three reports are beneficial, I have found that the leader's dark-side personality results contain a lot of aha moments. I think the reason is that this personality sneaks up on us when we are stressed and has free rein because we tend to drop our self-monitoring guards when we are mentally and emotionally strained. So, during a crisis, we are unaware that our thoughts, emotions, attitudes, opinions, and behaviors have changed under stress; it is often a seamless but consequential transition from one's normal, day-to-day bright-side personality to the dark-side disposition when a crisis hits.

A Stealth Change

According to the Hogan psychological studies, when individuals feel the immense pressure of a crisis, they tend to double down on and overuse their strengths—and what used to be reliable tools for their success suddenly begin to create the opposite effects. For example, the passion and energy that typically drives a leader to win might transform them to become volatile and ruthless under stress. Similarly, a leader whose strong suit is meticulousness and diligence may, when stressed, morph into someone obsessed with ridiculously high standards and unattainable perfection that cripples the organization.

Let us examine the two main ways a high-stress, high-risk, and high-emotion situation like a crisis may seamlessly and surreptitiously change you.

1) A different set of relational actions – According to Hogan, negative thoughts, emotions, behaviors, etc., appear and work in concert to form crisis-escalating behaviors that

   a) move you away from people (e.g., through social withdrawal, mistrust, hostility, etc.),

   b) move you against people (e.g., unhealthy competitiveness, manipulation, intimidation, etc.), or

   c) move you toward people (e.g., insecurities, eagerness to please, etc.).[182]

2) A different self-monitoring system is in place – While your bright-side personality is usually conscious of its impact on people, the dark-side disposition appears when you are NOT actively self-monitoring and managing how you show up. The dark-side personality is a temperament that thrives in stealth mode; often, everyone else but you will notice you have changed.

Using the sport of boxing as an analogy, your bright side is mostly about how hard you can hit and win, while your dark side is mostly about how hard you can get hit and remain on your feet. Emotional self-awareness and emotional literacy increase your capacity to hit harder and improve your ability to absorb stress-induced blows and keep pressing ahead.

The dark side of an individual's personality that covertly dethrones their bright-side personality is often the biggest culprit in the limitation or derailment of their career and life. But that does not have to be the case.

Start With the Person in the Mirror

As you understand the purpose and process of self-regulation to achieve control under fire, you must first acknowledge that you are the subject. If this is an art class, we are discussing you producing a self-portrait. You are the reflection in the mirror and the purpose of that reflection. You cannot self-reflect for anyone else or list things they need to do to improve.[183] You can only decide what you will do.

Some leaders admit that they do not practice self-reflection; such individuals jeopardize their successes due to the risk of their career-derailing behaviors. Self-reflection is a vital prerequisite for change. If you do not self-reflect, you cannot change.[184]

Before leaders can change others, which is the underlying belief of group regulation, they must start by changing themselves. Why? One reason is that you will be better prepared for group regulation because you know how taxing and messy change can be, having gone through the process of changing yourself. A second reason is that you will likely be more empathetic toward those going through a process of evolution, becoming a compassionate guide and a coach walking alongside them.

A third reason is that by going through the process of changing at a micro level, you will gain insights into what it takes to effect true and lasting change on a macro level. A fourth reason is that when you improve yourself first, you also model to your team how change happens. You will be modeling one of the most impactful approaches to leadership: leading by example. Doing so will reverse the normally cynical idiomatic expression into a results-oriented one: "Do as I do, not [only] as I say."

Steps to Process Emotions

With increased self-awareness and self-monitoring during a crisis, an individual is armed with the capability to methodically process emotions that would otherwise have gone under the radar. Below is a three-step process for emotional processing:[185]

1) **Seek out the emotions** – Emotional blindness is a common phenomenon in high-intensity situations like a crisis; emotions simply go unnoticed. During a crisis, everyone is subject to a degree of emotional blindness due to stress.

   But you can avoid being blindsided by your emotions. If you seek out your emotions, the chances are good that you will find them. Pause to ask yourself, "How do I feel about this debacle?" and locate your emotion(s) on the Emotion Wheel. If you feel a third-level emotion, walk it back to the core to understand the root and basic emotion. If you first recognize the basic emotion, move through the wheel to the outside to understand the broader meaning of that basic emotion to define it better.

2) **Sift through the emotions** – Take a moment to unpack and examine the emotions running through you that have now been identified. Even a five-minute exercise of writing about your emotions has been shown to have immense benefits.[186] The three-step process below can help:

   i)   Confirm your level of familiarity with the emotions. Is this feeling new? Has it happened before? In what prior situation(s) has it happened? In what context has it happened before?

   ii) Recall previous consequences of the emotions.

   iii) Review the onset and aggravating triggers of the emotions.

   In response to the question in #1 above, sifting through your emotions will enable you to respond with, "I feel _____."

3) **Search for solutions** – The question now is, "In what ways may I deal with these emotions?" Curiosity and exploration are the objectives, not precision and correctness. It is not a math problem

where you need exactness and where there is only one answer. The goal is to find *your* answer, not *the* answer.

It takes considerable courage to name, sift through, and search for solutions regarding your emotions, since ignoring them in stressful conditions is the default.

Why should we process emotions? Processing emotions helps leaders with:

1. **Identification** – This is recognition. If you can't recognize your emotions, you can't regulate them. Managers know this very

   "He who conquers others is strong. He who conquers himself is mighty." - *Lao Tzu, Chinese philosopher*

   well. You can't manage what you can't measure.

2. **Insight** – This is understanding. You will gain a deeper insight into your triggers, previous experiences, and how often you have these same emotions in the context of the current events in your life. You'll gain the understanding you need to see how your emotions are triggered and what aggravates them.

3. **Internalization** – This is meditation. The mulling-over process helps you measure these emotions with your values and recognize action items. Do these emotions represent your values, support your bright-side personality, and for what you want to be known? If these emotions contradict your values, etc., how can you turn them around? This is the point of personal growth.

Effective Leaders Exhibit Pragmatic Optimism

After experiencing the self-reflection process, understanding their emotional makeup, and calibrating their personality into a productive disposition, a leader responding to a crisis is well-positioned to project or externalize their pragmatic optimism mindset consciously, first to their team and second to external stakeholders. In other words, after getting a handle on self-regulation, pragmatic optimists pivot to group regulation, defined as the harmonization of a group's mindset, emotions, and behaviors to accomplish defined goals,[187, 188] and externalizing their optimism is one way to achieve it.

Though emotions can go through many stages and forms during a crisis, a leader can deliberately project their thoughtfully-crafted pragmatic optimism. In turn, the team connects with the leader and reflects or replicates the energy they give off, even during a crisis.

There are at least three reasons leaders intentionally externalize their pragmatic optimism mindset-driven behaviors during a crisis through the use of productive emotions that acknowledge the difficulty on hand yet highlight a solution-focused approach:

1. **Model** – Whether they are conscious of this organizational dynamic or not, leaders model behaviors for others to follow.[189, 190] Leaders are role models; if there is a gap between what they do and what they say, people will follow what they do. Pragmatic optimists are keenly aware of this responsibility even under high-stress conditions, so they knowingly showcase their productive personalities as a model for others to follow.

   A research participant from the aviation service industry reported, "Following the successful handling of a major crisis in my group, I asked my team about lessons learned and received much useful feedback. One of the lessons that has stayed with me all these years [after the event] was a comment by a direct report that others readily agreed to. He said, 'You were never down in the dumps despite the immense stress created by the crisis, [so] that helped us not be in the dumps, too.' From then on, I am more conscious about my role model responsibility with or without a crisis."

2. **Morale** – Another vital accountability of leaders is building and maintaining a healthy to high morale, defined as the mental state of an individual or team.[191] By projecting their pragmatic optimism, leaders can ignite morale in a team that is heavily weighed down by a crisis. Such leaders understand that a team with robust

morale is competitive, a go-getter, engaged, collaborative, productive, and solution-focused.[192, 193, 194] -

A senior decision-maker in the East African insurance industry
summed up the value of team morale during a crisis like this:
"Team members with high morale have a can-do attitude about
them; it doesn't matter the challenge they face. A leader can either
boost or deflate that morale. In my experience, nothing depletes
morale faster than a leader who focuses more on blame-fixing than
problem-solving."

3. **Mandate** – Every organization leader has both formal and infor-
    mal authority that they exercise through mandates to advance the
    collective cause. One of the most effective informal mandates a
    leader can project to the team is the expression of confidence in
    them during a crisis. A self-confident leader projecting pragmatic
    optimism instills confidence in the group that produces a creative
    mandate needed to navigate the organization out of a crisis.

A Central European leader in the shipping industry shared her experience with leadership mandate: "The crisis we were facing was
a first-of-its-kind and extremely mystifying; we didn't even know
where to begin. Then the [chief operating officer], having studied
the extent of the catastrophe, joined us in the 'War Room.' He
reminded us that we were chosen to work on the crisis because
we were the best in the business and that he believed we would
succeed. You could feel the sense of pride and positive energy
coursing through the room. He gave us the license to succeed,
supported us with the resources we needed, and succeed we did! It
was a grueling nine-month ordeal, but we succeeded. Since then,
I have become more conscious of my informal mandates and deployed them to achieve amazing feats."

Projecting pragmatic optimism is not about being phony or inau-
thentic. Self-reflection as part of self-regulation always precedes such
a projection of optimism. So, the leader is being intentional about it

because they believe it. As leaders adapt and adopt that constructive mindset, they can take the sting out of the initial negative emotional response to a crisis and bend their team's energy toward a solution. That is the skillset a pragmatic optimistic leader possesses. That is the transition from self-regulation to group regulation.

A Middle East-based telecommunications leader overseeing the operations of over ninety-five countries, reflected on the need for leaders to group-regulate by projecting pragmatic optimism to their teams after self-regulation: "Everyone [in the organization] is just going to follow your cue [as the leader]. It's psychological, right? Because, in the time of crisis, everyone you are leading is checking your body language, they're checking your tone, they're checking the pace at which you talk, and they're drawing strength from you."

> *"The mind is like water. When it's turbulent, it's difficult to see. When it's calm, everything becomes clear." – Prasad Mahes, author*

How NOT to Do Group Regulation

These are three common pitfalls that leaders will do well to avoid while trying to coordinate the mindset, emotions, and behaviors of a group:

1. **Excessive regulation** is where the leader overregulates, trying to control how the entire group thinks. This causes the team to get into either groupthink on the one hand or polarization on the other, causing the group to either ignore dangers or overlook new opportunities.[195] I have witnessed occasions where groups turned against the leaders in such a scenario out of frustration.

2. **Excused regulation** occurs where the leader ignores the emotional tensions in the team, whether caused by crisis or daily operations, and instead works around them. Individuals who intuitively prefer to avoid conflicts and difficult conversations regarding destabilizing behaviors on their teams fall into this category.

3. **Extraneous regulation** happens when a leader advocates for mindset, emotional or behavioral change that is either merely tangential or utterly unrelated to the organizational goals founded on the 3Ps. When there is a poor or nonexistent line of sight between the leader's team regulation tenets and the team's objectives, group regulation is bound to be fragmented and futile.

The Positives of Negative Emotions

Regarding negative emotions and self-regulation or team-regulation, pragmatic optimists do not throw away the baby with the bathwater because they recognize the benefits of seemingly pessimistic and undesirable views. While negative emotions are unpleasant, pragmatic optimists are known to find meaning in adversity by recognizing the value of negative emotions—fear, anger, surprise, and sadness—that are in abundance during a crisis.[196] They treat emotions as a valuable data source that should not be overlooked.[197]

How do pragmatic optimists benefit from negative emotions? They recognize that those negative emotions:

1. **Startle** us by hijacking our minds to focus on an occurrence that is high in urgency, importance, and gravity. Because stakes are high during a crisis, negative emotions grab a leader's attention. Pragmatic optimists see these negative emotions in themselves or team members as something to pay attention to, as warning signs that should not be dismissed.[198]

2. **Slow** us down to pay attention to details by increasing our awareness of hazards. This enables us to be more thoughtful and circumspect.[199]

3. **Spur** us to decisive action in the face of perceived danger. Negative emotions move pragmatic optimists from sitting on the fence to taking a position.[200]

4. **Stimulate** our perseverance and our willingness to persist through difficulties.[201]

5. **Sensitize** us to be open to behavioral changes that may otherwise be difficult to make or completely missed. For example, a senior decision-maker I know had a horrible sinking feeling of anxiety regarding a difficult situation. After going through the process of self-regulation, the leader discovered that the root cause of the worry was poor preparation. This led to a behavior change to build up the level of preparation, and the anxiety attack dissipated.[202]

6. **Supply** us with relevant information that we would otherwise have missed without self-regulation or group regulation.[203] For instance, one incident bound to elicit negative emotions from a leader toward a team member—ranging from anger to irritability—is to be surprised at an awkward moment by a piece of crucial data they should have known but didn't. Through self-regulation, the leader could realize the team's handling of data is ineffective, and through group regulation, create the desired behavioral changes around the proper escalation of crucial data.

7. **Stir** us up to work harder and better. When negative emotions rear their ugly head because a crisis has caused an organization to underperform its peers, pragmatic optimistic leaders tend to leverage them as a motivator to work harder at resolving the predicament.[204]

As counterintuitive as it sounds, the pragmatic optimist's goal is not to discourage or be dissociated from negative emotions but to process them advantageously. They recognize that negative emotions are natural and can be a healthy source of tremendous benefits when properly harnessed. Addressing the underlying trigger of a negative emotion causes a leader to focus, be more attentive, take action, persevere, change behavior, utilize relevant information, and work harder. As an individual does so, the negative emotion becomes dissipates.

However, pragmatic optimists also realize that negative emotions can be a slippery slope because when sustained over a long period, they are detrimental to mental and physical health.[205, 206] Studies have strongly linked some chronic diseases to prolonged sustainment of stressors due to negative emotions.[207] While leaders can reduce the amplitude of negative emotions, they may be unable to eliminate them in every case. But, as the amplitude of negative emotions is lowered, a leader can create a culture where these stressors have a negligible effect on the organization.

Crisis Displaces Empathy

One distinguishing personality trait is empathy, the ability to put ourselves in the shoes of others.[208] Empathy is central to interpersonal relationships across multiple contexts. Children seek empathy from parents, spouses from their partners, patients from their healthcare providers, and employees from their organizational leaders. The reverse is also the case in each of these relationships mentioned. Furthermore, the need for empathy is heightened during a crisis due to fear and anxiety from increased risk, impact, stress, (negative) emotions, uncertainties, and pressure (RISE-UP).

Ironically, during a crisis, when empathy is most needed, is when the ability to empathize is severely depleted.

"Empathy fatigue" is to blame for eating away at individuals' ability to empathize during long-drawn-out crises in personal lives, work, or at national and global levels.[209] In crises with shorter time frames, low self-awareness may cause people to demonstrate a diminished level of empathy.

According to a May 2022 report jointly produced by the Canadian Mental Health Association (CMHA) and the University of British Columbia, Canadians have lost significant ground in their empathy thanks to the prolonged COVID-19 pandemic.[210] Canadians reported a drop of 43% in their empathy compared to before the global health crisis. Ordinarily, the shared experience of a crisis requires interdependence among those impacted by the adversity. But when the social fabric is eroded by empathy fatigue, it creates a "concerning" situation, according to the national CEO of CHMA, Margaret Eaton.

When leaders lose empathy during a crisis, their bright-side persona goes out the window while their unwholesome dark-side personality walks through the door. With an eroded ability to empathize comes all forms of heat-of-the-moment inhumane, short-sighted, and unsustainable decisions. When team members lose empathy, there is apathy toward the leader, conflict among each other, and silo-building. All of this is bad news for an organization going through a crisis.

> *"Each time I think I've created time for myself, along comes a throwback to disrupt my private space." – Prof. Wole Soyinka, awarded the Nobel Prize for Literature*

Self-regulation and group regulation allow every member of the organization to safeguard their empathy by increasing their self-awareness, awareness of others, and the successful management of crucial relationships despite the onslaught of the crisis. That is because such positive relationship engagements are needed to capably navigate any crisis. An understanding of burnout, a phenomenon that depletes empathy, can help individuals protect their ability to understand the various stakeholders of a crisis.

Control Under Fire Is Courage Under Fire

Militaries award medals for "courage under fire." As any soldier, sailor, marine, or airman who has been decorated will tell you, "courage under fire" does not mean that you fight fearlessly; that is a myth. Brave troops feel fear. The difference between them and those who do not win medals for bravery is that they *control their fear*. They do not let fear dictate their performance.

No individual can multiply the organization's fear, uncertainty, and doubt faster than a leader who lacks self-control when under fire. That is because *"If you [the leader] are scared, terrified, hungry, and cold, they will be scared, terrified, hungry, and cold."* Similarly, if you are calm, confident, curious, creative, and calculated during a crisis, they will be calm, confident, curious, creative, and calculated.

Most times, your influence as a leader is so strong that all you need to model is self-regulation for group regulation to take the cue and align with your disposition.

The most famous American general of World War II, George S. Patton Jr., admitted feeling fear and told those he commanded that they would doubtless feel it, too. But he added this advice: "Do not take counsel of your fear." In other words, do not allow your fear— which is natural, even inevitable— to control your behavior under fire. Thus, fear is a necessary ingredient for courage; without being nervous you cannot be courageous.

We can put it this way: "courage under fire" is really *control under fire*.

The image in Figure 5-3 represents an intersection of the best of both worlds that the pragmatic optimistic mindset enables you to have in relation to control under fire.

To Achieve Control Under Fire, The Pragmatic Optimist Is Able To...

Control their emotions, yet not detach from them	Face the storm of a crisis, yet calm internal storms of fear, doubt, etc.	Be courageous, yet scared	Capitalize on their bright-side personality, yet minimize their dark side
Achieve group regulation, yet begin with self-regulation	Be exposed to negative emotions, yet benefit from them	Lower the amplitude of their negativity, yet boost the amplitude of positivity	Accomplish group regulation, yet avoid overregulation

Figure 5-3: Pairings of optimism with pessimism traits to form the pragmatic optimism mindset for achieving control under fire

Up Close and Personal

Consider the seven traits of the "tough leader" myth and their definitions: expressionless, affectionless, humorless, aloofness, blameless, heartless, and fearless. Are you susceptible to one or a combination of these, especially when you are under considerable stress?

_____

_____

_____

_____

What were the circumstances surrounding situations where you increased your emotional amplitude when you should have dialed it down and lowered your amplitude when you should have raised it? How could you manage those situations better in the future?

_____

_____

_____

_____

Review the list of seven benefits of negative emotions. Which ones resonate with you the most and the least? How can you improve the utility of the latter category?

_____

_____

_____

_____

CHAPTER SIX

Conviction to Act

Sooner or later, those who win are those who think they can.

– **Richard Bach**, author of the best-selling book,
Jonathan Livingston Seagull (1970)

What you will learn in this chapter:
- What is the conviction to act?
- Effects of a low conviction to act.
- Rebuilding your conviction to act from its four sources.
- The primary principles of the conviction to act.
- How leadership self-confidence produces "others-confidence."
- Six behaviors of leaders with a conviction to act.

Conviction to Act: The Leadership Confidence

Muhammad Ali was undoubtedly the greatest professional heavy-weight boxer of his generation and, some argue, the greatest of all time. However, his consummate ability in the boxing ring is only matched by his gift of gab. Ali had the extraordinary ability to get into his opponents' psyche with his legendary one-liners, zingers, and wisecracks.

Ali was the epitome of self-confidence. Asked by a journalist if a particular man had ever tried sparring with him (a form of boxing

"Self-confidence: The first requisite to great undertakings."
– Samuel Johnson, poet

training), Ali, who finished his career with fifty-six wins and five losses, replied, "If he dreamed it, he'd better wake up and apologize!"[211]

The third behavior found in pragmatic optimistic leaders is the conviction to act based on a belief known in psychology as self-efficacy. To possess a conviction to act, leaders must have a belief or perception of their competence or capability to succeed in a *specific* situation such as a crisis. In other words, self-efficacy is a more purposeful and task-specific form of a person's generalized self-confidence, but we will use them as synonyms in this book. Self-efficacy is based on Canadian psychologist Albert Bandura's[6] social cognitive theory that people are more likely to engage in an activity in which they perceive themselves to be competent.[212, 213]

Having a conviction to act starts with believing that you can overcome a particular challenge or obstacle or solve a problem. It is a belief that you'll be able to navigate through the maze you've been presented with. The conviction to act is not the ability to resolve a problem but the belief that one possesses that ability.

Even though you may have never faced a particular problem before, having a healthy self-efficacy means you have the mindset and the confidence to solve that problem.

Outcomes of a Low Conviction to Act

Based on decades of close working relationships with leaders across continents, sectors, industries, and organizations, I'd say that the part of leaders that takes the most direct hit during a crisis is their otherwise towering strength: their self-confidence in general and self-efficacy in particular as it relates to the turbulence at hand. A crisis lays bare the

---

6   In a study of the top 100 most eminent psychologists, Albert Bandura was ranked as the fourth with the most citations of all time after B.F. Skinner, Sigmund Freud, and Jean Piaget.

vulnerabilities of an organization and its management in a threatening way and consequently erodes the leader's confidence. This confidence erosion feeds into the emergence of the leader's destabilizing dark-side personality, as discussed in Chapter Five.

Unfortunately, many folks successfully conceal their low conviction to act and rarely admit that their self-efficacy has taken a direct hit. So, what are the telltale signs that a leader's conviction to act has become uncharacteristically low due to a crisis? Seven characteristics could become apparent in such leaders. They may become timid, tentative, transactional, tenuous, threatened, tiresome, and tone-deaf.

1. **Timid**: In times of extraordinary uncertainty, it is not an uncommon reaction to tread lightly, anxiously, and proceed with an abundance of caution. After all, the stakes are higher, and actions have far-reaching implications.

    While it's natural to initially be nervous during a crisis, it can sometimes stick around longer. From one of the participants interviewed for my research: "I am ordinarily a think-on-the-feet and clear-minded person. But I only recently realized that during crises, I become bashful and second-guess myself a lot, further complicating the fiasco I was responding to."

    After the initial nervousness, crippling fear will creep in and take hold if you allow timidity to fester. This is a deer-in-the-headlights moment where leadership becomes confused, disorganized, or ducks into hiding. In contrast, a crisis demands leadership characterized by clarity of thought and sharpness.

2. **Teetering**: As Chapter One explains, the heart of the Greek root word "krisis" is decision-making. A crisis forces decisions, while a low conviction to act causes teetering in decision-making. The organizational response may be prone to risk escalation, and the crisis may become more uncontrollable if a leader teeters when decisiveness is required.

Although most crises do not usually require hastiness, except for emergencies, all crises are time-sensitive. When leaders teeter and hesitate during a crisis, they lose opportunities and become susceptible to creating a new crisis within the existing crisis. Sitting on the fence and putting off making decisions will likely aggravate the crisis.

3. **Transactional**: Leaders who experience low self-efficacy are prone to being transactional in their thoughts and actions. They become locked in a loop of survival mode as they just want to outlive the crisis and become focused only on getting safely to the other side. Their short-sightedness causes such individuals to put blinders on and disregard the long-term consequences of their actions.

   Transactional leaders easily lose sight of the big picture projected by the organization's values, vision, and mission. I have heard uncomfortable statements like, "The company's values have to take a back seat until we get through this crisis." They take action that flies in the face of an organization's vision and culture, using the crisis as an excuse. In reality, trying to make up for a low level of self-efficacy causes individuals to reveal their dark-side personalities in this way.

4. **Tenuous**: Leaders who lose their conviction to act in adversity are unconvincing in their beliefs and half-hearted in their actions. This unenthused persona is usually a direct opposite of who they are on a day-to-day basis—convincing and committed—making them come across as cynical about the organization's chances of success in the crisis. When leaders project skepticism about the direction of and decision-making in an organization, they undermine the people's confidence. The team will

> *"The final test of a leader is that he leaves behind him in [others] the conviction and the will to carry on."*
> *– Walter Lippman, writer*

certainly take a cue from this new behavior during the crisis. From there, the execution of strategies falters and is doomed to fail.

A client of mine who runs a thriving division of a global tax consulting firm narrated a story that bolsters the points made about tenuous leaders in a crisis: "I recall an incident that occurred many years ago when I was a senior manager at a mid-sized financial institution that was showing early signs of [a] banking crisis due to significant NPLs [non-performing loans]. It was a solvable crisis. At the end of the first EXCO [executive committee] meeting to address the issue, members of the committee met with their various business groups and discussed clear and practical plans to address the NPLs. That was reassuring. Everyone was hopeful. That was until word got out that one of the senior EXCO members, immediately after engaging with his team, liquidated all his fixed-term investments in the bank, emptied all his DDAs [demand deposit accounts], and moved the funds to a bigger bank that was deemed safe. All hell broke loose. Employees who were once committed to resolving the NPL issue began moving their money from the bank to other banks and calling their family and friends to do the same. Within 72 hours, the bank was facing a run![7] The bank never recovered from that run due to the behavior and reaction of one EXCO member to a resolvable crisis." Remarkably, I have a firsthand experience similar to this story, and you may have a comparable version, too.

5. **Threatened**: Leaders experiencing low self-efficacy will feel threatened in their state of mind. Part of the definition of a crisis is that it creates threats. Most crisis experts focus on the threat to the company's operations and ignore the threat to the leader. This is a

---

7   A run on a bank happens when a significant number of the bank's clients, prompted by fear of the bank's solvency or soundness, withdraw their money within a short period of time. The fear of a bank's collapse drives a bank run. A run usually becomes a self-fulfilling prophecy as the bank's assets might be unable to meet the sudden liquidity demand, leading to a collapse.

big miss because threatened leaders who feel that their backs are up against the wall are prone to missteps in a crisis. When leaders live in a sustained state of threat, given the ominous and gloomy nature of a crisis, it is not uncommon for them to be thrown off their game—going from being self-assured to feeling insecure and panicked, taking down employees' morale with them.

Continuing in that state of insecurity will undermine their leadership. The ability to lead others diminishes because genuine leadership relies heavily on the manager's self-assurance. When leaders become insecure, they become suspicious of the team at a time when they need to believe in themselves and each other. A leader who feels threatened in a sustained way is prone to trying to protect their position and interest at all costs, including making decisions that are at best suboptimal and at worst detrimental to the organization.[214] They are susceptible to being selfish, creating conflict within, and looking out for themselves alone during a crisis.[215]

> *"The problem is not the problem. The problem is your attitude about the problem."*
> *– Coach Brevin, in The Sisterhood of the Traveling Pants by Ann Brashares*

6. **Tiresome**: Low self-efficacy may cause a normally charming, calm, and curious leader to rub others the wrong way and jeopardize relationships by becoming irritable, infuriating, and inflexible due to the exigencies of the crisis. Formerly inspiring professionals may transform under the enormous pressure of a crisis into uninspiring individuals who suck the energy out of the room.

A crisis aims to disrupt the operations of an organization but cannot fully accomplish that objective without first disrupting the leader. An out-of-control crisis ought to lead to an out-of-control response. Unfortunately, as leaders' self-efficacy wanes, they become less aware of their negative interactions with others. A low conviction to act may cause a leader to be pensive, uncooperative, and touchy because they are worried about the crisis.

7. **Tone-deaf**: As discussed in Chapter Five, sustained exposure to a crisis weakens an individual's ability to empathize with others, especially when combined with a "Tough Leader" persona. When that susceptibility is combined with a low conviction to act, and in some cases, an exaggerated view of one's capabilities, the leader becomes tone-deaf—i.e., unable to perceive or relate to organizational and external stakeholder sentiments and opinions. Many leaders lose their sensitivity to others by caving into the anticipatory dread of the crisis (the looming threat) by becoming inwardly focused, consumed by themselves and their inadequacies.

Several contemporary research studies have compared the scores of leaders' ability to perceive the sentiments of their team members to the results of the leaders' effectiveness.[216, 217, 218] The studies found significant relationships between the scores of both assessments. Tone-deafness can happen to the most empathetic leaders during a crisis when they don't self-monitor and instead focus primarily on themselves. By doing so, they miss out on opportunities to leverage the positive influences from others that could be deployed to address the chaos at hand. Those positive influences can come from a leader's team, professional network, and family that could help boost their conviction to act and help resolve the crisis.

You might have noticed that the seven characteristics of leaders with a low conviction to act may be rooted in their mindsets: either pessimism or unrestrained optimism. However, pragmatic optimists demonstrate a high conviction to act because they are solution-focused and concentrate on controllable elements of the crisis. Also, their level of self and

> *"'I can' is one hundred times more important than IQ."*
> – *Max Lucado, author*

other-awareness is elevated during turbulence because, as discussed in the previous chapter, they consciously externalize their confidence to achieve group regulation after self-regulation.

A Conviction to Act: The Can-Do Spirit

Demonstrating a conviction to act is a manifestation of self-belief that unlocks what we need to be successful; it reveals the can-do spirit that any leader can possess during trying times when the organization's survival depends on their leadership. Sports psychologist Dr. Jerry Lynch said, "When you believe and think 'I can,' you activate your motivation, commitment, confidence, concentration, and excitement —all of which relate directly to achievement."[219]

An extensive study published in March 2022 quantified the benefits of possessing a conviction to act. The authors analyzed the data of 3,500 publicly traded companies and their 7,800 CEOs over 20+ years, spanning 70 countries and 24 industries. They discovered that CEOs who demonstrate boldness in establishing a clear direction for their company generated $5 trillion more in value than their peers who lacked that attribute in their tenure.[220] These figures reflect the value of the pragmatic optimistic mindset that sustains a belief in one's leadership ability when calamity strikes—such boldness, when consciously projected by the leader, is reflected in every aspect of their organization.

Successful leaders understand that regardless of what life throws at them, what matters is that they meet it with their heads held high. That is what a conviction to act looks like in practice. It creates passion and enthusiasm in an individual and is a vital determinant in whether a leader can steer their organization out of a crisis. Physicist and Nobel Prize winner Edward Appleton understood the power of passion in the equation of success when he said, "I rate enthusiasm even above professional skill."[221]

The can-do spirit—the conviction to act—inflames enthusiasm in a leader and can ignite the much-needed energy for the team in a draining and long-drawn-out predicament. This is the intersection of self-efficacy and group regulation.

Everyone Is Susceptible to Self-Doubt

Task-specific self-confidence is sometimes misunderstood to mean that it is consistently at an elevated level among influential leaders. The reverse is true in reality—it is common for highly successful leaders to experience peaks and valleys, depending on several factors.

In 2010, US Supreme Court Justice Stephen Breyer said," "I do know my own first three years [on the US Supreme Court], I was frightened to death much of the time... [Scared about] how do I know I can do this? How do I know I won't make mistakes?" Despite Breyer's fear, he pressed ahead as though he had everything he needed to succeed. Though his self-confidence certainly varied as he experienced self-doubt, it is something that every leader will experience but can still push forward regardless.

"Fight as if you are right, listen as if you are wrong." – Dr. Robert I. Sutton, in *Good Boss, Bad Boss*

In his book *The 4-Hour Workweek*, Tim Ferriss wrote, "If you are insecure, guess what? The rest of the world is, too. Do not overestimate the competition and underestimate yourself. You are better than you think." It is hard to be confident when the alarm bells are going off, especially if you are susceptible to imposter syndrome, but it is a proven way to overcome self-doubt. If you plan to accomplish anything meaningful, then self-doubt is inevitable, and overcoming it will determine the quality of your success.

From Where Does a Conviction to Act Come?

According to the psychologist who developed the self-efficacy theory, there are four sources of the conviction to act.[222, 223] It is crucial to note that it is not these four elements that create self-efficacy, but *your* interpretation of them based on *your* belief system.[224] Consequently, one's optimism or pessimism mindset can heavily influence that belief system, and now we can add pragmatic optimism as an influential mindset option.

Based on long-standing studies, my research findings, personal experience in leadership roles, and my work with leaders, I have observed that people who have developed a pragmatic optimistic belief system extract the most value from these sources of self-efficacy. Here are the four sources and the subsequent discussion examines how pragmatic optimists maximize their significance:

- What you've done
- What you've seen others do
- What others say you can do
- How you feel

1. What you've done: Performance accomplishments.

John Singer Sargent, an accomplished American painter trained in Paris, had many esteemed works, including the paintings of US presidents Theodore Roosevelt and Woodrow Wilson. One of his art pieces, a panel of roses, received high praise from respected critics who regarded it as a masterpiece. Sargent, who took great pride in that particular painting, refused to sell it despite being offered a lot of money. So, what did he do with it? Whenever Sargent felt the onset of the symptoms of imposter syndrome—self-doubt, undervaluing oneself, disparaging one's performance, feeling unworthy, overcompensating for perceived inadequacy, etc.—he would bring out the celebrated artwork as a form of self-remembering practice[225] and say to himself, "I painted that!" By reviewing his past accomplishment, he regained his confidence and poise to continue painting.[226]

Likewise, you need your own "celebrated artwork," a previous performance that *you* consider to be a success. You need it as a confidence-boosting point of reference to counter days of self-doubt.

Pragmatic optimists interpret their past in a healthy, not haunting way. They recognize that they cannot change the past and avoid regrets. Instead, they own their past experiences, whether positive or negative, and can extract relevant lessons from them. They can determine how those moments will develop their perspectives, abilities, and personalities. Pragmatic optimists view a crisis as a furnace to mold their character, not as a wildfire to destroy them.

Even though no one can choose how life unfolds, pragmatic optimists can determine how they react to those events and how they will define them. They seek the most advantageous way to respond to a crisis by embracing past successes and failures and seeing them as valuable learning opportunities. They frame losses in a healthy way that shows growth and improved value. It is not uncommon to hear them say, "I am no longer the person who made that mistake—I have matured because of that experience." Blunders transform pragmatic optimistic leaders for the better.

Pessimists zero in on and exaggerate past mistakes, while optimists are inclined to focus only on the positives from their past. Unrestrained optimism causes people to gloss over their successes because they expected them, while they shy away from recalling failures. But like the painter John Singer Sargent, you need your

"An entire sea of water can't sink a ship unless it gets inside the ship. Similarly, the negativity of the world can't put you down unless you allow it to get inside you."
– Goi Nasu, author

panel of roses as a confidence-boosting point of reference; that is what pragmatic optimists do.

The confidence-boosting panel of roses for a longtime friend of mine, a senior decision-maker in the North American energy industry, goes as far back as the third grade when his teacher and peers affirmed him for surprisingly excelling in his most dreaded subject, mathematics. It was a turning point for him, even though the other people involved might have forgotten about the event. He said of that incident, "Decades have passed since then, but that remains my go-to experience for inspiration as I seek to repeat that performance. It is a constant reminder [for me], when I have self-doubt, fear, and anxiety about any situation, that when I put my mind to do something, I can excel."

Playwright David Storey puts it this way: "Have confidence that if you have done a little thing well, you can do a bigger thing well, too." It is not the scale of the confidence-boosting point of reference that matters. What matters is the magnitude of what that experience means to you.

2. What you've seen others do: Vicarious experience.

Humans are learning beings.[227] We learn by being a part of society regardless of the subset of that society and the different forms it can take. Ultimately, we learn by watching others and mirroring their behaviors; even when we are not conscious of it, we are doing so.[228], [229]

While the natural inclination when learning from others is to focus on their successes and what we can glean from them, that is only one side of the equation. Pragmatic optimists seek out and appreciate learning from the mistakes of others. An executive in my study stated,

> Bosses should talk about their failures. And from failures, people should learn how to do things better the next time. I'm seeing it happen even [in my organization], where [during] the senior management training program... senior [decision-makers are invited to] come and talk about their failures. And it's always a very positive thing to the people because they come back saying, "Oh, wow, this person failed before, this person did this, this person did that, amazing. Okay, I don't feel so bad." Because it builds the confidence of the person [learning about it].

Such learning opportunities build self-efficacy for crises in ways that learning from successes may never deliver. Seeing the failures of others has a way of reassuring us that if they can be successful in life after going through such cataclysmic events, then we can find the strength to pull through our own adversity.

While model learning can be a subconscious event, pragmatic optimists deliberately seek opportunities to maximize the vicarious experience. This is why true leaders ask many questions when they have opportunities to learn from others. They never assume they know the answers. They want to uncover the behind-the-scenes worldviews, opinions, motivations, sentiments, and values behind their visible actions. They desire to know their thought process, to understand what they were thinking and why they took action in the way they did. More importantly, they want to know how other leaders deal with failure and success and their processing method(s).

Conversely, individuals with a pessimistic mindset tend to focus mainly on the gaps, fears, inadequacies, and exaggerations of other people's failures.[230, 231] Being exposed to the failures of others also increases the pessimist's level of anxiety and apprehension as it may trigger a wave of negative expectancy biases—an inflated and hyperbolic concern about a harmful future.[232] In other words, they worry that "If they can fail, then I will most likely fail, too." Optimists, on the other hand, are easily inspired by the work of others but rarely dig deeper to learn the principles of success and are prone to embracing a one-sided view of these experiences—the positive side.

But pragmatic optimists *deliberately* seek a well-rounded view of other people's experiences, understanding that shortcomings are just as valuable teachers as triumphant outcomes. They are not afraid to ask questions from their peers and mentors. In fact, they recognize that most experiences have a combination of negative and positive outcomes.

3. What others say you can do: Verbal and social persuasion.
Oliver Wendell Holmes Jr. defined a word as "the skin of living thought."[233] Words have an essence, and they reverberate and linger

"The more you learn, the less you fear." – Julian Barnes, writer, The Sensing of an Ending

on in the consciousness but mainly in the unconsciousness of the audience. The higher the authority, the closer the affinity, and the stronger the speaker's credibility is to the listener, the greater the impact of the words. Words build up, and words tear down. That is why parents' words often haunt or motivate their children and shape who they become throughout their lives long after they have been spoken in anger, disgust, fear, joy, approval, and encouragement. The words of managers, teachers, coaches, mentors, family members, and close friends profoundly affect an individual's self-efficacy—thoughts, emotions, and actions—in both their personal and professional lives.

A pessimist will likely struggle to believe affirmative words said about them but will find it hard to forget negative remarks that sting.[234] I have met many professionals in the course of my career who exhibit this behavior—they simply blow off anything positive said about them. They never retain it and, therefore, rarely remember and build on those powerful words to strengthen their self-efficacy. Yet, they can quote verbatim mostly all the negative words that have ever been said to them going back decades.

Worse still, pessimists' tendency to assess negative data as more accurate than positive information causes them to believe put-down words that end up eroding their conviction to act.[235, 236] These are lost opportunities for personal and professional development created by an unproductive mindset and may be the source of leadership misbehavior during a crisis.

Inversely, an optimist is likely to dismiss and not believe words or incidents they consider discouraging by practicing what experts call "selective inattention,"[237] even when such words are said in good faith and could be helpful. Thus, if they are perceived by the optimist as negative, value-adding and self-efficacy-building statements to the optimist will likely be disregarded.[238, 239] That is a self-efficacy-building opportunity lost. Optimists will struggle to remember disapproving words but have a lopsided long-term memory for positive affirmations that come their way.[240]

However, pragmatic optimists learn from both demotivating and encouraging words. They are capable of evaluating themselves and seeing if there is anything that they need to change on their side based on feedback. Notwithstanding, they realize that some discouraging words, especially those meant to put them down, reflect the person speaking them more than themselves. They tend to place the responsibility of baseless discouraging words on the speaker (e.g., that the speaker may be having a bad day or is an unfair actor). At the same time, they personalize encouraging words and use them to replenish depleted self-efficacy.

Moreover, when pragmatic optimists receive positive affirmations, they look for evidence to support those reassuring words – Are there other leaders and peers saying the same thing, and there is a pattern, or is it a one-off comment? A one-off statement might be filed away as something that can be reviewed later or even developed to create a strong new attribute that might be more easily recognizable by others. A pragmatic optimist can undoubtedly build self-efficacy on both sides of positive affirmations and discouraging words because they are skilled in extracting maximum value by combining opposite mindsets.

4. What you feel: Emotional state.

Your interpretation of your emotional state will significantly shape your assessment of your conviction to act and the outcome.[241] For example, if the risk and pressure of a crisis cause you to feel highly anxious because you believe that you will fail, your self-efficacy will be noticeably weakened. Under this condition, the chances are that you will doubt yourself and question what you can accomplish.

Moreover, if you are prone to experiencing imposter syndrome, a time of turbulence is when the syndrome is on steroids, and your effectiveness is persistently hampered.[242] As one author plainly says, "No self-efficacy, no performance."[243]

In addition to feeling anxious and under pressure during a crisis, leaders also report experiencing stress, chronic fear, distress, shock, sadness, and anger. Leaders' interpretation of these emotional states might weaken their conviction to act by causing confusion, helplessness, and isolation.[244, 245] Therefore, it is vital to have a well-developed sense of self-awareness to realize when you are experiencing these negative emotional states and to steer away from self-efficacy-destroying thoughts and behaviors. Pragmatic optimists leverage their keen self-knowledge to adopt coping skills that counteract the negative impact of stressful situations.

> *"For this thing we call 'failure' is not the falling down but the staying down." – Mary Pickford, actress and producer*

A notable way pragmatic optimists steer away from negative emotions is their firm understanding that all emotions, negative or positive, are transient, and care should be taken so that they do not dictate long-term decisions.[246, 247] That is an uncommon approach because empirical research shows that, more often than not, temporary emotions form the basis for permanent decisions by most people.[248, 249] The motto of pragmatic optimists is the saying, *"Never make a permanent decision based on temporary emotions."*

Consequently, when emotionally aware leaders recognize that they are in a negative state of emotion, they pivot to other sources of conviction to fortify or rebuild their self-efficacy. Whether that source comes from your past accomplishments, what you see others do, or what others say you can do, drawing from other sources allows you to overcome a negative emotional state and its detrimental effect on your self-efficacy.

Finally, self-talk is another coping skill that leaders use to reinforce and reconstruct their crisis-battered self-efficacy due to a negative state of emotion. Decades of studies from sports psychology to business management and psychiatry prove that the nature of your internal dialogue—self-assurance versus self-criticism—dramatically influences your conviction to act and actual performance.[250] What you say to yourself about yourself determines how you perform, especially during a crisis.

Self-Confidence Triggers Others' Confidence

The self-efficacy of a leader goes beyond serving the purposes of the leader. Instead, when leaders visibly demonstrate a conviction to act, it serves as a prompt, a pattern, and permission to others within the sphere of influence of that leader.

First, leaders who exhibit self-confidence during a crisis **prompt** or signal calmness and composure that contradicts the chaos and confusion. A calm demeanor based on self-efficacy is authentic and relatable to others; they sense it as an indication that the leader can be trusted to regain control.[251] Leaders create on the outside who they are on the inside—chaotic leaders create chaos out of calmness while calm leaders create stability out of volatility. In leadership, you tend to replicate who you are.

Second, the principle of leaders as pace-setting models kicks in here.[252, 253] Leaders with a healthy level of self-efficacy during a crisis become a **pattern** and an archetype for how the organization should respond to the misfortune. As social learners, we absorb new knowledge by observing others, especially those with leadership authority. A leader lives in a goldfish bowl; all eyes are on you and many will likely emulate your behavior.

Third, when trusted leaders externalize their conviction to act, they give **permission** to those within that sphere of influence to develop creative solutions that will address the predicament. They achieve this by infusing self-confidence into their team, knowing that a self-confident team is a creative team. This shows a positive relationship between leadership confidence and group confidence. That is why a leader's self-confidence begets other people's confidence. The leader's confidence ignites a chain reaction that can be felt and utilized by the team during a crisis.

Let's consider behavioral examples from players in the capital markets. Optimism leads to confidence in companies' insiders[8] to buy the shares of the organization with which they are affiliated in the open market. The converse is also true: an insider's pessimism leads to doubt about the organization's future and may likely cause the sale of the company's stock. Such insiders' investing behaviors—the buying and selling of related companies' stocks —are so crucial to capital market participants that such transactions are regularly tracked and openly reported for all to access.

"Life shrinks or expands in proportion to your courage."
– Anaïs Nin, writer

When insiders, who invariably are leaders of companies, purchase their organization's shares, this expression of leadership confidence boosts investors' confidence in the company, generates positive sentiments in the market about the stock, and is viewed as a bullish signal. Inversely, when insiders sell their shares, investors view it as a bearish signal and will likely dump the stock.

The same goes for leaders and their organizations during a crisis. Leaders demonstrate contagious confidence when they express the conviction that their team can find a solution to the crisis, even when they don't yet have the answer. Leaders are multipliers, whether of confidence or doubt. A conviction to act is the ability to seek

---

8   According to the US Securities and Exchange Commission, an insider is a director or senior officer of a publicly-traded company, including any person or entity with more than 10% beneficial ownership of a company's voting shares. https://www.sec.gov/smallbusiness/goingpublic/officersanddirectors

opportunities and take action that creates a better future. How confident are you in chaos? When the chips are down, do you buy your own stock?

Six Behaviors of Leaders with Self-Efficacy

When pragmatic optimists demonstrate a conviction to act, they take these six actions:

1) **Determine** to be present and not ghost their team. It takes leadership confidence not to cut and run, physically and mentally, during a predicament. Through a conviction to act, a leader's presence is categorical in several roles and scenarios, resulting in the building of trust with the team. In the 2020 movie *Centurion*, the following dialogue ensued:

   > Centurion Quintus Dias: "I've never seen a general so beloved of his men."
   > Bothos: "Well, in training he is our scholar, at [the] feast he is our father, in the ranks he is our brother, and in battle, he is the [guide] we pray to save our souls."

   To be sure, the aim of leadership engagement aims is to earn trust, not seek to be liked. However, if you are trusted, chances are high that you will be liked.

2) **Diffuse** confidence throughout their organization in a deliberate fashion. Pragmatic optimists recognize that leadership confidence generates organizational confidence and that a leader's personal efficacy creates a groundswell of collective efficacy.[254, 255] Your team feeds off of your confidence.

3) **Distinguish** their confident self from the chaos of the crisis. One of my mentors was a lawyer in a large New English corporate firm. This lawyer once told me about a top client who would usually go to the law firm worked up, frustrated, and visibly upset about a legal issue. Unconsciously, my mentor began to mirror the client's agitation level whenever the client visited by being

visibly upset about the legal problem. One day, the client pulled my mentor aside and said, "Look, I am the client, and it is OK for me to be frantic and hysterical. But as my lawyer, you should be the opposite of that—calm and composed!"

A leader should be the opposite of a crisis, not mirror it. Don't be like a thermometer that reflects the heat of the crisis, but instead be a thermostat that sets the tone of a successful response.

4) **Decode** the external storm (the crisis) instead of being distracted by an internal storm of doubt, fear, and lack of confidence. Crises normally involve unique situations and uncommon challenges that require a healthy dose of self-efficacy to understand, unravel, and resolve. At the same time, crises undermine and weaken the self-efficacy of those involved. However, through the four sources of self-efficacy, leaders can reinforce and rebuild their conviction to act, thus calming their internal storms and focusing on the external turbulence.

> *"Part of being a champ is acting like a champ. You have to learn how to win and not run away when you lose. Everyone has bad stretches and real successes. Either way, you have to be careful not to lose your confidence or get too confident." – Nancy Kerrigan, Olympic figure skater*

5) **Delineate** responsibilities without scapegoating. From my experience, leaders who lose confidence in the face of turbulence tend to ignore their organization's blame attribution or culpability in a crisis but would rather devote considerable energy to attempting to pin the blame on a fall guy. They do so in a feeble and often failed attempt at absolving themselves of responsibility. But leaders who have a conviction to act will likely not look for someone to blame, a tactic that may lead to a backlash, particularly if a junior

employee, a smaller entity, or the consumer is scapegoated.[256, 257] Scapegoating can be extremely divisive and trust-eroding. Instead, pragmatic optimists are more focused on maximizing the strength of every one of their teams to tackle the crisis.

6) **Decide** with greater clarity. Decisions are always made in crisis, and confidence gives you lucidity. Having a conviction to act gives you a bias to take action. Taking action then becomes a part of your belief, mindset, and mission. The next chapter is dedicated to the decision-making behaviors of pragmatic optimists during a crisis.

Frank Wagner, a senior executive and practice leader at Marshall Goldsmith Stakeholder Centered Coaching, told the story of a memorable experience he had decades ago while consulting at an upstart East Coast bank that later became one of the largest financial institutions in the US. During promotion exercises, one of the most crucial questions the bank's management asked candidates was, "What risk did you take in the past year that failed, and how did you handle it?" That was the bank's way of testing the resilience of the candidates' self-efficacy and how it is rebuilt when damaged by adverse circumstances.

A conviction to act breeds self-confidence, not self-conceit, and pragmatic optimists recognize that thin line between assertiveness and arrogance.

To guide their organizations out of the darkness of a crisis, leaders have to generate their own light by creating hope in a hopeless situation, and a conviction to act is a dependable light source.

Figure 6-1 represents an intersection of the best of both worlds that the pragmatic optimistic mindset enables you to have in relation to the conviction to act.

To Achieve Conviction To Act, The Pragmatic Optimist Is Able To…

Exude confidence, yet avoid overconfidence	Be cautious, yet not timid	Be laser-focused on the crisis, yet not transactional	Admit to self-doubt, yet do not underestimate themself
Experience failure, yet interpret it in the most advantageous way	Learn from the failures of others, yet not trigger negative expectancy bias	Engage their emotions, yet do not base permanent decisions on them	Be a thermostat to set the tone, yet be a thermometer to be in the know

Figure 6-1: Pairings of optimism with pessimism traits to form the pragmatic optimism mindset for achieving a conviction to act

Up Close and Personal

Understanding the sources of your conviction to act allows you as a leader to harness that power to overcome self-doubt and rebuild self-efficacy. Referring to the four sources of information on the conviction to act, discover your own sources that you can use in the future to build your self-efficacy.

Which of your past performance accomplishments stands out as a confidence booster? What is your "panel of roses" that convinces you of your worthiness?

_____

_____

_____

_____

What did you learn from the failures of others (choose one or two individuals) and your own?

_____

_____

_____

_____

What do credible and authoritative figures say about you? How does this fuel your conviction to act?

_____

_____

_____

_____

Your emotional state is an important aspect of your conviction to act. What coping skills can you adopt to counteract the negative impact of stressful situations?

_____

_____

_____

_____

CHAPTER SEVEN

Concerted Decision-Making

It is because I alone, of all the Greeks,
know that I know nothing.
(Socrates' response, known as the Socratic Paradox, when told that
the Oracle of Delphi said he is the wisest of all Greeks)
– **Plato**, a paraphrase of the Apology of Socrates, set in 399 BCE

What you will learn in this chapter:
- The five common decision-making mistakes leaders make.
- The role of optimism in the search for information.
- Best practice for brainstorming sessions.
- The IKEA effect in decision-making and how to avoid it.
- The importance of improvisation.
- How pragmatic optimists handle information during a crisis.

Decision Time

The most critical official act you will ever perform during a crisis is
to make decisions. Everything we have discussed up until this point in
the book and everything left to discuss is to equip you for a concerted
or rigorous decision-making process. That is how central this chapter
is in the book.

Decision-making is central to crisis because, as discussed in Chapter One, the original Greek word "krisis" can be translated as "the point of decision." Krisis is derived from "krínnō," which means "I decide," "I discern," or "I separate." Thus, there are two notable emphases in the English translation of krínnō: an individual and an action. In an organization facing a crisis, that individual is everyone on all levels of leadership. The action is a rigorous and thorough process of separating the wheat from the chaff, also known as decision-making. In your personal life, that person is you or you and your partner, if any.

You are in a crisis to make decisions—nothing more, nothing less. Similar to the Hippocratic School's definition of a crisis as the turning point of a disease where the patient either gets better and recovers or gets worse and dies, the series of decisions you make while leading a crisis response creates a turning point for the situation to either get better or worse.[258] Such is the criticality of decision-making in a time of adversity.

As essential as decisions are in an organization and the focal point of any crisis, decisions fail a lot. Leaders struggle to make good decisions consistently, even on strategic matters. Multiple studies conducted over 20 years in medium- to large-sized organizations across the US and Canada show that *fifty percent* of managers' decisions fail.[259] That is staggering. It means that managers wouldn't fare better if decisions were based on a coin toss.

> *"For every complex problem, there is an answer that is clear, simple, and wrong."*
> – H.L. Mencken, journalist

It is noteworthy that the decisions reviewed by these studies were made as part of the regular course of business and not necessarily during a crisis. It is easy to guesstimate that the failure rate of decisions is higher than fifty percent in a crisis.

Recall the RISE-UP acronym from Chapter One. A crisis introduces risk, impact, stress, emotions, uncertainty, and pressure on the leader, the organization, and its stakeholders. Based on these severe conditions, it's not challenging to wager that 70% to 80%+ of managerial decisions fail during a crisis. The added exigencies of a crisis cloud managerial judgment and create enough distractions for leaders to derail the decision-making process. The question then arises: In what ways can decision-making go off the rails during a crisis?

Five Common Decision-Making Derailers

J.P. Morgan's love for yachts is well documented in his biography, *Morgan: American Financier*, by Jean Strouse. According to the 2014 edition of the book, oil tycoon Henry Clay Pierce asked the founder of United States Steel, the world's first billion-dollar company, how much it cost to maintain a large yacht. Morgan replied with the oft-misquoted[9] words, "You have no right to own a yacht if you ask that question."[260]

Owning and maintaining a yacht in the nineteenth century, a costly venture even then, was a fairly straightforward economic decision for multibillionaire Morgan. Unfortunately, leaders responding to make-or-break situations in their organizations have no such luxury of no-brainer decisions.

It is clear that during a crisis, decisions will often fail.[261] This is evident in the botched crisis responses we witness almost daily.[262, 263, 264] To understand why and how these failures happen, let's discuss the five most common derailers of decision-making to watch out for when the stakes are high, based on empirical data from my research and leadership experience:

1. **"I need complete information"** – A common difficulty encountered when developing a solution to resolve a crisis is a paucity of information.[265] There is rarely enough information. Due to the

---

9   Usually misquoted as "If you have to ask, you can't afford it."

heightened level of uncertainty and ambiguity that characterizes a calamity, much information is unknown—especially regarding the way forward. A lack of relevant knowledge is a cause of enormous distress to leaders in any crisis, and insisting on complete information severely hampers the decision-making process.

A pragmatic optimist's belief in and penchant for turning difficult and negative situations into desirable and positive outcomes makes them *seek* to make do with the best available information. In fact, pragmatic optimists tend to expect to encounter incomplete information when facing a crisis, so they are not destabiized by it.

"Be open to adjustments. There's nothing about this current moment in history that allows for stubbornness."
- Unknown

In turbulent times, ignorance is not bliss, but it should not be dismissed. To a pragmatic optimist in a crisis, ignorance due to a lack of information is not necessarily an enemy; it might be enlisted as an ally. Pragmatic optimists leverage ignorance to stimulate the innovation and creativity processes of developing solutions out of logjams.

Sydney Brenner, the 2002 Nobel Prize winner in physiology and medicine and a professor of genetic medicine at the University of Cambridge, believes that having a lot of information quenches the fire of innovation and creativity. So, he goes out of his way to create conditions where there is a lack of information, in a bid to spark innovative thinking. He made a compelling case for ignorance in the scientific process of innovation when he said,

> Biology got its main success by the importation of physicists that came into the field not knowing any biology and I think today that's very important.

> I strongly believe that the only way to encourage innovation is to give it to the young. The young have a great advantage

in that they are ignorant. Because I think ignorance in science is very important. If you're like me and you know too much, you can't try new things. I always work in fields of which I'm totally ignorant.[266]

2. **"I have to make a hasty decision"** – Without a doubt, a crisis demands a sense of urgency. A leader in the film industry put it this way to me, "There is a feeling that one is under the gun and a sense that [the entire] organization is waiting for [the leader's] next move. It can be unnerving."

That is because a crisis management process is in reality a change management process and timing is essential for such a process. A crisis is a process of forced change. Be that as it may, Harvard Business School professor John Kotter argues that change is doomed to fail without a sense of urgency.[267]

However, responding to a crisis is not a license to shoot from the hip. Hastiness or impulsiveness should be differentiated from a sense of urgency. Hasty decision-making introduces new risks into an already risky scenario. Meticulousness and a sense of urgency are not mutually exclusive approaches to decision-making under extreme pressure; concerted decision-making combines both.

Except for emergencies (including wars) where there is a threat to human life or property damage and snap decisions (normally sharpened through several hours of simulated training programs), are required, most organizational crises *allow* for thoughtful decision-making. Pragmatic optimists recognize that in decision-making, thoughtfulness does not necessarily mean slow, and being rigorous should not translate to being sluggish.

3. **"I don't need alternatives; the decision is clear"** – Sometimes, this faulty mindset follows from a desire to be hasty, while at other times, it's an outcome of a flawed decision-making process that has nothing to do with a crisis.

Paul Nutt, professor emeritus of management science at the Fischer College of Business at The Ohio State University, dedicated much of his research to decision-making and is a recognized authority in that field. One of his landmark studies shows that in seventy-one percent of all crucial decisions, decision-makers only considered a single option.[268] Just one option! Let that sink in. Imagine the level of presumptuousness, overconfidence, and know-it-all mentality required to make decisions in this manner.

You only need a few years of work experience under your belt to relate to the following scenario: You attend a decision-making meeting, but it becomes obvious to you (and others) rather quickly that the leader or an influential person in the room already has their mind made up on the way forward before having any meaningful discussion. The unstated objective of such a meeting was for the team to rubber-stamp the preconceived proposal. That is the stuff that botched crisis responses are made of—in noncrisis times, such an approach could be suboptimal at best, but during a crisis, it could lead to a whole new round of fiasco.

No matter how convinced you are about your proposed line of action, you stand to benefit immensely from combining seemingly contrasting viewpoints, like a pragmatic optimist, to create a more rigorous and hybrid solution. A study conducted by the aforementioned Professor Nutt followed the decisions of a group of tech industry leaders for ten years and discovered that the participants made successful decisions six times more often when they considered two alternatives instead of one. [269] That is an exponential benefit from a single addition.

4. **"I'll go with my gut"** — Several neuroscience studies have declared that the gut is the "second brain" of the body.[270] The human digestive system is home to a less-talked-about nervous system called the *enteric nervous system*. There are about 500 million neurons in your gut with connections to your brain via the nervous

system, so both organs are in constant communication.[271, 272] Long before science proved its connections to the brain, the gut has been relied upon as a reliable but crude guide, as evidenced by age-old sayings like "Trust your gut" and "What does your gut tell you?" In his 1976 book, *The Metaphoric Mind*, author Bob Samples said,

> Albert Einstein called the intuitive or metaphoric mind a sacred gift. He added that the rational mind was a faithful servant. It is paradoxical that in the context of modern life we have begun to worship the servant and defile the divine.[273]

I believe intuition plays a vital role in leadership and decision-making. A lot of what goes into crafting a vision is rooted in a leader's intuition. I have experienced intuition at all levels of leadership; its manifestation ranges from flashes of insights to the fluidity and creativity in executing a rigorously developed strategy.

"The truth is that many people set rules to keep from making decisions. Not me." - Mike Krzyzewski, basketball coach

I can also confirm that my intuitive leadership experiences and those of the professionals I've worked with over the years align with the position of prominent cognitive psychologist Gary Klein, that intuition grows over time from lived and learned experiences.[274]

So, by all means, listen to your gut instinct during critical decision-making but do not go with your gut without first road-testing the intuition. The stakes are simply too high. Pause to validate and kick the tires on your intuition. Have the courage to share it with others as an option, not *the* option, and allow others to pick it apart—that is what it means to analyze. Purposefully create an environment that allows for new and superior information that contradicts your intuition to come forward. Avoid treating your gut feel as sacrosanct or unimpeachable.

Pushing ahead with untested intuition can lead to grave missteps and mishandling decision-making in a crisis. Remember that your intuition is prone to be compromised due to the intense stress and emotional roller coaster of a crisis. Therefore, treat your gut feeling as a hypothesis that needs to be tested.

5. **"There is no need to involve others"** – It is almost instinctive for decision-makers to seek to limit the size of the decision-making body and in many cases constrain other people's exposure to the decision-making process. Arguments in support of this approach center around achieving efficiency.

On the size of the decision-making body, the adage "two heads are better than one" may be more poetic than it is always valid. Scientific experiments that studied decision-making show that there is no significant improvement between decisions made by one person or two people, especially if the latter is a homogenous group.[275] More importantly, decision-making teams of four prove to be the sweet spot as they are shown to outperform solo and duo decision-makers.[276]

My conclusion from these studies, the data from my research, and my experience is that homogeneity of decision-makers, regardless of the group size, leads to underperformance compared to a more diverse or heterogeneous group of equal size. Therefore, when a leader decides that they do not need anyone else to make a decision, or severely limit the decision-making to a team of homogenous people, they not only risk missing out on the bigger picture of the crisis, but they are alienated from the needs of their stakeholders.

Involving diverse and relevant individual stakeholders, an approach favored by the pragmatic optimistic mindset, does not slow down the decision-making process as some fear.[277] Instead, doing so leads to a concerted, well-rounded, and rigorous decision-making process that a high-stakes scenario like a crisis demands.

When leaders involve others in decision-making, those participating feel a sense of ownership of the final decisions and tend to collaborate better in executing the decided strategies and solutions to the crisis. A leader cannot and should not do it all alone. There is always time to involve others because it results in a group effort to resolve the crisis; the approach distributes the burden of crisis resolution to others beyond the leader.

I have never been involved in a crisis where the entire solution came from the leader. More often than not, the solution is generated when the leader

   i.   Asks questions,

   ii.   Leverages their relationships, or

   iii.   Inspires the team to succeed with "group confidence."

Optimism and the Search for Infomation

A vital aspect of a systematic decision-making process is the methodical search for information that will aid the selection of a course of action.[278] Key studies from the field of medicine have found that people's pursuit of discovering information relevant to resolving chronic health crises is greatly influenced by their optimism.[279] Optimists tend to possess the readiness and zeal to search out information pertinent to decision-making. That is because optimists are more curious about and drawn to exploring new experiences than pessimists.[280] Pragmatic optimists selectively exhibit this trait of optimism.

> *"The time to take counsel of your fears is before you make an important battle decision." – General George Patton, WW2 combatant commander*

In addition, pragmatic optimists respond positively to the fear of failure common in highly uncertain situations, like a crisis. High achievers like leaders are especially prone to one or more of the following multifaceted impacts of the fear of failure:[281]

1. Ambiguity about the future—relates to the unknown
2. Disgrace and humiliation—relate to a view of oneself
3. Loss of self-worth—relates to a view of one's value
4. Loss of confidence by influential people—relates to validation by others
5. Loss of interest by influential people—relates to connection with others

In a crisis, virtually all five aspects of the fear of failure converge. Nevertheless, pragmatic optimists convert their fear of failure into motivational pressure to seek out new information that may help resolve the logjam because of their desire to overcome challenges. It is this motivation to search for information that researchers have discovered is an association between optimism and goal adjustment or goal resilience—the ability to keep pursuing one's goals in the face of daunting challenges and the flexibility to amend them in the light of a crisis.[282, 283]

Conversely, pessimists tend to disengage from their goals when the going gets tough and do not exert as much energy on information search. At the same time, wishful and naïve optimists are nonchalant or casual about searching for information because they simply expect difficult situations to resolve themselves. Both approaches—pessimism and naïve optimism—are rejected explicitly by pragmatic optimists.

A participant in my doctoral research, a senior vice president overseeing a thriving business group that covers almost 100 countries in the trading sector, emphasized that the pragmatic optimist's drive for information to resolve a crisis does not guarantee success. Yet, the resolve to keep plugging away remains undeterred because information search is also about covering all the bases and leaving no stone unturned:

> …If I think the [crisis] is not going to be favorable, I want to be able to stand up as an authentic leader and say, 'You know

what? We did everything humanly possible. We explored every angle under the sun, [and] did our best, but unfortunately, it ended the way it did, so hands-off.' [It means] we couldn't avoid it. [But] I don't want [a crisis] to end unfavorably because we didn't cover all the bases.

Brainstorming and Cooperative Criticism

The decision-making process during a crisis requires producing new ideas through brainstorming to tackle the problems and bring the organization back on course.[284] For most of my career, criticism during ideation and brainstorming has been considered harmful, damaging, and counterproductive, and, therefore, should be withheld entirely from the process.[285, 286] Records show that this well-established practice of not criticizing during brainstorming and creativity is often regarded as the most important rule for ideas generation and goes back over seventy years.

However, a recent experiment led by an MIT Sloan professor, Jared Curhan, shows that this long-held view is not always true—it all depends on whether the organizational setting is cooperative or combative.[287] Curhan's study shows that criticism adds substantial value to the breadth and depth of ideas generated in **cooperative settings**—usually characterized by a high level of trust, selflessness, competence, and positive intentions. In the experiment, independent observers noted that criticism improved idea generation by 16% and the quality of the proposals by 17%.

Those outcomes represent significant improvements that can make the difference between a mediocre proposal that barely gets the organization out of the roadblock and a game-changing solution that opens

"On the plains of hesitation bleach the bones of countless millions who, at the dawn of decision, sat down to wait, and waiting died."
– Sam Ewing, writer

up new opportunities from the crisis while future-proofing the business.

On the other hand, in **combative settings**, generally characterized by distrust, selfishness, manipulation, unhealthy competition, adversarial engagement, and hostile intentions[288]—where help offered could be misinterpreted as hurting or interference—criticism during brainstorming is negative. In short, they are toxic work environments. Such antagonistic settings produce 16% fewer proposals and 23% poorer-quality proposals. That is an astounding 32-point and 40-point swing, respectively, compared with results from a cooperative setting.

It must be noted, however, that a cooperative environment is neither inherited nor spontaneous. It doesn't just happen; it is the outcome of intentional investments by the leader to generate and promote interpersonal trust. Why intentional? It is because the way to a high-trust environment is through deliberate and consistent leadership actions and management policies that constantly promote relationship-building.[289]

Thus, when a crisis hits, the time to create your organizational setting—whether cooperative or combative—is past. A crisis is a time to test whether your organizational setting is cooperative or combative. The adversity will reveal the setting you have built as a leader. Pay attention to the signals and objectively evaluate whether what you have is a cooperative setting or a combative one. Then, adjust your brainstorming approach accordingly.

Although criticism during brainstorming in a cooperative setting is recommended since it yields the best results, it is wise to avoid criticism if you assess that your environment is combative.

Watch Out for the IKEA Effect

The business model for the Swedish multinational furniture company, IKEA, is broadly well-known and simple to grasp. In order to offer low-cost furniture, IKEA introduced "flatpacking" in 1956, a system of selling furniture in modular forms or unassembled pieces. This successful approach has fueled the company's aggressive expansion into several countries as IKEA saves on high operating costs like assembly, transportation, and inventory.

IKEA consumers purchase unassembled furniture and follow the assembly instructions at home using basic tools provided to put the furniture together. The assembling process requires a basic level of creativity, nothing more. Interestingly, this simple furniture-assembly activity creates a bias in the consumer's mind toward the assembled furniture.

That was the core reported finding by Harvard professor of business administration Michael Norton in his *Harvard Business Review* article, "The IKEA Effect: When Labor Leads to Love."[290] The IKEA effect is a cognitive bias that causes an individual to value an item more simply because they put it together. The extra effort needed to assemble the furniture makes the individual feel invested in the output, leading to an inflated valuation.[291]

I have observed and experienced a cognitive bias similar to the IKEA effect in leaders during decision-making in general and especially in a crisis. When leaders invest effort in generating ideas to resolve a crisis, they risk falling in love with them and dismissing ideas from other credible sources. That is the IKEA effect in decision-making. It is an unjustified overvaluation of one's proposal simply due to the effort invested in developing it. Most people are susceptible to it, but a leader backed by formal authority can easily push through their substandard ideas in the heat of a crisis.

Individuals with a "tough leader" persona will likely prefer to take on the crisis resolution challenge singlehandedly or with minimal input but could be tripped up by their blind spots. Such leaders aggravate crises instead of resolving them. It becomes an intensely personal process.

In contrast, pragmatic optimists have a realistic and practical view of their strengths and weaknesses; they know how to maximize the former and minimize the latter by fostering a melting pot of ideas and viewpoints to tackle the crisis. While pragmatic optimists fully accept and are vested in the responsibility for leading in a crisis, they are also mindful of the tremendous value in those they are leading.

Decision Fluidity—Stumbling into Success

Pragmatic optimistic leaders seek to take advantage of unplanned situations in a misfortune. Decision-making in a crisis is like building a new road into uncharted territory; it will be full of surprises, and the pragmatic optimistic mindset is primed to improvise and benefit from them. Leaders should be sensitive to and ready to maximize fortuitous opportunities in their decision-making process to resolve a crisis, even though it might not follow their original plan. This is the improvisation and flexibility that a pragmatic optimistic mindset activates.

"The fact that man knows right from wrong proves his intellectual superiority to the other creatures; but the fact that he can do wrong proves his moral inferiority to any creature that cannot."
– Mark Twain, in What is Man?

The story of sildenafil, a chemical compound, is relevant here.[292, 293] A large pharmaceutical company developed this compound to address two major health issues: angina pectoris, a cardiovascular disease, and hypertension or high blood pressure. After several unsatisfactory clinical trials, the compound did not improve any of the health conditions for which it was intended and was assessed as a failure. "This was a cardiovascular project, and we were very disappointed in the cardiovascular studies where we saw very little [positive effects]," said Simon Campbell, a chemist at the pharma, during a BBC Discovery interview. The only logical thing to do was to scrap the project and write off the losses.

However, the pharma's leaders took a decision to conduct one final clinical trial for ten days "at the maximum tolerable dose, and let's see what we find," continued Campbell. The result of this last trial was equally disappointing. Nothing had changed. The compound had negligible effects on the cardiovascular issues it was developed for—bad news.

When asked about side effects reported by the all-male volunteer group that participated in the final trial, the study director replied, after listing some side effects, "Oh, yes, one of the nurses noticed erections [as reported by participants in the clinical trial]." That was puzzling. Yet, five out of eight volunteers reported that side effect.

The leadership team had to challenge their thinking in light of the consistency in the side effects. The pharma aggressively pursued this new line of thinking by conducting "twenty-one clinical trials in patients with erectile dysfunction. The drug … was effective in every single one of those trials," said Dr. Peter Ellis, an executive director at the pharma. He worked on the biological properties of the drug. Ellis continues,

> We had to think, "Is this a side effect, or is this actually a genuine action of the drug that could have clinical utility for the treatment of erectile dysfunction?" We had patients who refused to return [the drugs], who lied whether they had any tablets left or not. They were not willing to give them back. Forget about statistical analysis. Forget about the full details of the study. The patients themselves said, "I'm keeping my tablets!"

That is the origin story of Pfizer's "little blue pill" sold commercially as Viagra, the all-time fastest-selling drug in the world.[294]

The decision-makers at Pfizer demonstrated what I call **decision fluidity**, the ability to adapt decision-making protocols to unexpected roadblocks and unplanned opportunities. What presented as a side effect, aftereffect, or by-product of their investigation's principal focus turned out to signal an unplanned solution with massive market size. Pfizer's leaders could have easily dismissed the new signal due to disappointment from failing in their original intention. Instead, they set aside their initial plan, thoroughly investigated the new signal, and maximized new information to uncover the solution to a major problem. I can tell you from experience that such a pivot is difficult for organizational leaders to attempt and accomplish in the face of a serious letdown like failed clinical trials.

"Often greater risk is involved in postponement than in making a wrong decision." - Harry. A. Hopf, business thinker

Improvisation, an attribute of pragmatic optimists, is a necessary ingredient of decision fluidity. Leaders must be adept enough to "change the tires on a moving bus" during decision-making. Dead ends and disappointments are inevitable when seeking a solution; don't pout over it but expect it. A dead end may be the place to change directions like flowing water does when it encounters a rock. Leaders should build a system that can fine-tune decision-making to pursue unexpected opportunities without being bogged down by red tape.

The mindset of a pragmatic optimist leans heavily on iteration in the same way that decision fluidity is an iterative process, not a rigid or inflexible one. Settling on effective solutions during a crisis is rarely a linear process.

Pragmatic optimism is a departure from the permanence and mutual exclusivity of pessimism and optimism and an embrace of changeability, improvisation, and fluidity. Remember that your decision-making process predates the crisis, so it may need to be tweaked due to the difficulties of the crisis for it to be effective. Such openness about decision-making will yield better results than a rigid approach that most organizations have.

Mishandling of Crucial Information

Generally, an attribute of a crisis is that it alters people's behaviors long after the predicament has passed. One of the relics I expect to linger long after the COVID-19 pandemic is handwashing. Apparently, before COVID, people were not handwashing as often as they are now. A 2009 study showed that 69% of men and 35% of women did not wash their hands after using a public restroom.

While the world now knows that handwashing is the easiest and cheapest way to halt the spread of several diseases, there was a time in human history when not even doctors washed their hands between procedures while tending to patients. Physicians could move from teaching students with cadavers to tending to expectant mothers without washing their hands. This practice resulted in "childbed fever," the most common killer of women related to childbirth in Europe through the millennia until WWII.[295]

In 1846, Dr. Ignaz Semmelweis, a Hungarian obstetrician who would later be known as "the savior of women," became the chief resident at the First Obstetrical Clinic of the Vienna General Hospital, a university teaching hospital, at the age of twenty-nine.[296] Semmelweis' primary duties included teaching obstetrics to medical students and overseeing problematic deliveries.[297]

He was enormously bothered by the high number of deaths of mothers at the clinic and worked tirelessly to find a solution. His breakthrough came after connecting a disease he discovered in the autopsy of his late friend and fellow physician with an infection in dying mothers in his maternity clinic. He concluded that he and the medical students somehow transmitted the disease between cadavers and women in the delivery room. This was before the discovery of germs as disease-causing microorganisms.

Semmelweis was the first doctor to implement the practice of handwashing when transitioning from handling corpses in the autopsy or anatomy class to attending to pregnant women in the maternity clinic. The result was as astounding as it was immediate—the death rate of mothers fell by 90% in just a few months, and the clinic recorded no deaths from the disease a year later—All because he instituted handwashing.

While this was a major potential breakthrough in medical practice, the scientific and medical community rejected Semmelweis' solution presented in his academic publications and mocked him for it. In the absence of the knowledge of germs, the idea that the cleanliness of doctors could solve such a fatal and perennial crisis sounded too fanatical and outside the realm of possibility in the minds of medical practitioners of the day.[298, 299] The scientific community did not bother to test his hypothesis until well after his untimely death.[300]

A few years after Semmelweis' death, chemist Louis Pasteur confirmed the germ theory, and Semmelweis' handwashing proposal was eventually vindicated.[301]

Just like the scientific and medical community during Semmelweis' time, leaders, too, can mishandle information—such mismanagement of information is worse during a crisis. Some leaders are prone to rejecting information that

i.   does not come from them (the IKEA effect),
ii. does not originate from their homogenous circle,
iii. is a simple solution relative to the complexity of the problem,
iv. is unproven even when it is successfully tested, and
v.   they have little knowledge in or exposure to.

The mishandling of information by otherwise smart and highly accomplished leaders is all too common in a crisis. Adopting the pragmatic optimistic frame of mind can help leaders maximize instead of malign useful information.

7 Ways Pragmatic Optimists Respond to Information

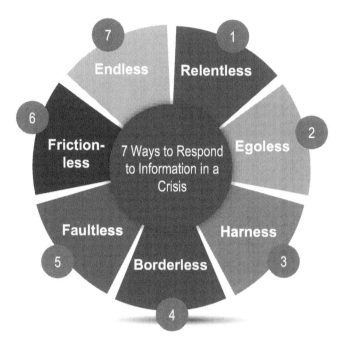

Figure 7-1: Seven ways to respond to information in a crisis

Pragmatic optimists respond to information in seven effective ways (see Figure 7-1). Let's look more closely at each of these.

1. Relentless

Pragmatic optimistic leaders understand how important it is to be **relentless** during a crisis because engaged optimists are persistent. My experience working with several leaders shows that a crisis is a good revealer of a leader's level of relentlessness.

A leader's sincerity in uncovering and searching for new information during a crisis will reflect their relentlessness to create a better outcome for the organization. A leader's relentlessness in a

"The straight line, a respectable optical illusion which ruins many a man." – Victor Hugo, in Les Misérables

189

crisis bolsters their authority within the team. Without it, a leader cannot be trusted, and their influence starts to disappear.

Semmelweis was so driven by finding a solution for the long-standing unexplained deaths of mothers that he admitted that the situation got him "so miserable that life seemed worthless."[302] He was consumed with finding a solution. Before his eventual break-through, Semmelweis relentlessly attempted several tests and experiments to resolve his maternity clinic's childbed fever death crisis. He further demonstrated this persistent trait in his failed attempt to convince the scientific and medical community to adopt the simple practice of frequently washing hands. He was so persistent about persuading others of his life-saving discovery that his professional colleagues were convinced that he was mentally ill. He persevered until the end. He understood his findings' value, which later became a critical part of patient care.

Pragmatic optimistic leaders do not falter in their beliefs in the face of adversity. Instead, with a measured dose of optimism combined with deliberate pessimism, they can create a new path forward with new information and utilize available resources to advance their causes. Leaders have to choose to be relentless when it comes to their vision, which is one of the biggest things that comes under attack during a crisis. If you do not fully believe in your vision, as some leaders are wont to do, you will not be disciplined in the decision-making process, and your indifference will be evident for all to see in a time of turbulence.

2. Egoless

The medical professionals of Semmelweis' time felt personally attacked by his suggested solution of physician cleanliness as the panacea for an enduring crisis in maternity clinics across Europe. Their egos clouded their scientific reasoning that advocates for testing a hypothesis under the conditions with which it was proposed.

In the same way, organizational leaders need to be **egoless** in the decision-making process, especially in handling potentially game-changing information that is fed into the process by those with firsthand knowledge of the issues but who may lack seniority in the hierarchy. Solutions to crises are not respectful of organizational hierarchies; they can come from the lowest levels in the organization.

Some leaders get stuck in the rinse-and-repeat mentality of, "I did it today, and it worked, so I can do it again tomorrow and succeed." Physicist William Pollard warned, "The arrogance of success is to think that what you did yesterday would be sufficient for tomorrow." Leaders should not presume that which worked yesterday will continue working today—the presence of a crisis confirms that fact. Therefore, pragmatic optimists put their egos aside and embrace the humbling nature of a crisis.

A leader's current belief system is another roadblock to the flow of new and useful information into the decision-making process. How leaders respond to new information that contradicts their beliefs is critical to decision-making. All too often, a leader's ego can get in the way of receiving such critical but contradictory information. Leaders who do not self-monitor due to the stress of a crisis are prone to dismissing new information that does not align with their beliefs or the prevailing belief system in the industry, also known as "best practices."

> *"Waiting hurts. Forgetting hurts. But not knowing which decision to take can sometimes be the most painful." - José N. Harris, in Mi Vida: A Story of Faith, Hope and Love*

Semmelweis' campaign to save the lives of countless mothers through the simple practice of handwashing by attending physicians contradicted the personal belief systems of his colleagues.

Also, it was out of step with the prevailing industry best practices. They got in their way. Egoless leaders *get out* of their own way.

More often than not, newly sourced information that can help neutralize a crisis does not come from the top of the organizational hierarchy. Therefore, leaders with a pragmatic optimistic mindset who receive new and relevant information, regardless of the rank or title of the source, will process it, test the hypothesis, and, if found valid, change their minds and their thinking. The decision-making process during a crisis relies on information to change the current thinking because "we cannot solve our problems with the same thinking we used when we created them."[303]

3. Harness

Accepting new information is not enough; the manner of processing the information matters. Leaders need to **harness** information to its fullest. They do this by drilling down through the layers of that information. Semmelweis tested new data he generated in several ways and kept drilling down on it until he found the solution. Unfortunately, the pressures of a crisis can distract leaders from peeling back the layers of new data received and therefore make them prone to assessing potentially useful information as unusable.

"The people who get on in this world are the people who get up and look for the circumstances they want, and if they can't find them, make them."
– George Bernard Shaw

Pragmatic optimistic leaders appreciate that information is divergent in nature. The heterogeneity and variability of information contribute to the quality of information. Semmelweis searched for and collected data from the two maternity clinics in the hospital and even went outside the hospital to gather information about women who chose to give birth on the streets (known as "street births" in those days) rather than in the clinic due to high death rates in the hospital.[304, 305] Semmelweis shockingly found that street births had a far lower death rate than hospital births. It turned out that the clinic's main clientele, mostly uneducated and low-income women, already knew what the physicians of the day struggled to understand: that the hospitals were the problem. This diversity of information sources and depth of analysis helped him narrow the primary origin of deaths from childbed fever to the hospital.

Leaders need to expect information to come from different and nontraditional sources, especially in a crisis. The ability to thoroughly analyze and synthesize information is crucial to decision-making. In doing so, information is maximized and not taken lightly.

4. **Borderless**

The very structure designed to ensure the smooth operation of organizations by assembling individuals with similar expertise into the same team—vertical business groups and horizontal support functions—is the main culprit in creating organizational borders, more commonly known as silos. On the contrary, successful leaders are **borderless** in their thinking as they move seamlessly across functional teams to source relevant information for decision-making.

The silo effect means an organization's groups, departments, and functions work autonomously instead of interconnectedly.[306] More damagingly, the silo effect is the root cause of information hoarding, lack of communication, and the pursuit of conflicting goals. That explains why the silo effect is one of the major causes of internal crises. In her 2015 book *The Silo Effect: The Peril of Expertise and the Promise of Breaking Down Barriers*, author Gillian Tett traced how silo-inspired internal crises snowballed into the 2008 global financial crisis.[307]

Silos manifest in curious ways. Operations might withhold relevant information from human resources. Finance might not have respect for the marketing department. Technology might prioritize building its empire at the expense of the product team. The sales division might be distrusted by everyone else in the organization. Silos create partitions that weaken the interdepartmental flow of information—it is a source of disunity that undermines the organization's mission, vision, and values.

Trying to source pertinent information from such a divisive and combative environment is like pulling teeth. Forget about contending against external competitors in your industry—the most brutal wars professionals face are mostly within the organization. Pragmatic optimists find a way to step across silos, overcoming these challenges by taking time to build cross-functional partnerships and trust long before the crisis strikes. They do this by

i.   showing respect to other departments and their worldviews,

ii. finding common ground with other teams in a collaborative style, and

iii. defining their goals in a manner that, if achieved, will help other teams accomplish their objectives.

They live by the sage words of Zig Ziglar, "You can have everything in life you want if you will just help other people get what they want."[308] This relationship-building approach should be incorporated into day-to-day operations and habitually practiced to step over silos successfully. I have seen several sporadic attempts to destroy silos and one-time events focused on "silo-busting" — unfortunately, they don't work.

Finally, the devastating crisis of the 9/11 attacks in the United States is a testament to the damaging nature of silos. General Stanley McChrystal's book, *Team of Teams*, recorded testimony to the US Senate Committee on Homeland Security and Governmental Affairs on Homeland Security & Governmental Affairs that described the silo-thinking behavior of the US Intelligence Community as "secretive pockets of the nation's most valuable information."[309] If various units shared information, that crisis, like many other organizational crises, would have been avoided or its impact greatly minimized.

5. Faultless

New Information is rarely **faultless**, and the pessimistic part of the pragmatic optimist expects that. Without having this expectation, leaders who discover errors or inconsistencies in new data may be tempted to discard the information and discredit the source.

> *"It's not about making the right choice. It's about making a choice and making it right." – J.R. Rim, writer*

While new information might not be fully usable in its original form, some parts of it may still contribute to a solution. Leaders must learn to glean the most useful part of any new information to succeed in decision-making.

Recall that one of the original definitions of a crisis is "I discern." This is where the leadership skill of separating the wheat from the chaff comes into play in handling new information.

Leaders should anticipate receiving fragmented information while searching for the best available information that feeds into decision-making. This sifting process usually involves the leader raising their hand to ask for help from subject-matter experts and relevant teams in understanding the information.

Also, it is critical to seek collaborative data that supports the new information while demonstrating a willingness to test the hypothesis to identify the useful part of the information and run a pilot that simulates real-world scenarios.

6. Frictionless

This is where a borderless view of cross-functional sources of information (discussed earlier in this section) is tested. Generating new information cannot be **frictionless**. Leaders need to become comfortable with the compartmentalized parts of an organization and the chaos that comes with it.

Coalescing as homogenous groups has always been a characteristic of the evolution of the human race. So, as much as silos and compartmentalization are burdensome, attempting to permanently eliminate such a fundamental characteristic of humans may be a pipe dream.

A manifestation of the friction in organizations is group-based bias. All information you receive will be tainted by the bias of the department that generated the information. Therefore, leaders may use expository questioning like the "Five Ws and How"—who, what, when, where, why, and how[310]—to tease out the bias and gain a proper understanding of the value of the information.

Leaders who expect information generation across departments and functions to create friction are prepared to step in and smoothen things over. Also, they are not thrown off by the often-chaotic process of extracting pertinent cross-departmental data. A pragmatic optimist expects such chaos in pursuing information and is prepared for it.

7. **Endless**

The search for information to aid decision-making cannot be **endless**. Management in noncrisis times usually requires making decisions with incomplete information—how much more during a crisis.[311, 312] At some point, a leader must determine that enough is enough, even when what they have is not enough. They must decide when to stop searching for new information and utilize what they have already discovered. At that point, a decision is made on how the organization will proceed with an action plan.

Leaders must differentiate between a perfect plan and an optimal solution to accomplish this. While perfection is rarely a reasonable goal, except when dealing with binary issues like the presence or absence of infectious disease, there is often an optimal solution that is discoverable with incomplete information in many organizational scenarios.

Figure 7-2 represents an intersection of the best of both worlds that the pragmatic optimistic mindset enables you to have in relation to concerted decision-making.

To Achieve Concerted Decision-Making, The Pragmatic Optimist Is Able To...

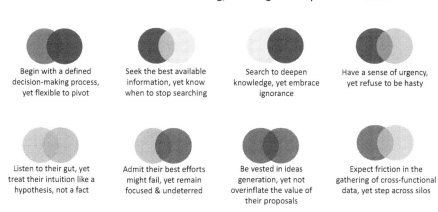

Begin with a defined decision-making process, yet flexible to pivot	Seek the best available information, yet know when to stop searching	Search to deepen knowledge, yet embrace ignorance	Have a sense of urgency, yet refuse to be hasty
Listen to their gut, yet treat their intuition like a hypothesis, not a fact	Admit their best efforts might fail, yet remain focused & undeterred	Be vested in ideas generation, yet not overinflate the value of their proposals	Expect friction in the gathering of cross-functional data, yet step across silos

Figure 7-2: Pairings of optimism with pessimism traits to form the pragmatic optimism mindset for achieving concerted decision-making

Up Close and Personal

To which of the five common decision-making derailers are you most susceptible? Why? How might you counteract it?

_____

_____

_____

_____

Based on a recent survey that measures the point of view of employees in your organization, would you say you lead (or belong to) a cooperative or combative team? How will you handle brainstorming in the future?

_____

_____

_____

_____

Being vested in one's ideas is a common cognitive bias—how would you minimize the IKEA effect in your decision-making process?

_____

_____

_____

_____

Of the seven ways pragmatic optimists respond to a crisis, which one resonates with you the most as an area of development? What will you do differently?

_____

_____

_____

_____

CHAPTER EIGHT

Conscientious Communication

*Communication. It's the first thing we really learn in life.
Funny thing is, once we grow up, learn our words, and really
start talking, the harder it becomes to know what to say. Or
how to ask for what we really need.*
– **Dr. Meredith Grey**, in *Grey's Anatomy*[313]

What you will learn in this chapter:
- The centrality of communication in leadership and crisis.
- How crisis breaks down communication in a team.
- Effects of poor communication.
- Leaders' personalities shape their communication.
- Mode matters—choosing the right communication channel.
- Leadership is measured in communication.
- Communication principles of pragmatic optimists.

The topic of communication is commonly discussed in the world of crisis. From my reckoning, it is the most researched area of crisis management by far. Leaders are forced to make decisions and must communicate clearly and strategically during a crisis. When leadership communication is poor, the crisis can be made worse. My goal is to shed new light on this deeply researched crisis area by focusing on the pragmatic optimistic behavior of conscientious communication.

The conscientious level of communication is thoughtful, well planned, and properly executed. At this level, leaders know how they come across, to whom they are messaging, and how that message affects a diverse audience. They are also aware of the best methods to communicate that are appropriate for the situation without relying on often contradictory and hollow clichés like, "If it can be said in an email, it doesn't require a scheduled meeting" or "When in crisis, overcommunicate!"

The Criticality of Communication

The numbers are in, and the avoidable cost of poor communication to organizations is stunning. In an October 2021 survey of 1,252 US-based professionals—1,001 knowledge workers and 251 business leaders—conducted by The Harris Poll for Grammarly, the annual loss due to communication is estimated at $1.5 trillion for US businesses.[314] To put this preventable loss into perspective, Spain's 2021 GDP is $1.4 trillion. Whichever way one cuts it, it is a humongous loss.

Many leaders erroneously underrate their strategic role in communication and undervalue their communications team. Two telltale signs of such undervaluation are the communications team having a catch-all responsibility for all things considered nonstrategic and being left out of crucial decision-making deliberations.

"Be sincere, be brief, be seated." - Franklin Delano Roosevelt, former US president

Yet, communication is the most prevalent activity of leaders, the most practical way to disseminate direction, goals, and ideas, and the best way to achieve sensemaking:

1. **Most prevalent** — Communication is by far the most common of all a leader's activities. A Harvard study that analyzed 60,000 work hours of some CEOs by accessing their scheduling data around the clock for three months revealed that the participants spent 72% of

their time in meetings.[315] This study excluded other forms of communication, such as email and phone messages. However, if you included these messages, it would be easy to estimate that CEOs easily spend over 80% of their workday communicating.

Thus, the higher an individual is in the organizational hierarchy, the larger the communication component is in their daily tasks. Communication is an essential aspect of a leader's responsibility because virtually everything you accomplish is through others.

Unfortunately, as prevalent as communication is, well-handled communication, especially with the added exigencies of a crisis, is not as widespread. Like the words of Samuel Coleridge's poem, it is a case of "water, water, everywhere, [and not a] drop to drink."[316]

One factor that drives the mishandling of communication is what I call the *reverse spotlight effect*. Let's first discuss what the spotlight effect is. It is an egocentric bias that creates a tendency to feel that all eyes are on you and a feeling of being closely watched under a spotlight.[317, 318] Some define it figuratively as feeling like being the center of the universe. The spotlight effect was a major source of social anxiety I overcame when I faced my fear of public speaking in 1998.

Thus, the *reverse* spotlight effect in communication results from low self-monitoring and deficient social awareness that causes you to underestimate how much others pay attention to you and value your message as a leader. Leaders who succumb to the stress of a crisis are prone to undervalue the importance of their presence and their message, instigating the mishandling of communication. Mathematician and physicist Blaise Pascal is quoted as saying, "Kind words do not cost much. Yet they accomplish much." Coming from a leader who is engaging with anxious, bewildered, and distressed stakeholders, kind and empathetic words genuinely expressed may mean the world to them.[319, 320, 321]

2. **Most practical** — Communication is the foundation of sharing information within an organization and between the firm and the community.[322] Long ago, I heard a speaker say lightheartedly that communication is a method for transferring ideas from one person to another without brain surgery. It is the most practical way of exchanging information.

Organizations trade in communication. Their products and services are merely the outward expression of receiving, processing, and creating an edge with information. That is how powerful and practical communication is.

Even though organizations typically have communication departments, everyone is in the business of communicating. Information is the DNA of an organization and crucial during uncertainties.[323] Leadership is measured by the effectiveness of communication. It is the leader's responsibility to communicate their results in a form that allows colleagues and external stakeholders to understand vital parts of the message.

> *"I'm not convinced that the world is in any worse shape than it ever was. It's just that in this age of almost instantaneous communication, we bear the weight of problems our forefathers only read about after they were solved."*
> – Burton Hillis, columnist

But most leaders struggle with communication. A survey of a sample of US managers published by the *Harvard Business Review* shows that nearly 70% of them admitted to being uncomfortable communicating with employees.[324] According to the survey, managers are uneasy about giving difficult feedback, exhibiting vulnerability, and delivering corporate messages like a change of course. Because managers struggle to communicate in noncrisis scenarios with employees with whom they have considerable social power, it is not surprising that during a crisis, communication with employees is often bungled, and engagement with powerful external stakeholders is typically botched.

3. **Making sense of it all** — Sensemaking is the process of ascribing meaning to shared experiences, especially those that are new, perplexing, uncertain, ambiguous, and unexpected.[325, 326] If you think the list of experiences reads like characteristics of a crisis, then you are right. While not only applicable to turbulent times, this definition makes sensemaking a central part of dealing with a crisis.

Sensemaking involves the purposive construction of reality with the intention that it will be adopted as a shared reality by the target audience.[327] While much attention is placed on the top-down flow of sensemaking, successful managers recognize the power of a bottom-up flow to achieve a 360-degree view.[328] Since sensemaking is the process of articulating circumstances into coherent expressions that motivate action, it means that communication is its backbone.

Thus, effective communicators construct a convincing expression of reality from the circumstances the target audience is experiencing or has recently experienced.

More than at any other time, a crisis period calls for deploying a leader's best communication skills in sensemaking. While responding to a predicament—a time when virtually nothing makes sense—pragmatic optimists recognize that communication is their most powerful sensemaking tool for constructing reality aimed at getting the target audience to buy in.

This is because there is a total breakdown of what is—and what is not—during a crisis. Without a leader swiftly and categorically composing a comprehensible reality to achieve sensemaking, internal and external stakeholders are prone to conjuring up multiple realities because nature abhors a vacuum. Sensemaking fails, and crisis management begins to unravel when leaders fail to create a convincing expression of reality, causing various stakeholders to adopt numerous versions of realities.

Pragmatic optimistic leaders also set the stage for creating future realities in terms of where the organization is headed, based on the organization's mission, vision, and values. Such leaders intentionally define how the future of the organization should be envisioned.

In summary, you might notice that the Harris Poll study referenced at the beginning of this section showing a $1.5 trillion annual loss by US businesses due to poor communication did not focus specifically on times of crisis. This period is known for immense pressure, a torrent of negative emotions, and significant stress that combine to make leaders prone to mishandling communication. It is, therefore, reasonable to assume that potential losses from poor communication will increase during a crisis. Nevertheless, the pragmatic optimistic mindset helps a leader to cushion the impact of a crisis on their own and their stakeholders' psyches through the execution of self-management and group regulation approaches discussed in Chapter Five.

When Leaders Lose Their Voice – A Case Study

Abe is a high-flying food and beverage executive whose previous experience before joining his present organization spanned the military and industrial sectors. He was winding up his third assignment overseas and looking forward to his next move to a C-suite role in the head office. In fact, preliminary discussions had commenced, and he was a shoo-in for two likely roles. The board saw him as a contender for the CEO role at the right time.

Abe is the type of person who commands the stage when he speaks. His towering strengths are his warmth, eloquence, and ability to express complexities in relatable terms. His reputation for having a strategic approach to communication is solid within the media community and among various stakeholders.

Abe's breadth of responsibilities is wide. He oversees the company's end-to-end business in 30+ counties with a total population of well over two billion people who speak 500+ languages. In addition, he is responsible for the P&L that covers the company's entire value chain in the region.

His seemingly perfect world began to unravel on the fateful day that has been etched in Abe's memory forever. He and the region's management team met over a few days at a serene resort to plan for the following year. While Abe presented his exciting vision of growth to his team, he noticed his executive assistant (EA) answer a phone call. He made little of it until he saw the horrified look on the EA's ordinarily calm countenance. He knew he had to pause the meeting to learn what had happened.

> *"The biggest mistake is believing there is one right way to listen, to talk, to have a conversation-or a relationship."*
> *- Deborah Tannen, communications expert*

It was a mess. Labor unions representing manufacturing and supply chain employees at the company's primary production and distribution hub had just announced an indefinite strike! They walked off the job. An ongoing negotiation suddenly took a turn for the worse. This had never happened before in the company's 30+-year history in that region.

The impact of this crisis was immediate. Production and distribution of *all* the company's products ground to a halt. Also, since the regional hub was impacted, it meant crippling operations in the company's 30+ regions in other countries.

Abe promptly assembled a multifunctional crisis intervention team comprising senior managers in human resources, internal labor disputes, legal, operations, supply chain, manufacturing, brand management, employee and public relations (PR), and finance.

Before the end of that day, the impact of the walkout had already been felt across the region. The media picked up the story, and the competition started to target the company's now-disturbed distributors. The stakeholders were in a panic. The company's market value began to drop precipitously.

Abe quickly called headquarters to send in the cavalry. But he soon learned the hard way that using the services of a foreign-based labor dispute consulting firm sent by headquarters would cause more harm than good. This crisis consumed Abe's every waking moment. His goal was clear, straightforward, and focused: resolve the sticking points of the labor negotiations and reopen the business.

In doing so, he expectedly deprioritized what he considered non-essential activities. Unfortunately, communication was one of them: Abe had no strategy for communication and stakeholder engagement. Also, he delegated most of the decision-making and execution to his communications team. The consequences were ugly.

Abe explains the biggest mistake on the stakeholder front: "Apart from the obvious powerful stakeholders—decision-makers at the labor unions—I did not identify and cater to the needs of other powerful stakeholders in the market, including distributors, local government boards, and consumer advocate groups because one of our products was designated as an "essential commodity." I missed the opportunity for direct engagement and an opportunity to shape the story with these powerful constituents."

Admitting to dropping the ball in the area of communication, Abe said,

> I had no time to carry along the nonunionized employees, as my full attention was on the squeaky wheel—employees participating in the walkout. By doing so, firstly, the leadership team and I lost a lot of credibility with nonunionized employees.
>
> Secondly, I missed an opportunity to rally internal allies who had strong informal relationships with union leadership and could have helped resolve the industrial action faster, even though they had no official title in that regard.

Lastly, my uncharacteristic disengagement caused major distractions for nonunionized employees [who were not on strike], leading to a greater loss of productivity. I did several things right, but missed the boat in those critical areas. Developing and leading the execution of a communication and stakeholder engagement plan could have saved me a lot of headaches and the company tremendous losses.

The multiple fiascos that emerged within the labor strike crisis did not stop there. There was also a breakdown in communication within his team. The labor dispute consulting firm dispatched from headquarters to assist Abe and the region despite having limited knowledge of the market, strongly encouraged the company's lead ne-

> *"Once a human being has arrived on this earth, communication is the largest single factor determining what kinds of relationships he makes with others and what happens to him in the world about him."*
>
> *- Virginia Satir, therapist*

gotiator in the dispute to take what Abe described as "an ill-advised [and] culturally insensitive action that blew up in our faces! Things went from bad to worse pretty quickly." The misguided lead negotiator failed to obtain Abe's approval before implementing such a drastic and insensitive action, which accounted for the breakdown in internal communication. Needless to say, had Abe's approval been sought, he would have stopped the implementation of the inconsiderate action.

Eventually, the negotiation yielded the desired results, and the labor unions called off their strike.

Dire Consequences and Lessons Learned

In Abe's post-crisis reflection, he singled out poor communication and weak stakeholder engagement as the Achilles' heel of his crisis leadership. In his estimation, the losses generated by these two poorly handled areas made him appear like a shadow of himself: "Executive presence and strategic communication have always been my strong suit but [looking back], it's like I became a different person. I lost my voice when it mattered most and [was] sort of mentally detached even though I was physically present. I allowed others to tell our story when that was my [number] one job."

Poor communication and sloppy stakeholder engagement caused the crisis to last 40% longer, dragging the brand down, and costing the company over 120% more. Abe's career also took a hit; the exciting job opportunities waiting for him at headquarters evaporated, his prospects in the organization dimmed, and his leadership brand was irreparably damaged. He accepted a severance package and left the organization about eight months after resolving the labor dispute crisis.

In addition to Abe's reflection discussed above, there are at least three other lessons to learn from his experience. First, never deprioritize communications as it is a critical pillar of your leadership responsibility in a crisis. Abe's rationale was, "I focused most of my attention on the technical aspects of the industrial action like labor laws, health and safety implications for the plants, manufacturing and supply chain management, human resource issues, etc." I must admit that Abe's approach is uncommon based on my experience; I see the other extreme more often than not—many organizations improperly equate their communications team to their crisis management team and disproportionately focus on communication during a crisis. It surely does not hurt to focus a lot on communication, but it shouldn't be done to the extent that it excludes other pertinent functions.

Second, how you feel influences how you lead and communicate. A towering quality of Abe's bright-side personality is his renowned and exceptional strategic communication competency that demonstrates his industry knowledge, sociability, infectious passion, and go-getter mentality. Unfortunately, he buckled under the enormous pressure and stress of the large-scale debacle. Due to low self-monitoring and inadequate self-regulation, his derailer dark-side personality surreptitiously took over, causing his effectiveness to fall off the cliff. Furthermore, he did not engage in group regulation, as even nonunionized employees who did not participate in the strike action felt alienated by him during the crisis.

Third, always take the lead in telling your own story. Abe lost control of the narrative by delegating communication and stakeholder engagement to his capable PR team. That's because the competence of a PR team cannot make up for the void created by a disengaged leader. The leader is the Chief Storytelling Officer. No one else can successfully fill those shoes in a crisis. The people want to hear from you—don't shun them.

> *"The best way to show that a stick is crooked is not to argue about it or to spend time denouncing it, but to lay a straight stick alongside it."*
> *- D.L. Moody, clergy*

In summary, based on what we have covered thus far, I can surmise that there are at least three roles that a leader cannot successfully delegate during a crisis. I have witnessed several leaders delegate them, but it always ends badly. The three nondelegable leadership roles in a time of crisis are direction, decision, and dissemination:

i. **Direction** – establishing mission-vision-values-driven goals that provide clarity in chaos.

ii. **Decision** – sourcing the best available information, analyzing it, and making concerted decisions.

iii. **Dissemination** – purposefully engaging with stakeholders through effective communication that listens, shapes the narrative, and tells your organization's story. In a crisis, your ears are as important as your mouth.

When there is no direction, division is inevitable. In the absence of decisions, there is dysfunction. When dissemination is lacking, disconnection is widespread.

Personality Shapes Communication

Let's dive deeper into how people's personalities shape what and how they communicate. Decades of research on which the Myers-Briggs model was based show that the exchange of information within an organization is influenced by the personalities of individuals involved more than company policies.[329] Information that might seem innocuous to you can be seen as threatening to someone else and yet creative to another, depending on the personalities involved.

Why is information so easily interpreted differently by various people? It is because the information is filtered through each person's mindset, emotions, and personal preferences.

Let's consider the extroversion-introversion view of personalities. Extroverted individuals are energized by being outgoing and engaging with others because "they think, feel, and act in relation to external factors rather than the subjective."[330] Thus, extroverted leaders typically prefer working with their team to understand problems and collaborate to work out a solution. Doing so makes them appear to be open, forthright, and candid in the way they resolve organizational issues.[331]

On the flip side, introverted individuals direct their energy inwardly because their "energy tends to expand through [self] reflection and dwindle during [social] interaction."[332] So, when faced with a troubling challenge like a crisis, introverts tend to go to their energy source, their minds. They are prone to withdrawing to intensively think through the issues and turn the matter over in their minds.[333] Consequently, introverted leaders may be erroneously perceived as quiet, hard-to-read, disengaged, and even indifferent to resolving crises.

Now, let's consider the effect of personality on leadership and communication from the optimism-pessimism lens. A leader's level of optimism will influence the content, timing, delivery, and direction of information. Optimistic leaders, due to their positive view of the future, tend to boost the morale of their team and are generally rated as better leaders by their teams.[334] This is crucial since employees are normally demoralized by the stress of a crisis.[335] However, as discussed in Chapter Two, leaders who demonstrate unrestrained optimism can escalate and complicate a crisis if they minimize the crisis's impact on the organization, ignore future negative repercussions of the crisis that need to be addressed, or downplay its adverse effect on stakeholders.

Pessimists, on the other hand, expect failures and disappointments. Thus, their assessment of a crisis is likely to be accurate, factual, and less embellished. Such an approach can be a breath of fresh air to an organization due to the leader's candor and clarity about the challenges at hand.[336]

However, pessimistic leaders' bleak view of the future is prone to stalling creativity and hampering innovation within their team—their gloomy future view in a chaotic situation like a crisis can trigger the "why try" syndrome that kills initiatives in their team. Pessimists like Abe in the case study discussed earlier in this chapter tend to disengage during a crisis. When that happens, the team will also likely disengage from finding a solution because innovative thinking is negatively correlated to pessimism.[337]

> *"The ability to simplify means to eliminate the unnecessary so that the necessary may speak."*
> *- Hans Hoffmann, painter*

Consistently negative communication from a pessimistic leader can cripple the entire organization and discourage stakeholders.[338, 339] Pessimism erodes the will to fight and communication (or a lack of it) exposes that condition.

In contrast, leaders with the pragmatic optimist mindset fuse together the best characteristics of both optimism and pessimism to create conscientious and engaging communication that is grounded in the reality of the damage, but convincing about solutions to address the issues, and inspiring to envision a better future in the post-crisis world.

Similarly, your relationship with information is skewed by your view of the future; that is, whether you are optimistic or pessimistic.[340] This connection is crucial because a leader's relationship with information will influence their communication strategy. Therefore, the consciously developed pragmatic optimistic mindset shapes how you will internalize, interact with, and interpret information:

  i.   Internalize – relates to how you receive information,
  ii. Interact with – relates to how you process information, and
  iii. Interpret – relates to the judgment and decisions you make from processing the information.

The Channel Matters—A Case Study

Better.com is a New York-based mortgage origination tech company whose growth exploded during the COVID-19 pandemic. Mortgage rates were historically low, spurring huge business volume and helping the company's valuation hit $6 billion by April 2021.

However, by the fourth quarter of 2021, the company's leadership believed it was facing a business crisis due to drastic changes in the homeownership industry. This crisis created significant issues for Better.com in the areas of "market efficiency, performance, and productivity," according to CEO Vishal Garg.[341] Management needed to address this crisis by taking action and communicating with employees.

On December 1, 2021, Garg invited almost 10% of the company's workforce to a Zoom call and opened the meeting with the now-infamous twenty-four-word announcement delivered in a monotone: "If you're on this call, you are part of the unlucky group that is being laid off. Your employment here is terminated effective immediately."

The more than 900 employees on the call were stunned by the mass firing announcement for two reasons. First, only seven months before the notorious Zoom call, in May 2021, Softbank-funded Better.

com had received a massive cash injection of $750 million ahead of the deal closure. That is normally a great sign, and the company's leadership did tout the funding as good news. In an upbeat email to all employees following the cash injection, CFO Kevin Ryan wrote,

> We pulled forward the funding of our SPAC [special purpose acquisition company][10] deal... With this new structure the company will fortify our balance sheet and position us as extremely well capitalized in a tough mortgage market... We will continue working through the process of public listing but the most important step has been taken (getting the money).[342]

CFOs are known to be cautious and meticulous. So when a CFO strikes such an optimistic tone as recently as Ryan did, you can't blame the laid-off employees for being shocked.

Second, the impersonal channel of communicating the firing—a terse three-minute Zoom meeting—chosen by the company's leadership left much to be desired. A former employee who was on the Zoom call summarized it this way, "They dumped us like trash."[343] Another employee aimed squarely at the CEO's manner of communication and described it as showing a "lack o humanity."[344]

The ill-advised channel of communication, heartless timing (just three weeks before the Christmas holidays), and the cold manner in which Garg communicated to the affected employees turned a typical business crisis into a massive leadership crisis that gained the attention

"The problem with communication is the illusion that it has taken place." - George Bernard Shaw, playwright

of global media and unleashed a heavy dose of negativity toward the company.[345] Better.com's board called the developments "very regrettable," and Garg said to the remaining employees, who rightly felt

---

10 A special purpose acquisition company (SPAC) is a publicly listed shell corporation with the aim of acquiring an existing private company as a way of bypassing the traditional initial public offering (IPO) process.

nervous, "…in communicating [the layoffs], I blundered the execution. In doing so, I embarrassed you."[346]

One week after the botched communication of the mass layoff, the board abruptly announced that Garg would proceed to go on leave. He returned to work over a month later.

Significantly, the company is still reeling from the fallout of the failed communication. After seeing how the leadership treated their former colleagues, the remaining employees lost confidence in the organization's management. Several executives and staff resigned from Better.com following the December 2021 communication debacle.

Likewise, the general negative market sentiments toward the company continued to depress revenue and business prospects. In early March 2022, it became public that Better.com planned to lay off an additional 4,000 employees, or about 50% of its workforce across the US and India. This time, the actual mass firing did not make the news as communication appeared to be better managed in comparison. But it seems it's too little too late.[347]

As of the writing of this book, Garg is being sued by a former executive vice president of the company for misleading investors to facilitate the SPAC deal.[348]

A Better Approach Than Better.com

When a crisis hits, all communication elements are impacted in one shape or form —context and environment, sender, encoding, channel/medium of transmission, receiver, decoding, and feedback.[349] All the components interrelate and create a loop (see Figure 8-1).

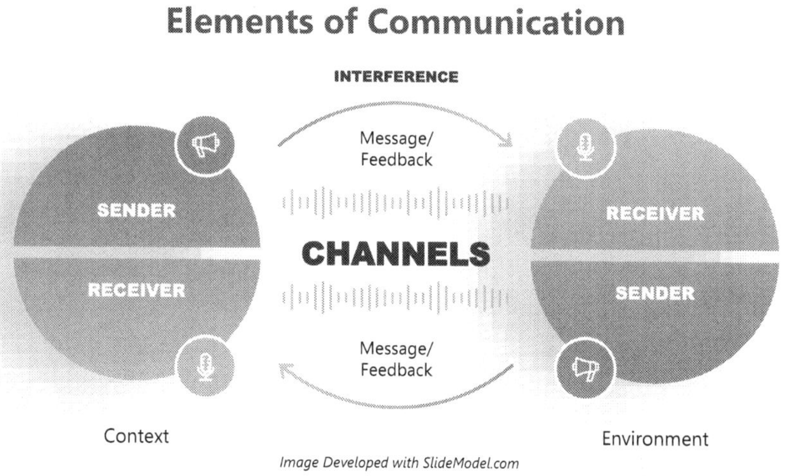

Elements of Communication

Image Developed with SlideModel.com

Figure 8-1: The elements of communication

In the example of Better.com, the business crisis was the context and environment. Garg was the sender whose mindset, perceptions, emotions, and behaviors went into encoding the message. The channel was Zoom. The receiver was the group of 900+ employees who decoded the message and provided scathing feedback. Each of these components of communication was impacted by the crisis.

The context and environment were supercharged with the business risks articulated by management and the enormous task of firing so many people. Plus, it was close to the holidays. Garg, the sender, was so stressed that he admitted on the

> *"Leadership is communicating to people their worth and potential so clearly that they come to see it in themselves."*
> – Stephen Covey, author

Zoom call, "The last time I [laid off employees], I cried. This time I hope to be stronger."[350] Thanks to the COVID-19 pandemic, Zoom has been warmly embraced as a mainstream communication channel; however, the sensitive nature of Garg's message and the expected impact on employees made it a poor choice, devoid of humanity. The affected employees (the receivers), in their decoding and feedback, felt devalued and dehumanized.

No element of communication escapes the impact of a crisis.

It takes a conscientious communicator—as demonstrated by the mindset and attribute of pragmatic optimists—to *painstakingly* reflect on all the elements of communication, *meticulously* encode an apt message, and *carefully* choose the most appropriate channel of communication that will ensure that the encoding and feedback that are done by the receiver produces the results envisioned by the sender.[351] Such leaders clearly understand what parts of communication they control—sender, encoding, and channel. Similarly, they are not confused about the elements of communication that are out of their control but not beyond their influence—receiver, decoding, feedback, context, and environment. Lastly, they look out for and reduce "noise" that can be a form of interference. Noise is anything that can distort the message. Garg's cold message and poor channel choice generated tremendous noise that interfered with decoding and feedback.

Pragmatic optimists bring to the table a highly developed sense of self-awareness that recognizes the impact of a crisis on their mental and emotional states and work to limit their dark-side personalities. They consciously combine pessimism and optimism to achieve self-management. Following that, their group regulation acumen equips them to read the room and take the pulse of their intended audience. Above all, they understand the power of a leader's empathy, especially during chaos and disorder.

Crisis Impact on The Receiver

As discussed earlier, decoding and feedback occur on the receiver's side of the communication framework. A deeper understanding of how these three communication elements are impacted by crisis is necessary for senders to achieve their message objectives.

The RISE-UP characteristics of a crisis discussed in Chapter One affect receivers, who are usually also stakeholders, primarily by changing:

1. **How they absorb the information.** The way they hear information is the first part of decoding. The channel heavily influences this process as methods of successfully transmitting messages in noncrisis may likely fail during a crisis. The leader/sender must choose the most appropriate channel of information (on a case-by-case basis, depending on the nature of the crisis), considering the context, environment, sensitivity of the message, and possible effect on the stakeholder/receiver.

   When it comes to communication, the channel is as important as the message. Choosing an unsuitable channel increases the noise level, distorts the message, and leads to a failure to meet the sender's objectives.

2. **How they administer the information.** The way stakeholders process information is the second part of decoding. This is where the brain of a stakeholder sorts out the information and assigns meaning to the message.[352] For the sender to interpret the message, the word choice, sender's emotions, message content, and symbols are translated into the stakeholder's life experiences.

   "When everyone is against you, it means that you are absolutely wrong or absolutely right."
   - Albert Guinon, playwright

   The latter is influenced by the receiver's view of life (optimism or pessimism) and emotional state, all of which are profoundly influenced by the exigencies of the crisis. Stakeholders process information differently during a crisis.

   For leaders in a crisis, the themes that run through their mission, vision, and values need to align with what they transmit for the receiver's processing to yield the appropriate feedback. If a new message no longer aligns with the big picture, then there must be clear reasons for the misalignment.

3. **How they act on the information.** The way stakeholders react to a sender's message is known as feedback. The crisis impact on this final part of the communication flow (before restarting the loop) is immense. If the context and environment are volatile, uncertain, confusing, or emotionally charged (characteristic of a crisis), feedback required in such a scenario is typically instantaneous. This setting allows the sender to explain, clarify or justify their message based on the receiver's feedback. Thus, a sender will be wise to utilize face-to-face oral channels that facilitate such interaction. A pragmatic optimistic leader thinks ahead and walks through each communication component before initiating the process. One way they do this successfully is through empathy. They put themselves in the shoes of diverse receivers and simulate receivers' experiences through the decoding and feedback process. This mindset also allows you to consider the best word choice, intonation, pace of speech, and channel for your message to produce the desired feedback. Regarding communication, pragmatic optimists do not "shoot first and ask questions later."

In summary, envisioning how their core messages will be transmitted, translated, interpreted, and acted upon by stakeholders is what pragmatic optimists do. It is shocking to see many leaders ignore this proactive approach and mess up communication, creating dire consequences. The pragmatic optimistic mindset methodically caters to the elements of messaging to produce conscientious communication that delivers value to the organization.

Three Communication Principles of Pragmatic Optimists

The following three communication principles guide pragmatic optimists:

1. **The relatability of empathy** — Let's start by looking at two definitions of social power. First, it is defined as having the ability to influence the thoughts, feelings, and actions of others.[353] Second, social power also means creating legitimacy by establishing customs, setting standards, and developing values others adopt without intimidation or inducement.[354]

If we combine these two definitions and consider the workplace context, it becomes clear that leaders wield significant social power in their organizations. The larger the teams they lead, the more substantial social power they possess.

One of the main advantages of social power is the ability to operate in an executive function with a strong focus on goal setting and goal attainment and influencing others to take desired actions to achieve certain objectives.[355] Unfortunately, a major downside of having social power can upend your communications strategy. That shortcoming is a lower level of empathy. Simply put, possessing social power alters the brain's ability to empathize.[356] Organizational leaders are prone to suffer from an inadequacy that blocks their ability to sense and make sense of what others are feeling.[357]

I find it ironic and a strange twist of fate that empathy, the ability to experience and explain what others feel,[358] is impaired in leaders (due to their social power) even though they depend entirely on others to be successful.

Also, social power erodes a leader's sensitivity to their environment, and those around them, especially when they are intently focused on achieving a goal.[359] This is due to a phenomenon known as tunnel vision, the inability to see the bigger picture due to a narrow focus on an idea, a process, or a goal.[360]

How does a pragmatic optimistic leader overcome these shortcomings? First, increase your self-awareness. Admit that having social power is a two-edged sword that enables you to function and achieve goals, yet inhibits your ability to empathize. It is crucial to embrace these contradictions and deficiencies in how the human brain is wired.

Second, increase your perspective-taking, the process of seeing the world through the eyes of others.[361] You can accomplish this by actively seeking and documenting the viewpoints of subordinates, cross-functional colleagues, and external stakeholders about a situation, e.g., a crisis and its impact on them. The perspective-taking process will help you to form a more rounded view.

Third, increase your sensitivity to others. Pulse checking is a frequent sensitivity check-in with stakeholders that is both formal (using survey instruments) and informal (a casual chat). I call it "stakeholder listening." One of the primary objectives of pulse checking is to pick up on the general mood and feelings of the target stakeholder about broad or specific matters. But one caution about the informal pulse-check: avoid becoming an unwitting "grapevine clearinghouse" to whom unsubstantiated and malicious rumors are fed and extracted. Unfortunately, some paranoid leaders consciously power and participate in the grapevine to know what is happening. Such leaders are easily manipulated and prone to being stage-managed to make strategic decisions based on hearsay.

2. **The repairability of positivity** — What is clear from my study and was extensively discussed in Chapter One is that unrestrained optimism and unhelpful pessimism do more harm than good.[362] Communication founded on unrestrained optimism will inflict additional damage to the organization's already-battered reputation because

> *"Many attempts to communicate are nullified by saying too much."*
> – Robert Greenleaf, author

the leader will come across as disconnected from reality or lacking sincerity. Similarly, nothing drains the morale of a team battling a crisis faster than its manager's pessimism. "It's like being heckled, or worse still, tackled by your teammate while playing a team sport," said one of the executives in my study. They described how such an experience led to a protracted crisis by ruining the organization's chances of quickly resolving the situation.

However, when leaders combine optimism and pessimism to create a pragmatic optimistic mindset, they report success in deploying communication as a tool to repair the damage done to the positivity-powered goodwill and brand by a crisis.

Using communication as a tool to repair an organization's crisis-damaged positivity requires the following three leadership behaviors that are powered by the pragmatic optimism mindset for it to be successful:

i. **Shun overpromising** – The temptation to overcommit is an optimistic trait that a pragmatic optimist reins in. Overpromising undermines leadership integrity and authenticity and may ignite a new round of crises.

ii. **Strive to exceed expectations** – Pragmatic optimistic leaders ascertain stakeholder expectations, then aim to exceed them. This is particularly crucial in a crisis because doing so helps to rebuild trust, one of the early victims of a crisis.

iii. **Stay visible** – Pragmatic optimists understand that their mere physical presence, without saying a word, is a source of formidable communication during a crisis. A leader's physical presence in a crisis conveys at least three key nonverbal messages to stakeholders:

   • **Association** - "I am here with you."
   • **Obligation** - "I am committed to you."
   • **Collaboration** - "I am ready to support you."

These vital messages reassure and anchor stakeholders and build trust between the parties. This nonverbal aspect of communication is one of the most overlooked powers of leadership that research participants told me they learned to appreciate through experience after many years. Thus, this confirms the criticality of nonverbal messaging in a leader's communications toolbox.

3   **The replicability of optimism** — Chapter Five discusses how pragmatic optimists consciously externalize their thoughtful confidence to replicate optimism in internal and external stakeholders. That is because they appreciate that optimism (like pessimism) is highly contagious and recognize that communication effectively transmits the mindset during a crisis.

Figure 8-2 represents an intersection of the best of both worlds that the pragmatic optimistic mindset enables you to have in relation to conscientious communication.

To Achieve Conscientious Communication, The Pragmatic Optimist Is Able To...

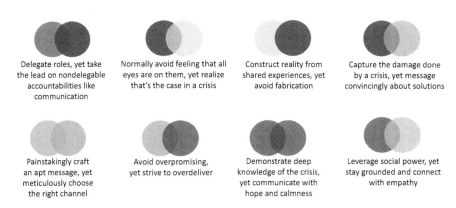

Figure 8-2: Pairings of optimism with pessimism traits to form the pragmatic optimism mindset for achieving conscientious communication

Up Close and Personal

Reflection Activity: How would you rate your level of communication during your last crisis? In what way could you have used conscientious communication instead?

_____

_____

_____

_____

_____

_____

Of the three nondelegable leadership roles in a time of crisis—direction, decision, and dissemination—which ones do you struggle with the most?

_____

_____

_____

_____

_____

There are three ways a crisis affects receivers of a message—the way they absorb, administer, and act on information. Which of the three impacts stands out to you in a recent crisis you handled and why?

_____

_____

_____

_____

_____

CHAPTER NINE

Connection to Caring Systems

In everyone's life, at some time, our inner fire goes out.
It is then burst into flame by an encounter with
another human being. We should all be thankful for
those people who rekindle the inner spirit.
- Albert Schweitzer, in *Out of My Life and Thought: An Autobiography*[363]

What you will learn in this chapter:
- The lone wolf leader.
- The symbiotic relationship between optimism and social networks.
- The power of human-to-human connections and relationships.
- The value of asking others for help.
- The barriers to asking others for help.
- The sacrifice of vital relationships.
- The cost of relationships and social capital.

When The Fire Goes Out

A participant in my postdoctoral study, a leader in the real estate sector who oversees a multinational division with over 30,000 employees, has a rags-to-riches origin story. Born into poverty, the fourth of seven children to a janitor father and factory-worker mother, this leader started working at age ten, like his siblings, to contribute to the family's meager finances. Having barely finished high school and due to many family and financial distractions, college was simply out of the question—it was unaffordable.

Through the experiences of several menial jobs, including dumpster diving, this leader was eventually hired as a property maintenance worker. Real estate unlocked this young laborer's passion, and he rose through the ranks to become a senior vice president of a global multibillion-dollar commercial property management firm, heading multiple business groups. That is a significant accomplishment given this individual's background.

While reflecting on an unforgettable crisis that threatened to wipe out a major business group within the division, the leader said,

> Contrary to what people might think about me, I am not always pumped and fired up. Sometimes, my fire literally goes out when I am under intense pressure and [dealing with] a swim-or-sink situation [with] a heavy dose of uncertainty.
>
> [But] I don't wait for the fire to go out completely. Once I feel my baseline passion diminishing because of a stressful situation, and my [inner] fire turns into embers, I turn to my trusted social network—family, friends, mentors, colleagues, and industry contacts—before the walls close in. The biggest lesson from my trusted social network is [that] my crisis experiences are not unique as they share their relatable experiences, support me, and broaden my horizon. What a relief that is. A helpful network [like that] frees me up to learn and grow. [And] before I know it, my fire is back, raging like an inferno!

When the inner fire goes out due to stress, negative emotions, failure, pressure, and uncertainties, an individual's leadership competency may take a direct hit. When that happens, the risk of missteps rises considerably, especially during nerve-racking situations like crises.

When the fire goes out in a person, it often takes another person's support to help rekindle the flame.

This chapter is about the power of human-to-human (H2H) connection during a crisis. The value of a leader's connection to caring social systems in a crisis is by far the most surprising of my research findings. I did not find sufficient literature discussing the topic prior to data gathering, so it was unexpected from an academic perspective. However, when I put on my practitioner's lens as a global executive leader, I was not surprised that research participants consistently highlighted the value of this pragmatic optimistic behavior.

The Lone-Wolf Leader

I have observed in practice a large and influential school of thought that believes "leadership is the loneliest job in the world." It is a highly pervasive perspective that many leaders intuitively believe and unconsciously practice. A highly respected leader and author once said, "The price of leadership is loneliness... I think it is inescapable."[364] Ernest Shackleton, a pillar of the Heroic Age of Antarctic Exploration (spanning 1897 to 1922), was resigned to the viewpoint that "loneliness is the penalty for leadership."[365] Finally, some point to the arts for evidence, quoting a popular line from a William Shakespeare play, "Uneasy lies the head that wears the crown."[366] That is the "lone wolf" depiction of a leader.

Without a doubt, individuals with a high level of commitment to some issues are confident enough to stand alone. As Zig Ziglar said, "Most people who fail in their dreams fail not from lack of ability but from lack of commitment." Also, it is not uncommon for *"One foe is too many and a hundred friends are too few." – Native American proverb* such leaders to find themselves in a one-person minority when they make unpopular decisions. Similarly, when their purpose and vision take them down a road less traveled, they may be hard-pressed to find a travel companion.

However, evaluating those scenarios and similar situations to mean that leadership is a lonely vocation or that leaders must be lone wolves is a gross misunderstanding of the concept and purpose of leadership. From my experience, some who embrace the leadership-is-lonely doctrine express their personal preference for working alone, as captured in the Merriam-Webster dictionary definition of a lone wolf: "a person who *prefers* to work, act, or live alone."[367] So, it may all be down to the individual's preference. Furthermore, while your vision may spur you to take the unbeaten path, your true leadership capability is demonstrated when you convince enough other people to follow you on the journey. If you are alone, you are not leading anyone.

The increasing speed, size, and seriousness of crises nowadays have raised the stakes for lonely leaders. In a world riddled with fiascos, adversities, and turbulence, lone-wolf leaders are increasingly caught helpless and don't make it through the night. Wolves in the wild are highly social and avoid the risk of being alone. According to the Wolf Education & Research Center, wolves do not prefer to be alone and are only alone as a transitory rite of passage to form their own packs[368]—wolves are alone on a journey to not being alone. As the lone wolf is a misnomer in nature, so is the concept among leaders in human-based organizations. As a fully functional ship cannot but be surrounded by water, so a fully functional leadership is not built to be alone. Leadership is designed for the benefit of other people. So how can you be lonely on a job that only has meaning when it's impacting others?

"Leadership in Progress: Please Keep Off!"

Too many leaders have been practicing social distancing long before COVID-19. Some were highly social and engaging as individual contributors but transformed into loners as they went higher in the hierarchy. Why? Here are four reasons driving the lone wolf-approach of leaders who keep others at arm's length.

1) Some do it to be respected—**the scarcity mentality**. If you believe that you need to deprive the team of your presence so that when you do show up, after the team has yearned for your presence, you will then be respected, you have what I call a scarcity mentality. This type of leadership mentality, fairly common among "tough leaders" (discussed in Chapter Five), believes in trading presence for respect. Even when physically present, such leaders may be withdrawn or adopt other avoidance tactics to achieve the same purpose.[369, 370] The basis of this faulty viewpoint is that when leaders are easily accessible, they will not be as respected as when they are scarce—like a commodity versus a high-value item scenario.

   In reality, the opposite happens. When a team is deprived of a leader's presence and engagement, the leader's value is quite negligible, even though such a leader rarely fails to claim the credit. I have observed that loner leaders create a widespread situation in mid-to-large corporations where a team is flourishing *despite* the absence of leadership. A deliberate disengagement of leaders negatively impacts the team's productivity if it is unable to function at an optimal level without appropriate guidance.

2) Some do it to be feared—**the threat mentality**. This is the domain of individuals who exhibit the "tough leader" syndrome. Wielding fear as a weapon to ensure an autocratic leadership system may require the leader to limit interactions with the team.[371] And on rare occasions when they show up, they deliberately instill anxiety and apprehension in their colleagues. They believe that a leader ought to be feared, so they walk around with a frown. Unfortunately, fear-based leadership destabilizes organizational creativity, a valuable attribute needed to successfully navigate a crisis,

because employees react with damaging coping mechanisms like withholding efforts, "defensive silence,"[11] and knowledge hiding.[372, 373, 374]

> *"Try to be a rainbow in someone's cloud."*
> – Maya Angelou, writer

Some leaders incorporate this approach in the design of their offices. I recall meeting a CEO in his office, and the social distancing barriers (this was many years before COVID-19) were not lost on me. First, the visitors' chairs were at least 20 feet away from him (no, he is not a germophobe). In addition, I noticed that when we were both seated, he towered over me, so I looked closely and realized that his sitting area was raised at least two feet higher than my side of the room. His employees, who noted that he changed the office design when he became the CEO, later confirmed what I had deduced—he rules with an iron fist, finds alternative proposals insulting, and desires to be feared.

3) Some do it because they prefer operations to leadership—**the expert mentality**. Some individuals are more interested in the operational and technical details of the business than in leading people. Like most people, they cut their teeth and qualified for leadership by being subject-matter experts in human resources, finance, sales, marketing, or information technology. However, they never stepped out of the expert domain and did not embrace their role as people leaders. This type of leader will have their hand in many areas of the business's operations except the people they are supposed to lead. This leader avoids engaging with people.

A friend of mine, who is an executive in a multinational company, admitted that the part of the job they dislike most is dealing with people. While they love their job otherwise, interacting with and

---

11 Defensive silence is defined as a conscious and proactive behavior adopted by employees to protect themselves from perceived external threats and avoid conflict within an organizational context. It involves holding back potentially valuable information if an employee perceives a backlash from sharing it.

leading people often causes them a lot of angst and frustration. The most mind-blowing part about this story is that this leader is the head of human resources! It makes you wonder how leaders with that mindset progress so far in organizations—I believe it is most likely because this flawed mentality is more prevalent than thought.

4) Some do it because that's their preference—**the self-absorbed mentality**. Individuals in this category fit the Merriam-Webster dictionary definition of a lone wolf because they "prefer to work … alone." Ironically enough, this is not necessarily an intro-vert-only mentality. While some introverts identify as loners, the reality is the two attributes should not be conflated. Introverts gain energy from within but don't need to be loners. Broadly speaking, introverts invest in and cherish deep relationships and are more likely to be more empathetic and thoughtful about others than the general population.[375] That is the opposite of being self-absorbed. The self-absorbed mentality is about wanting to do your own thing in your own way and primarily using people to accomplish your objective even when it undermines the common good.[376, 377] Self-centeredness and a low level of empathy characterize such leaders.[378] This means extroverts can also have a self-absorbed mentality if inclined to the distinguishing attributes discussed. I have come across some extroverts who fit into this category. At the end of the day, their high level of social interaction is more about themselves than others.

We can further regroup the four reasons some leaders embrace the fictional lone-wolf concept into two broad root causes. First is their misconception of the true essence of leadership, as evidenced by scarcity and threat

"It's better to hang out with people better than you. Pick out associates whose behavior is better than yours, and you'll drift in that direction."
– Warren Buffett, investor

mentalities. The second is a failure to adjust their personal preferences to meet leadership demands, as manifested as expert and self-absorbed mentalities.

On the contrary, pragmatic optimists avoid these four drivers of lone-wolf leaders. That is because they recognize that life in general, and leadership in particular, is built to be experienced as a member of a pack of wolves, not as a lone wolf. So, pragmatic optimists strive to identify their pack because they believe doing so will help them reach their full potential. Find your pack, and you will find your spark—especially when your fire goes out.

The Interplay Between Optimism and Social Networks

Research shows a reciprocal relationship between an individual's optimism and their H2H connections. The interplay is demonstrated by the influence of optimism on an individual's approach to building, investing in, and maintaining a social network and the latter's impact on one's level of optimism.

Contemporary research shows that an individual's level of optimism can either strengthen or weaken their H2H connections. That is because an optimistic leader is more likely to desire the creation of new social networks and tend to invest in strengthening the existing connections.[379, 380] In addition, compared to pessimists, more optimistic leaders will also be more enthusiastic and proactive about leaving behind old connections and moving into new ones.[381]

Furthermore, a scientific experiment found that one's level of optimism is a "significant predictor of future depressive symptoms."[382] Thus, a low level of optimism (or high pessimism) indicates that the individual is more susceptible to depression in the future. This is important in considering optimism's influence on H2H connections because it has long been established that social isolation or disconnection from one's social network is the most telling symptom of depressive behavior.[383, 384, 385]

On the other hand, a healthy social network greatly boosts an individual's optimism. A wholesome network of H2H connections reinforces the commonality of pain and success and is a constant reminder that we are not alone. Eminent modern-day media artist Liat Segal puts it this way: "One thing that is clearer to me every day is how much we all have in common, and one of those commonalities is that we all think we are alone." Similarly, a person's caring network of H2H connections plays an immense role in their mental health and overall well-being. The size of this network and how well a person can rely on those in their network can influence the person's mindset toward optimism or pessimism.[386, 387]

In addition, leaders who can rely on their network of family and friends for emotional support are less distressed and more optimistic during crises. In other words, the mere existence of such a reliable and caring system of H2H connections is sufficient to enhance the optimism of a person facing a stressful situation. Moreover, perseverance, a trait of optimism, is further strengthened in individuals who constantly interact with their social network while facing a predicament.[388]

The Power of an H2H Network

This section provides further evidence that building and staying connected to a social network of caring systems is rooted in established science and not merely feel-good advice. I believe offering additional proof in this section is necessary because of the widespread dismissal of the value of social interactions in today's organizations. In spite of this, the extensive social isolation experienced during the COIVD-19 pandemic and its negative effects have challenged the erroneous relationships-belong-on-the-back-burner perspective. Still, some professionals say, "I'm in a highly specialized field; people close to me have no idea about what I do, so what value can they add to me?" That is one way to look down on and forfeit the value of their network. Let us closely examine the power of H2H connections.

In a popular 2015 TED Talk with total views of over 42 million, Robert Waldinger, professor of psychiatry at Harvard Medical School, spoke about the value of a strong social network for the individual.[389] Waldinger's discussion relied heavily on the results of what is touted as the world's longest-running research about happiness. At its commencement, 724 males entered the study as teenagers and have been monitored for over eight decades and counting. Subsequently, in 2005, their spouses were included in the research. Each year, Harvard researchers will conduct extensive interviews with and administer surveys to the surviving participants to monitor the statuses of their social networks, home lives, careers, health, well-being, and happiness, among other factors.

> *"In prosperity, our friends know us; in adversity, we know our friends." - John Churton Collins, literary critic*

About 8% of the original participants were still alive at the time of the TED Talk in 2015. Research participants have had various career roles, including bricklayers, lawyers, factory workers, and doctors. One of the initial participants became the president of the United States (John F. Kennedy).[390] The results of the study discussed below were shared at the 75th-year milestone of the ongoing research by Waldinger, the current director of the study:

> The clearest message that we get from this 75-year study is that good relationships keep us happier and healthier. We've learned three big lessons about relationships.
>
> The first is that social connections are really good for us and that loneliness kills—people who are more socially connected to family, to friends, to [the] community, are happier; they are physically healthier, and they live longer.
>
> The second big lesson that we learned is that it's not just the number of friends you have, and it's not whether or not you're in a committed relationship, but it's the *quality* of your close

relationships that matters. Living in the midst of conflict is really bad for our health... And living in the midst of good, warm relationships is protective.

And the third big lesson that we learned is that good relationships don't just protect our bodies, they [also] protect our brains...The good life is built with good relationships.

To answer the question of whether or not investing in H2H connections to create caring systems is just feel-good advice—it is sound and science-based advice that helps you feel good and be at your best. These connections give you the best odds of success when you face inevitable crises. It is also a practical and tangible solution for leaders who experience loneliness in their day-to-day operations—a fulfilled life needs the right company.

The Value of Asking for Help

Generally, humans have a tendency to go to great lengths to hide the adversities and challenges we are going through from those around us who may be willing to help. According to a British survey conducted on behalf of the WKD brand of drinks, the most common lie people tell is, "Nothing is wrong—I'm fine." We are inclined to want to solve problems ourselves instead of asking for help, a trait that we develop early in life.[391, 392] Socialization plays a role in strengthening this proclivity because kids who take on tasks without seeking help are praised and rewarded as "independent," while those who call for assistance may be labeled as "needy."

Nonetheless, to achieve any significant goal, chances are high that you will need help. Your vision is likely too small and uninspiring if you don't need help achieving it. Not needing help to accomplish your vision could be a telltale sign that you need to broaden and deepen that vision because a characteristic of a formidable and influential goal is that you cannot do it alone.

A few years ago, I stumbled on an eighty-four-second video of Steve Jobs from 1994, featuring a Silicon Valley Historical Association interview. At that time, Jobs was at Pixar/Disney, and the recording occurred three years before he rejoined Apple Inc. In the brief but highly revealing interview, he expressed his firm conviction that people sell themselves short when they do not ask others for the help they need. To Jobs, remarkable success is often only achievable through asking others for help:

> Most don't get those experiences [because] they've never asked. I've never found anybody that didn't want to help me if I asked them for help...I called up Bill Hewlett [co-founder of Hewlett-Packard] when I was twelve years old... got his number from the phone book. He answered the phone himself, he said, "Yes?" I said, "Hi, I'm Steve Jobs, I'm twelve years old, I'm a student in high school, and I want to build a frequency counter—and I was wondering if you have any spare parts I could have."
>
> And he laughed. He gave me the spare parts to build a frequency counter and he gave me a job that summer at Hewlett-Packard working on the assembly line, putting nuts and bolts together on frequency counters... I was in heaven!
>
> Most people never pick up the phone and call; most people never ask. And that's what separates, sometimes, the people who do things from the people who just dream about them. You got to act. And you've got to be willing to fail.

I have found that when you ask for something, you usually get more than what you ask for. This is what Steve Jobs experienced. The phone call was meant to result in just some surplus spare parts to build a frequency counter. Not only did he receive the spare parts he asked for, but he also received a head

"Be a friend to thyself, and others will be so too."
– Thomas Fuller,
clergyman and historian

start in the technology industry with a summer job at HP. So, set aside your misgivings about asking for help and simply ask.

Generally, infants need help. Of all mammals, human infants are born the most helpless.[393] Without the support of a caregiver, they will not survive. Moreover, children battling chronic health crises definitely need help, and research in the healthcare sector confirms the value of such help. "There is international consensus that sick children should receive care in their homes as far as possible."[394] In the same vein, studies indicate that help from multifaceted sources like "extended family, the church, and healthcare professionals is crucial to parents' endurance when their children are battling illnesses."[395] That is the reason "When families stay together, sick children get stronger" is the slogan for the Ronald McDonald House Charities, a nonprofit organization formed in 1974 to facilitate the power of H2H support to improve the well-being of sick children. We need the help of others to go far in life.

Why We Don't Ask for Help

Let us dig deeper into why we are reluctant to ask others for help. There is no point connecting to a caring system if you don't extract value from it by asking for help. That is because the value of a social network does not automatically flow to individuals connected to it. Such is the irony of human connections—we can have a wide breadth of connections to various networks but remain disadvantaged if we don't draw from those resources. This section is best read as a form of self-assessment to identify which of the seven points below may be hindering you from maximizing the benefit of your existing social network.

Participants in my research reported that when they struggled with asking for help, it was for the following reasons:

1) **Inbred** - Some individuals seem to be hardwired and socialized to be insular, independent, and motivated to get things done and

resolve challenges independently. It doesn't matter if the individual is an extrovert or introvert; this is simply an inclination to want to resolve issues ourselves. Those who identify with the category trace their go-it-alone mentality as far back as they can remember. But the pragmatic optimistic view of raising one's hand to ask for help is usually learned in the school of hard knocks and that it is worthwhile. The first step to embracing this new behavior is that participants recognize how much value they missed out on by not asking for help. These life lessons help moderate the inbred tendency, shifting that mindset to a pragmatic optimistic approach. Experiencing appreciable results from reaching out reinforces the new behavior of asking for help.

2) **Inconvenience** – If you do not want to impose, intrude, and be seen as a burden by others, you belong in this category. Individuals hold back from asking for help because they don't want to be seen as a nuisance or a source of inconvenience. But the reality is that more often than not, we make up reasons why people don't want to help us without asking them. For example, we may reason, "Oh, she must be busy with the acquisition project that she's leading and will not have time for me."

> *"Don't make friends who are comfortable to be with. Make friends who will force you to lever yourself up." - Thomas J. Watson, founder of IBM*

However, pragmatic optimists appreciate that when relationships are genuine, people see it as a privilege or source of joy and not a bother or burden to help others in their network. Pragmatic optimists not only recognize the value that others have but their own value to the network. In addition, people are happy to be asked for help because they are seen as valuable.

3) **Insecure** - Some individuals hold back from asking others for help for fear of being rejected and the consequences of such expected

rejection. This kind of insecurity may be triggered by anticipatory humiliation, a powerful but unpleasant sensation of shame that negatively influences our view of ourselves.[396] Thus, the risk of going out on a limb keeps them from seeking help.

Pragmatic optimists have discovered through experience that most people are willing to help when you are

i.   clear about what you have done so far,

ii. what you need help with, and

iii. what the help means to you.

In the short telephone conversation between Jobs and Hewlett, young Jobs hit the mark on all three requirements when he asked for help. In response, Hewlett was happy to help Jobs with what he needed and then some.

4) **Inadequate** – Not wanting to appear vulnerable, especially to peers, forms a major barrier that keeps many people who need help from seeking it. Individuals who fear being seen as inadequate, needy, and weak when they ask others for help and so pull back from asking fall in this classification. They are held back by their perceived negative portrayal before others when they ask for help. This is particularly true for individuals who have built a "tough leader" persona that exhibits self-sufficiency and no weakness.

Mostly through experience, pragmatic optimists understand that receiving help and giving help is a two-way street where both the receiver and the helper benefit from the exchange. For example, asking for help is a powerful expression of input required to create the desired output that helpers find motivating. Furthermore, research confirms that helpers end up helping themselves even when they did not expect a reward.[397] The long list of benefits to helpers includes gaining a reputation for being supportive, an increase in hope, a stronger connection to the community, a deepening of trusting relationship with the receiver, an increase in social reliability, and a boost in one's positive mood.[398, 399, 400, 401] Thus, asking and helping produce a win-win scenario.

5) **Indiscernible** – People in this category do not ask others for help because they don't know what to ask. The fog of a crisis can make it difficult for you to articulate your needs. For example, a professional colleague of mine was in dire straits. Her husband had been suddenly hospitalized with a serious health condition, and she had three kids to care for. Offers for help started pouring in from her network, but none of them met her needs, so she kept rejecting them. Gradually, the offers to help dried up. Then, she realized that her needs were indiscernible to her social network because she didn't even know what request to make. So, she took the time to articulate her needs and shared them with her network—the responses from her family and friends were as instantaneous as they were positive.

Earlier, we discussed how clarity of asking could counter the asker's insecurity. In this case, the person in need of help is not insecure about asking but is so caught up in the confusion of the crisis that they do not ask for help with clarity. People eager to help you may be clueless about what you need.

Pragmatic optimists have clarity of purpose that helps clear the fog of a crisis (as discussed in Chapter Four). Therefore, they can articulate their needs and purposefully engage with potential helpers systematically. They begin seeking help from individuals in their direct social network but are open to extending the search for assistance to second-and third-degree connections if required.

6) **Insurance** – Some people will not consider asking for help as a shield to protect themselves from being hurt. This is because trust is needed to ask for help; if the helper betrays that trust, willfully or by omission, it can lead to hurt and heartbreak on the asker's part. People who have suffered betrayal in the past shy away from creating, investing in, or trying to benefit from a social

network.[402] Such people find it protective to push others away rather than risk exposing themselves to being heartbroken again. Thus, the wronged individual takes out an "insurance policy," swearing off social networks to protect themselves. They are willing to stew in a problem instead of asking for help.

"When we try to pick out anything by itself, we find it hitched to everything else in the Universe." – John Muir, renowned environmentalist

Pragmatic optimists learn to walk through the hurt. They don't sweep it under the carpet; instead, they work through their hurt to overcome it, which could mean cutting off those who hurt them with malicious intent. After that, they learn to trust again by starting small and gradually increasing their trust as individual members of their network earn their trust again.[403]

7) **Invested** – Many empaths, who are heavily invested in helping others, struggle to ask others for help.[404] In the middle of the COVID-19 pandemic, I conducted a series of development sessions via Zoom with leaders in a hospital network across multiple cities in the Greater Toronto Area. Almost 400 healthcare professionals participated in a survey I conducted during the training sessions. While it was not shocking that virtually all of them scored high on the empathy scale, I found it interesting that more than 75% of them admitted to struggling with asking others for help even though they help others for a living. Helpers struggle to ask for help.

Pragmatic optimistic thinkers use self-awareness to understand that being empathetic comes with a huge weakness: the unwillingness to ask others for help. Change begins with self-awareness and self-reflection. The survey result was certainly an eye-opener for the healthcare professionals, allowing them to come to terms with that weakness and become more open to asking for help. As one of the training participants said, "Now that I know I am not alone in this weakness, [that] I'm not weird. From now [on], I will push aside the nervousness I feel when I need to ask for help." It gets better with practice as the awkward feeling decreases with each attempt.

Regardless of the reason for not seeking help, what was universal among the research participants in my work was their willingness to overcome their misgivings about tapping into their social networks. The comments below by a research participant who is an executive with an extensive background in the consumer packaged goods industry summarized the transition from skepticism about asking for help to a full-throated endorsement.

> Oddly enough, I would say that I probably, looking in hindsight, would have managed certain crises in my executive and professional development better if I were to raise my hand and reached out for support faster than I actually did. And it's funny that we all mature in a certain way that, now that I'm older, I reach out [to others for support] much more. Now that I'm older in more senior jobs, I reach out [to others for support] much more than I was younger. And it makes life so much easier.

The Negative Value of H2H Connections

Even though I presented arguments and evidence that encourage leaders to build their network of caring systems before they are in dire need of assistance, I am aware that H2H connections are not always positive. In fact, some social connections can have pretty negative consequences. That is because not all social networks are created equally; some will significantly increase your risk of failure.

Here is an example of what I mean. In countries where I have accessed reliable data, it is universally known that teenage drivers are involved in more car crashes, including fatal ones, than adults. In the

US and Canada, teenagers are involved in about three to four times more collisions than adults ten to fifteen years older. This wide disparity in crashes between teenagers and adults may be conveniently ascribed to a lack of driving experience. However, I dug deeper and found a social network component to teenage car crashes.

A 2012 study published by the US AAA Foundation for Traffic Safety examined fatal car crashes involving teenage drivers with passengers and contrasted them with data of teenage drivers with no passengers.[405] The results were stark. Young drivers with young passengers are a fatal combination (see Table 9-1).

Teenage Driver Plus	Driver's Risk of Death Per Mile vs. No Passenger
One passenger under 21 years old	Up 44%
Two passengers under 21 years old	Up 100%
Three passengers under 21 years old	Up 300%
One passenger 35 years or older	Down 62%

Table 9-1: Teenage driver's risk of death when compared to driving alone (Source: AAA Foundation for Traffic Safety)

The risk of a teenage driver's death per mile increases by 44% when the young driver has one passenger under 21 years old in the car. That is a dramatic increase in fatality risk, but it gets worse. The risk of a young driver's death increases by 100% and 300% with two and three passengers under 21, respectively. However, the risk of a deadly car crash that kills a teenage driver falls significantly by 62% when only one passenger is 35 years of age or older.

Inferring from the teenage driver fatality study, I propose below the characteristics of social connections that are more likely to create negative value for leaders:

1) **Distracts you from your drive** – A relationship is toxic if it diverts your attention from your 3Ps: purpose, path, plans; overall, your vision. Such social connections are counterproductive. When

you take your eyes off the road, representing your vision, terrible things happen.

2) **Dissuades you from being disciplined**. The reason teenage passengers are bad news for young drivers is not farfetched; they tend to influence the driver to make risky decisions. So, if your social connections encourage you to be careless, impulsive, and imprudent, they are toxic and will likely derail major aspects of your life. Relationships in your social network that egg you on to succumb to your most destructive tendencies should be avoided. Finally, another sign of toxicity in your H2H connections is an urge to prove yourself and impress others. If there are people that bring such energy into your life, mark them and keep them at arm's length. That is what pragmatic optimists do.

> *"Nothing makes one feel so strong as a call for help."*
> – Pope Paul VI, clergy

The Cost of a Social Network

Social capital is an important concept in the field of leadership development. The concept can be defined as the total of the advantages accruing to an individual who taps into a network of relationships to accomplish objectives.[406] Because we work in social settings, social capital is one of the most potent resources a leader can have.[407] This resource complements other companies' resources, such as innovation and expertise.[408] Social capital grows with use and shrinks from disuse. Therefore, social capital is the outcome of activating your H2H connections.

The deployment of this vital resource is influenced by a leader's skill set, personality, and knowledge. Social capital adds to a leader's characteristics because it ties together common threads binding leaders and organizations.[409, 410] While most publications about social capital are limited to relationships within the organization, this book takes a much broader view to extend social capital to all relationships in your social network. That is because, during a crisis, you will also need support from outside the organization to be successful.

Building a formidable social network that can deliver substantial social capital will cost you. Below are seven resources you can expect to invest in while building a strong social network:

1. **Relational**: A prime investment needed to build and maintain your social network investment is your engagement in the relationships themselves. That is the running investment for virtually all relationships. This is where mutual caring and shared respect are built into the relationship.

   Since extroverts are energized by engaging with others, this investment may not be a high barrier for them. However, a significant commitment for extroverts is demonstrating sincere empathy and being genuinely interested in other people. On the other hand, introverts are generally empaths who connect deeply with others but deliberately limit their engagements. Being relational is a massive drain on them psychologically. A participant in my research put it this way,

   > I literally have to psych myself up to meet friends, colleagues, and clients for drinks. I learned to do that [as a way to] advance my career because as a younger professional, I used to avoid [such meetings] completely, and that stalled my career progression. Don't get me wrong, I always enjoy the company when I go and make a lot of progress with those relationships. Still, I always get back [feeling] completely drained mentally and emotionally. It is a lot of work for me. Still is, even after over thirty years of leadership experience.

2. **Influential**: More often than not, your influence lies dormant until you need it or others activate it. Your influence could lead to a tremendous breakthrough and untold opportunities for your connections. Leveraging your professional status, social power, and goodwill to open doors for others creates a multiplier effect of

your influence. This is a resource that most people don't recognize that they have.

3. **Intellectual:** Some of your connections simply need to tap into your wealth of experience and knowledge. When initiated by someone in your social network, the request usually comes in the form of "Can I pick your brain on so and so?" Similar to your influence that remains dormant until deployed, your robust knowledge founded on your distinctive life experiences could benefit others immensely.

"As to diseases, make a habit of two things—to help, or at least, to do no harm."
- Hippocrates

You've already been through several experiences and have been shaped by them. That knowledge is something that your connections could use to avoid the same challenges or mistakes. A couple of years ago, a close friend introduced me to an executive in the supply chain technology industry who wanted to pick my brain about his plans to enroll in a doctorate program while working full time. In 75 minutes, I shared my experience (and those of several colleagues) who did the same thing. As we wrapped up the Zoom meeting, he looked down as he flipped through four or five pages of notes he had written during our call, looked up at the camera, and said, "Thank you so much for saving me unimaginable hardship. Having attended the information sessions of a few schools, I thought I knew what I was getting into before this meeting. Whoa! This [meeting] has been an eye-opener for me."

Please note that the tendency is for you to underrate the real value of your intellectual capacity. Unless hubris is your vice and you believe that you are the universe's gift to mankind, it is hard to see the value that others see in you. So, trust them when they identify valuable intellect in you and share what you know. Your intellectual capital boosts your social capital.

4. **Personal**: Your presence and time are crucial investments appreciated by individuals in your social network. Your involvement and presence in the moment of need are of great value to your connections. This is a powerful resource that can help others through their difficult patch. This is what "just being there" looks like.

5. **Confidential**: This is about being a trusted sounding board, even if you don't have any of the answers. Being someone others can confide in causes your relationships to thrive and grow. This is not using your intellectual knowledge to help a friend or spouse solve a problem. It is simply being able to listen and keep what's been shared confidential. People need someone they can rely on and with whom to share yet-to-be-fully-formed thoughts, without the fear of their issues being aired out to others. Many leaders are problem-solvers, so they miss opportunities to listen without simply jumping in to try to solve problems.

   A Tokyo-based executive I met when I led a global business group surprised me when he asked me to be his mentor. It was surprising because we only had a superficial relationship before then. I soon realized that this executive only needed a sounding board for his thoughts and ideas. Every session was like a brainstorming exercise. We constantly interacted for over six months, and in the end, this executive expressed that the mentoring experience had been beneficial as it increased his self-confidence. I also learned a lot from the discussions.

   Having this type of interaction deepens a relationship. However, be highly selective with whom you choose to confide. Also, be careful to keep in confidence things shared with you—few things destroy relationships faster than disclosing a person's confidential matters to others. It will help your standing in your social network if you don't betray other people's confidence. As the World War II-originated idiom states, "Loose lips sink ships," including friend*ships*.

6. **Financial:** From buying a cup of coffee, paying for a meal, contributing to a family member's down payment to buy a house, to investing seed capital in a friend's entrepreneurial venture, maintaining a healthy social network sometimes carries a financial tab. It would be best if you didn't break the bank to do this and seek expert financial advice for substantial monetary commitments.

7. **Material:** Material investments in relationships are tangible. While they do not cost you money directly, most material investments can be assessed in financial terms. An example of this investment is rendering your professional service pro bono to help get your friend's business off the ground.

"We eat with a friend because of the pleasure of friendship not because we lack." – Yoruba Proverb, from West Africa

To recap, the objective of this section is to highlight that building and maintaining a healthy social network requires investments. Another aim of discussing these seven relationship-building investments is to encourage you to be deliberate about allocating and expending these valuable resources to build and nurture relationships well before you need them. It would help if you considered having a "social network budget" consisting of all seven investment components. Maximizing your connection to caring systems requires you to show that you care. Life is not a gift you own, but a loan you owe; a loan that is serviced when we serve others. I recall the following words from a plaque I saw some years ago:

Nothing in nature lives for itself
Rivers don't drink their own water
Trees don't eat their own fruit
The sun doesn't shine for itself
A flower's fragrance is not for itself
Living for each other is the rule of nature.

Figure 9-1 represents an intersection of the best of both worlds that the pragmatic optimistic mindset enables you to have in relation to connection to caring systems.

To Achieve Connection To Caring Systems, The Pragmatic Optimist Is Able To...

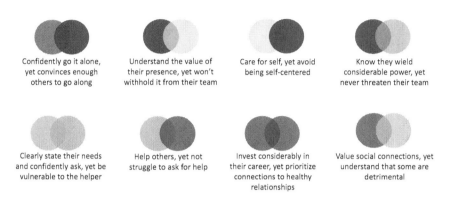

Confidently go it alone, yet convinces enough others to go along	Understand the value of their presence, yet won't withhold it from their team	Care for self, yet avoid being self-centered	Know they wield considerable power, yet never threaten their team
Clearly state their needs and confidently ask, yet be vulnerable to the helper	Help others, yet not struggle to ask for help	Invest considerably in their career, yet prioritize connections to healthy relationships	Value social connections, yet understand that some are detrimental

Figure 9-1: Pairings of optimism with pessimism traits to form the pragmatic optimism mindset for achieving connections to caring systems

Up Close and Personal

Reflection Activity: On a scale of 1 to 5, with 1 being *strongly unwilling* and 5 being *strongly willing*, how willing have you been in the past to ask others for help, and why?

_____

_____

_____

_____

Which of the seven reasons leaders are reluctant to ask others for help resonates with you? Why does it resonate with you?

_____

_____

_____

_____

What are the top three things you can start doing now to improve your willingness to ask for help?

1) _____

2) _____

3) _____

If you identify as an empath, you will likely struggle to ask other people for help. If so, what are three practical things you can do to begin to work on asking others for help in your social network?

1) _____

2) _____

3) _____

Successful professionals tend to give something up to progress in their careers. What have you given up, and how can you redress the situation?

_____

_____

_____

_____

CHAPTER TEN

The Leadership Roundtable: *In Their Own Words*

No matter what anybody tells you, words and ideas can change the world.
– **Tom Shulman**, Screenwriter

In this final chapter, I share excerpts that I found striking and memorable from my in-depth interviews with a diverse group of seven highly experienced leaders who reflect a diversity of professional and personal backgrounds across the Americas, Europe, Africa, and Asia. For consistency, the interview questions were the same as those used for executives who participated in my doctoral study but with less emphasis on sensitive information.

The chapter is organized by the major themes discussed in the book:
- Defining a crisis
- Leaders' optimism and pessimism during a crisis
- Unrestrained optimism
- Pragmatic optimism
  - Clarity in chaos
  - Control under fire

- o Conviction to act
- o Concerted decision-making
- o Conscientious communication
- o Connection to caring systems

I hope these curated words and ideas resonate with you as you reflect on your key takeaways from this book.

Defining a Crisis

Christine Elliott, Chief Corporate Affairs Officer, Moody's Corp.

"A crisis usually requires a significant and out-of-cycle adjustment of your priorities or [at least] a real-time review of your strategy. Generally speaking, a crisis has some form of stakeholder impact, and those stakeholders could be internal or external, or both.

"While there is a lot of attention on external crises that affect organizations, e.g., COVID-19, obviously leaders face significant crises that can occur inside the organization."

Thomas Kolditz, Brigadier General (retired), author of *In Extremis Leadership,* and former head of the Department of Behavioral Sciences and Leadership at the US Military Academy, West Point

"One of the things you'll hear me say over and over about crisis is that there's a lot of uncertainty. That's really what makes it a crisis.

"Consequently, *in extremis* [or in an extremely difficult situation], leaders learn optimism early, and they practice it often. No wonder Napoleon [Bonaparte] is credited with saying, 'Leaders are dealers in hope.' There are good psychological reasons for that."

Ann Cairns, Executive Vice Chair, Mastercard Inc.

"While there are external triggers for crises, many times, crises arise from within companies. In some cases, crises build up slowly in companies until they get out of control because leaders delay [taking] corrective actions.

"In my opinion, it's not that leaders are asleep at the switch or they are derelict—from what I have seen, it is usually because leaders underestimate how damaging a potential crisis can be. Leaders will do well to monitor critical metrics that act as the bellwether or leading indicators. Every industry has them. Leading indicators in the financial industry are different from retail."

David Curmi, Executive Chairman, Air Malta Plc

"Leaning on my insurance background, I'd describe one type of crisis as an event with a very low probability but a very high impact—they are mostly external in origin, like the COVID-19 pandemic, and the world always resolves it. However, a more concerning crisis, in my view, originates from within and is traceable to extensive mismanagement and a sustained lack of remedial action. I call it the 'creeping crisis' because the underlying issues run deep and are multifaceted yet remain unattended until they explode into a crisis.

"A crisis worsens existing difficulties an organization is facing."

Caroline Stockmann, Chief Executive, Association of Corporate Treasurers

"I see many forms of crises, but they can broadly be grouped into internal and external crises. In the category of internal crisis, I often see poor or no leadership as a catalyst where people are running around like headless chickens and chaos ensues.

"Also, in this group, a misfortune like a plane crash killing staff members, a reputational crisis where a staff member is in the public eye for a crime or misbehavior, or an operational turmoil leading to a major product recall due to defects."

Dr. Johannes Boroh, Airline Pilot (Captain, B737 Fleet), Singapore Airlines, and Course Director of BSc in Aviation Operations, Kingston University, London

"From a pilot's point of view, a crisis is a situation which may lead into an unfavorable condition, be it loss of assets or loss of life, or it may damage the brand or the image of the company.

"Of course, when the safety of an aircraft is threatened, that is a major crisis. However, the reputation damage component of a crisis is crucial and multifaceted for us since it has a higher chance of occurrence—it can happen from an unpleasant or volatile interaction between the crew and passengers captured and shared on social media or an emergency stop on the runway that ends up in the news painting the organization in a bad light.

"Things usually look beautiful before a crisis strikes!"

Leaders' Optimism and Pessimism During a Crisis

Thomas Kolditz, Brigadier General (retired), author of *In Extremis Leadership*, and former head of the Department of Behavioral Sciences and Leadership at the US Military Academy, West Point

"Following shocking losses suffered by Allied forces in a surprise attack by German forces on December 16, 1944, at the start of the Battle of the Bulge, Eisenhower summoned all his top commanders, and he opened the meeting by announcing, 'The present situation is to be regarded as one of opportunity for us, and not of disaster. There will be only cheerful faces at this conference table.' The Allies rallied and won that battle.

"When you're in crisis as a leader, you have to restore that loss of certainty. The way you do it is by getting people to trust you, and you gain trust by being confidently optimistic, which is forward-looking.

"If you are not optimistic about the future, as a leader, you just fired yourself."

Ann Cairns, Executive Vice Chair, Mastercard Inc.

"To me, optimism is practically an indispensable mindset for a leader—and you don't need to be in a crisis to see the evidence of possessing a positive outlook. The broader the scope of your responsibility as a leader—wide-ranging geography, multiple products, diverse employees, and many strategic customers—the more vulnerable you are to crises, and the more crucial is an optimistic mindset. Stuff is going to happen.

"Therefore, it is absolutely clear to me that leaders' optimism will help them emerge better from a crisis. If you dwell on bad news, you cannot move forward."

David Curmi, Executive Chairman, Air Malta PLC

"I firmly believe that a leader needs to think positively, both during and after the crisis. A leader needs to think positively throughout. Positive thinking leads to positive results, whether you are in a crisis or not in a crisis.

"The tone at the top is very, very important for leaders. The job of a leader is to inspire and galvanize, not to share distraught thoughts—better to keep those to yourself and meditate on them and reflect on them, and find ways to resolve them."

Christine Elliott, Chief Corporate Affairs Officer, Moody's Corp.

"My former CEO, [ex-CEO of American Express] Ken Chenault, has a phrase that he uses all the time: 'The role of a leader is to define reality and provide hope.' When effective leaders take on crises, the reality may be so bleak that they cannot honestly guarantee a win, but they demonstrate a tenacious willingness to fight for what the organization stands for. It takes optimism to do that.

"However, care must be taken not to get caught up in the type of optimism that is too lofty and unrealistic.

"I find that the aura of optimism creates followership and camaraderie. If people have a choice between negative and positive leaders, I would think that human nature will steer them to follow a more optimistic path."

Kola Adesina, Group Managing Director, Sahara Power Group

"Leaders must not forget that their teams are looking up to them. They're following your decisions. They're following your emotions. They're following your words; meaning they believe in you. For you to truly inspire them, it means that your vision must be clear. It means that you must be able to inspire them.

"The moment you, the leader, do not demonstrate optimism with regards to the outcomes you seek, then you've lost the game."

Caroline Stockmann, Chief Executive, Association of Corporate Treasurers

"I believe that being optimistic is important as confirmed by several studies in neuroscience. The optimistic mindset impacts what goes on in the subconscious, and how visualization and mantras really work in my experience.

"To me, the criticality of leaders' optimism has to do with its impact on people around them. If the leader is positive, then others will feel reassured. But it's got to be honest and authentic. You have to really mean it.

"I believe you can train yourself to be genuinely more positive. That may sound a bit odd, but by smiling, you release hormones like serotonin and dopamine, and by saying mantras, you get your mind thinking more positively."

Dr. Johannes Boroh, Airline Pilot (Captain, B737 Fleet), Singapore Airlines, and Course Director of BSc in Aviation Operations, Kingston University, London

"An airline captain needs to expect positive outcomes during a crisis—I was trained that my actions must be based on the expectation of a positive outcome. The training for airline captain is not so much about flying a plane because you would have excelled in that already, but it is a leadership training program, among others.

"We cannot act or decide without expecting a positive outcome. We can't think, 'Oh yeah, this action will fail,' because human lives are at stake! A pilot must be 'a reasonable optimist.' Through several hours of training, we are conditioned to develop that mindset."

Unrestrained Optimism

Thomas Kolditz, Brigadier General (retired), author of *In Extremis Leadership*, and former head of the Department of Behavioral Sciences and Leadership at the US Military Academy, West Point

"Leaders need to avoid denying reality because it is negative. Don't ever write a check you can't cash. You don't say something stupid like, 'The crisis is just going to magically disappear!'

"Your optimistic promises cannot keep failing; else, you will overdraw your trust. You can't be wrong most of the time. Nobody follows a loser into combat."

Ann Cairns, Executive Vice Chair, Mastercard Inc.

"Believing that you will be successful at every turn when managing a complex crisis takes optimism too far is one sure way of getting bogged down emotionally, and setting up oneself to fail woefully. Such leaders are likely to get stuck on a failed decision and struggle to be in the best frame of mind for the next series of decisions that need to be made."

David Curmi, Executive Chairman, Air Malta PLC

"Obviously, optimism has to be bounded by reasonableness. It can't be unbounded. There's no point in being too optimistic because that could also lead you into a different kind of crisis. Unbounded optimism is not good because you could be leading people up the wrong path."

Christine Elliott, Chief Corporate Affairs Officer, Moody's Corp.

"Leaders must make an honest assessment and are well-served to avoid anything that appears unduly optimistic. But certainly, confidence and a reasonable expectation of success are important, giving employees a reason and drive to keep pushing toward a solution."

Pragmatic Optimism

Ann Cairns, Executive Vice Chair, Mastercard Inc.

"It is expected that one will feel down and not particularly optimistic when leading an organization… facing a major headwind. So, there is a pessimistic pull in a crisis, [which] gets leaders to think in a certain way to prevent or limit losses, etc. You just have to accept that some of your best efforts may fail.

"But to give the organization a fighting chance, leaders must also be positive and optimistic because that encourages creativity, perseverance, etc. So, in my view, it is hard to be 'either or' in a crisis because you need both mindsets to successfully navigate the difficult terrain of adversity."

Thomas Kolditz, Brigadier General (retired), author of *In Extremis Leadership*, and former head of the Department of Behavioral Sciences and Leadership at the US Military Academy, West Point

"Throughout my military career, I developed my personality so that I am the guy in the room who immediately goes to the worst possible outcome. In fact, I always go to the most likely and dangerous outcomes, and you've got to be ready for both. But [my team] won't know I'm doing that. There is no way for me to share that with my people without introducing negative emotion into it. So, don't engage in it as a matter of interpersonal communication. You can sit on it yourself and analyze it. That's just one of the crosses that leaders have to bear.

"There's an argument that, if you allow everyone else to help you with this pessimistic analysis, then it might be better. And in my experience, it ain't worth it."

Caroline Stockmann, Chief Executive, Association of Corporate Treasurers

"From my experience, there are different leaders for different times or seasons in an organization's lifecycle. Some people are very good in a crisis mode, others are strong in a recovery mode, and other leaders are brilliant when things are in a stable mode, and they can pursue growth. In the past, the competencies needed in each mode were not usually found in the same person. But, nowadays, leaders must acquire and pivot among the unique competencies needed to excel in each mode.

"If leaders are only competent in noncrisis periods, but they can't manage in a crisis, particularly as we see with our current [COVID-19] environment, probably we're going to experience more crisis over time. So, managers need more firepower in their crisis leadership arsenal and [to be] better prepared."

Dr. Johannes Boroh, Airline Pilot (Captain, B737 Fleet), Singapore Airlines, and Course Director of BSc in Aviation Operations, Kingston University, London

"When I worked as an instructor evaluating pilots who were training to become captains, I looked for these three qualities recognized across the aviation industry as the gold standard for professionals in such leadership roles: skill, knowledge, and attitude, or SKA for short. Some airlines shuffle the letters in the acronym as KSA.

"The quality of attitude includes listening to and acting on feedback including negatives, being open to critiques, knowing one's limitations and understanding when to depend on others, having a vision, and doing one's best to produce desired outcomes.

"There is a saying among some aviators that pilots earn their money in crisis."

Kola Adesina, Group Managing Director, Sahara Power Group

"The natural demand from the people with regard to leaders is for the leaders to inspire them to get the results. If you are going into any venture as a leader, you must be optimistic. When you realize that you cannot deliver expected results, please yield the space for others to take over.

"Also, when facing a deep crisis, you need to have an objective view of the situation based on several measures, including taking on a ton of negative news and not just seeking one-sided optimistic views. However, I think as a general rule, a leader should be positive and think of successful outcomes."

Christine Elliott, Chief Corporate Affairs Officer, Moody's Corp.

"A leader's aura of optimism produces followership. If you had to choose between a leader who immediately cuts the losses versus another who recognizes the challenge, but believes the team can overcome it—Someone who's determined to acquire as much knowledge as possible and develop a reasoned strategy. Naturally, I would think human nature is to follow that more optimistic, supportive path."

David Curmi, Executive Chairman, Air Malta PLC

"I think human nature motivates people to avoid being overly pessimistic because pessimistic leaders demotivate their people—I frankly don't like it at all. But at the same time, I wouldn't want to follow an overconfident optimist blindly. So, I want to be convinced that a leader's optimism is based on facts and has considered probable worst-case scenarios. Optimism based on sound arguments, counterarguments, principles, and an understanding of organizational strengths and weaknesses is more believable and thoughtful than building castles in the air.

"Most successful leaders are in the middle of the pessimism-optimism spectrum. This is how I see it. I think successful people avoid the very high or very low end of the spectrum. I believe we are somewhere in the middle where we have a bit of both pessimism and optimism. So, I think this is a balance that great leaders strike."

Clarity in Chaos

Kola Adesina, Group Managing Director, Sahara Power Group

"A lesson I learned from handling an industry-wide crisis is the importance of adaptability in strategy. In response to the crisis, I led my team to revise our strategy and overhaul our plans while staying true to our vision. That's how we became even more successful after the crisis while other organizations in the industry collapsed under the weight of the crisis.

"I believe the first thing a leader should do after being hit with a crisis is to practice critical listening. You need to open your mind immediately by bringing together the thinker and the doer."

Caroline Stockmann, Chief Executive, Association of Corporate Treasurers

"Some leaders I've seen struggle with being true to their vision and strategy when a crisis strikes—so maybe they're not [true] leaders. They show a complete lack of commitment to the organization and its cause by jumping ship when it gets complicated.

"I talk a lot about personal resilience—leaders with low resilience are prone to mental health issues, but leaders who've upheld their personal resilience levels fare the best in the achievement of their organizational goals despite a crisis."

Christine Elliott, Chief Corporate Affairs Officer, Moody's Corp.

"Storytelling is a critical leadership skill that takes center stage in a crisis. You've got to be able to tell your own story in a cogent and compelling way to the stakeholders. While the way that you might explain a crisis to your board is going to be in much greater detail and significant than [how] you might describe it to the media, importantly, it's the same story. You've got to understand your purpose and objective and what is the desired outcome. What's the best-case scenario you're looking for from this [crisis], and how do you get from where you are right now to where the outcome is?

"So, the only way to really have that narrative is if you are very, very clear about who you are as a company and what you exist for.

"In times of crisis, whether you're talking about individuals or corporations, character counts. You can't create an image of a company that's very open or a person that wears their heart on their sleeve, and then when a crisis hits, things turn 180 degrees and shut down lines of communication. That's not authentic, and it will undermine your character and brand."

David Curmi, Executive Chairman, Air Malta PLC

"A crisis always exposes the flaws and uncovers the weaknesses of leaders. So, you will be exposed if you decide to fight a crisis on your own. I know my flaws; therefore, I try to always surround myself with the best people who compensate for my weaknesses so that I can listen to them—I don't see many leaders doing that.

"I notice several leaders push top-down solutions in erratic and incoherent forms. No matter how strong the leader is, I don't believe one person could run an organization without increasing their risk of failure. And that risk of failures blows up exponentially during a crisis."

Ann Cairns, Executive Vice Chair, Mastercard Inc.

"It is essential to be clear what the objectives are—some leaders do not have well-defined objectives, and that gets exposed during a crisis. The objectives must be clear enough to translate to either activity or inactivity; yes, at critical times, your deliberate inactivity can be just as effective as your conscious activity.

"Owing to the high rate of change and substantial pressure that happens in a crisis, it is important to hold regular meetings at the start of a crisis, sometimes several times a day, to clarify and recalibrate objectives. In a fast-moving crisis, it is not uncommon for your objectives at 9:00 a.m. to be obsolete by 4:00 p.m. on the same day."

Dr. Johannes Boroh, Airline Pilot (Captain, B737 Fleet), Singapore Airlines, and Course Director of BSc in Aviation Operations, Kingston University, London

"Airline captains can regain perspective and clarity when a crisis severely threatens their objectives by soliciting colleagues' views on the flight deck—copilot, senior first officer, first officer, and even a trainee. This speaks to the 'A,' which stands for attitude in 'SKA'; the best captains consult in a crisis to sharpen their view of the way forward.

"Unfortunately, as seen in flight safety reports worldwide, a small number of captains might have a less-favorable attitude or mindset. They do not engage others on the flight deck, leading to errors in judgment."

Control Under Fire

Caroline Stockmann, Chief Executive, Association of Corporate Treasurers

"I think showing vulnerability at times is a strength. But you don't want to be a kind of emotional mess in front of people because that doesn't necessarily help people to follow you and to feel good.

However, showing your own concerns and that you are human, especially during a stressful time like a crisis, increases trust between leaders and their people. I think society is now waking to this view that I've always had that a leader that shows that they're human is much more acceptable and trustworthy. People don't connect with leaders who seem too perfect because it is hard to relate to them.

"You don't make good decisions if you are panicking—I know this from safety training I've done before visiting harsh environments. When you've got your adrenaline going, you don't hear or see as well. It's a fact. In the midst of chaos, calmness is required for clear and innovative thinking."

Dr. Johannes Boroh, Airline Pilot (Captain, B737 Fleet), Singapore Airlines, and Course Director of BSc in Aviation Operations, Kingston University, London

"When leaders come under enormous pressure and stress and fail to manage their emotions, many of them tend to shut down others, refuse to take input, and say things like 'Just do what I say,' although under certain conditions this may help. They become dictatorial and overbearing. This kind of disruptive behavior might be observed during a simulator assessment when the pressure is high. A crisis is not an excuse to be a dictator. As in this case, that could lead to a failure in the assessment.

"Similarly, in the absence of a flight simulator, organizational leaders can reflect on their behavior during a recent crisis and note opportunities to improve their emotional management. Leaders must consciously and constantly assess their emotions until it becomes a habit because they greatly influence their team's emotional health and stability."

Ann Cairns, Executive Vice Chair, Mastercard Inc.

"A leader's emotional management in a crisis goes a long way to create a collaborative and supportive environment or a chaotic and stressful atmosphere. It is extremely important that leaders get the hang of their emotions through self-care, like getting enough sleep at night during a crisis. Leaders who neglect self-care are prone to losing it under stress. Yelling at people or succumbing to other negative emotions distracts the team from its primary responsibility: finding solutions to the crisis.

"Calm leaders do better in a crisis. However, it is vital to differentiate between productive calmness [which] helps to foster clarity of thought, and lethargic calmness, making the organization docile and unresponsive to changes that characterize crises. Being calm yet having a sense of urgency helps you to respond thoughtfully and not react hastily; there is a big difference [between the two]."

Kola Adesina, Group Managing Director, Sahara Power Group

"Leaders create the culture in their organizations based on what they do every day, not necessarily what they say. People believe more in what they see [in leaders] than what they hear [from leaders]. The retention rate for what they see is higher than what they hear. So, they don't want to hear you say it, [as much as] they want to see you do it.

"Therefore, for me, you need to manage your emotion as a leader because a lot of people are paying attention to you. They're watching you and they're watching you most especially in moments of crisis."

Christine Elliott, Chief Corporate Affairs Officer, Moody's Corp.

"Most people in leadership positions will imagine that they are self-aware, but we all have room for improvement. A way leaders can improve their self-awareness is to remember to seek and be open to feedback. Surround yourself with people you trust to be honest with you.

"So, the big lesson here is to have people close to you that you listen to; it is very important."

David Curmi, Executive Chairman, Air Malta PLC

"Emotions are a product of human nature. They are challenging and difficult to simply set aside. But in a crisis, it is essential to be very rational and to try to put your emotions under the control of your rational mind. I find that it is a conscious and mindful process.

"I know of people who took the crises they faced very personally because their emotions took over. They took it to heart and suffered. Their health suffered and they failed to manage the crisis, even though they were in relatively important positions.

"In noncrisis, you can't let your emotions rule you, let alone in a crisis when everything is so much more pronounced."

Thomas Kolditz, Brigadier General (retired), author of *In Extremis Leadership*, and former head of the Department of Behavioral Sciences and Leadership at the US Military Academy, West Point

"I constantly remind my clients of this truth: leaders are always on the record. How you do what you do reflects your emotional state, and it is never lost on your team, especially during a difficult time like a crisis."

Conviction to Act

Christine Elliott, Chief Corporate Affairs Officer, Moody's Corp.

"It takes time for leaders to learn to dissociate one's self-confidence and self-worth from the failures of a crisis, but that's what seasoned leaders do. They do not internalize a crisis to the point where their self-confidence takes a notable hit. Any crisis is stressful, [and] it takes a toll personally and professionally, but that dispassionate leader can be most effective when it is needed most.

"The reason I said this skill is learned is that the natural tendency of leaders is to insert themselves in the crisis, put it on their backs, and feel personally responsible. But the best leaders have learned to take a step back, bring in subject-matter experts, and empower them. That way, the burden of the crisis is shared, and the handling is more robust and systematic."

Caroline Stockmann, Chief Executive, Association of Corporate Treasurers

"You need to have flaws and faults as a human being for other people to trust in you. But, if during a crisis, you, the leader, are not convincing, then it's not going to work. Listening hard to a diverse group of experts is a key element, and taking their views on board can help you build up your confidence.

"Leaders must think, 'It's not all down to me because I will tap into the commitments of others. I didn't create this crisis, but I will do my utmost best and be very pragmatic about resolving the crisis.'"

Thomas Kolditz, Brigadier General (retired), author of *In Extremis Leadership*, and former head of the Department of Behavioral Sciences and Leadership at the US Military Academy, West Point

"A leader that lacks confidence is screaming to others, 'Don't follow me!' Why should anybody else be confident in you if you don't appear confident in yourself? So, I think leadership confidence is very critical, and it begins with committing.

"I'll give you an example from parachuting. I made more than a thousand jumps at West Point. I went through [the US Army] HALO [high-altitude low-opening] school. I've done that for a long time. And there's something that I learned early on about parachuting: That you can be really worried right before you step out of that plane, and the moment you leave the step of that plane, you quit worrying because you are committed. At that point, the parachuting is on. And so, you do what you know you need to do. You do it confidently. You get the job done. Poof! Your parachute opens, and you get to the ground, and you're fine. None of that would have happened if you didn't commit."

Kola Adesina, Group Managing Director, Sahara Power Group

"Your confidence as a leader is only as good as your acknowledgment of what your weaknesses are, and you find the right people to cure your own weaknesses. Once you're able to do that, your confidence will never wane.

"Personally, I'm not shy about admitting my vulnerabilities. My team knows my areas of strength and weaknesses; I am not a jack-of-all-trades. In turn, I celebrate them in their areas of strength. My job is to bring it all together. To connect the various people's strengths and weaknesses to produce the result I desire to see and achieve the vision."

Dr. Johannes Boroh, Airline Pilot (Captain, B737 Fleet), Singapore Airlines, and Course Director of BSc in Aviation Operations, Kingston University, London

"A crisis-prepared pilot is a self-confident pilot during a crisis. Airlines strive to achieve this level of preparedness and competence for pilots through continuous evidence-based training programs based on past crisis scenarios worldwide. Assessors will then evaluate the pilot's decision-making under pressure. This kind of consistent exposure boosts a pilot's confidence to take on the challenge of a crisis when it arises.

"If we observe gaps in a candidate for the position of a captain, and we don't see improvements after further training, we say, 'Okay, you can't be a captain; you will have to continue as a first officer.' That shows the importance of having in place a self-confident pilot with crisis composure before a catastrophe strikes."

Ann Cairns, Executive Vice Chair, Mastercard Inc.

"A crisis stacks the odds against an organization. But leaders need to believe that they're going to win. They need to teach themselves to believe that. Because once you commit, once you really commit to dealing with the issue, dealing with the problem, whatever course of action it is, you have to do it boldly, not hesitating or doubting.

"You need to go into a crisis having a clear sense of what you are very good at and what you are not so good [at doing]. That way, you can concentrate on your strengths and allow others in the organization to step up in areas where they are outstanding. It is tempting for leaders to want to do it all during a crisis; that approach rarely works out well."

David Curmi, Executive Chairman, Air Malta PLC

"To protect your confidence from eroding, do not be tempted to outdo yourself in response to a crisis. Instead, be sensitive to the difficulties of the crisis and do what is required by the situation. Let the crisis inform your action.

"You must also keep your self-awareness grounded by connecting it to the outer world [where the crisis is happening]. I think when you do that, you avoid overreacting to certain situations just because your self-awareness is telling you to do that. I practice and recommend *integrative awareness,* i.e., incorporating your emotions with a rational thought process to produce intentional calm."

Concerted Decision-Making

Thomas Kolditz, Brigadier General (retired), author of *In Extremis Leadership*, and former head of the Department of Behavioral Sciences and Leadership at the US Military Academy, West Point

"Leaders need to show competence and downward loyalty during crisis decision-making. We did a study in Mosul [Iraq], and our findings revealed that the two most significant capabilities for leaders making decisions to order soldiers into combat were number one, competence by a wide margin. But competence was not sufficient. It had to be paired with number two, downward loyalty. Your people need to know that when you're making decisions, even if they're hard decisions, even if you might put them at risk, you are genuinely concerned about them.

"Those two capabilities—competence and downward loyalty—were required to build trust. Integrity was number three or number four. Other capabilities did not register as that important; for example, courage was number six down on the list."

Kola Adesina, Group Managing Director, Sahara Power Group

"You must respond as quickly as possible, but don't be impulsive. Adapt your decision-making to the speed of the crisis—[which] may mean not adhering strictly to your established chain of command. Remember, there is no existing pattern to follow in a crisis; creative thinking is what you need to lean on.

"Don't lean on just the process, which is why I said often processes are suspended in crises, usually because [existing] processes can't deal with all the crises. Most crises are outside of existing processes.

"Every crisis is a critical opportunity for you to create something novel, something unique, something beautiful. Don't miss that opportunity."

Ann Cairns, Executive Vice Chair, Mastercard Inc.

"While there is usually a need to make several decisions during a crisis, not every decision is as weighty or as far-reaching as the other. What I find useful is to make less critical decisions relatively quickly and take as much time as the crisis allows on the weightier and more far-reaching ones.

"You need to bring other people to the table; people from diverse backgrounds, cultures, genders, and expertise, because problem-solving requires new thinking and diverse perspectives."

Dr. Johannes Boroh, Airline Pilot (Captain, B737 Fleet), Singapore Airlines, and Course Director of BSc in Aviation Operations, Kingston University, London

"As part of the decision-making process, leaders need to know when to call for help from those outside their immediate team. During a flight, a captain can determine that an ongoing crisis has escalated to an emergency beyond what their team on the flight deck can handle and declare Mayday,[12] a call for others—an air traffic controller or a pilot in another plane—to help, for instance by giving priority to the aircraft in distress, relaying messages, and so on.

"When you make a decision in a crisis, realize that uncertainties remain, and you have to assume that the decision could be wrong. You have to. So, you should constantly monitor the execution of the decision to be sure it's yielding expected outcomes and be prepared to amend the decision as required.

"A good captain differentiates between being hasty and having a sense of urgency. The former is haphazard while the latter is thoughtful. I used to remind my trainees [by saying], 'Hey, the fact that you have a crisis does not mean the plane will drop immediately. There's always enough time to think of a reasonable response.'"

Christine Elliott, Chief Corporate Affairs Officer, Moody's Corp.

"We do tabletop crisis simulations in my organization. We make up crazy and sometimes not-so-crazy scenarios to test the system. The most important part of that simulation is knowing who the owners are of different decision points, who needs to be informed, and who is responsible. Having that clarity and identifying those systems in advance is incredibly good for time-saving during decision-making in a crisis.

"Here is a best practice I follow for decision-making during a period of uncertainties: Give me all the bad news or just all of the news, give me everything that you know, give me all the knowable facts, don't hold back, and then I can make an educated decision based on that.

---

12 Mayday, according to Merriam-Webster, is comparable phonetically to French's M'aidez, meaning "Help me," and was adopted in 1923.

"Overall, avoid creating chaos when responding to a crisis. Two sure ways leaders create a crisis while trying to solve the primary crisis are [first] assuming you know everything about the crisis at the onset, and [second] not showing humanity by refusing to accept blame for an obvious fault or not empathizing with stakeholders who bear the brunt of the issue."

David Curmi, Executive Chairman, Air Malta PLC

"This is far from cliché, but no matter how devastating a crisis is, decision-making should always explore opportunities during and after a crisis to restructure, create better value, and think differently. I don't like to think of crisis resolution as returning to normalcy; I don't believe in that. Going back to normalcy is not the answer. Going back to normalcy means that we will continue to do business the way we were before the crisis, and we don't want to do that. We want to do business differently now that the crisis has taught us huge lessons.

"Apart from trying to retain the status quo, the worst thing a leader can do is not to decide. The decision-making process needs to be very agile. You become a leader by the quality of your decisions. If your decisions are weak or nonexistent, then your people will say, 'Well, I mean, this person is a weak leader.'

"Finally, a failure to listen is the root cause of many leadership fiascos. I have learned to listen a lot to gather the information necessary to make decisions. So, listen seriously and critically, then make your own conclusions."

Caroline Stockmann, Chief Executive, Association of Corporate Treasurers

"There is usually a need to consult with internal or external experts because a crisis normally goes beyond the capacity of a single leader. Therefore, practice critical listening and be open to changing your mind when presented with superior proposals. So, consult widely, but act swiftly and decisively.

"Remember that you've got to be agile because you need to be able to respond quickly. The most effective leaders I've seen gather as many facts as possible, but accept uncertainty. You'll never get the 100%, you've got to employ the 80/20 rule and not keep trying because you'll be too late if you try to get all the facts."

Conscientious Communication

Thomas Kolditz, Brigadier General (retired), author of *In Extremis Leadership*, and former head of the Department of Behavioral Sciences and Leadership at the US Military Academy, West Point

"When I did some of the research for my book, I realized that in crisis, people don't want rational or emotional communications; they want transformational and forward-looking communications. They just want to be carried forward by that leader, and not with a detailed, rational calculation of the probabilities.

"So, I think this ability to authentically and genuinely show consideration for other people is very pronounced. And I've never seen [a lack of this ability] in a combat-experienced, three- or four-star general; I've never seen a lack of that. Never.

"You have to be precise when you communicate; never mislead. If you can't be trusted to tell the truth in a situation where people's lives are on the line, that is unforgivable."

Christine Elliott, Chief Corporate Affairs Officer, Moody's Corp.

"The best-handled crises I have experienced share similar communications themes. Here are the critical ones in my mind:

"[First,] leaders developed a communications strategy early and stuck to its core principles from the beginning of the crisis until the end, no matter how long it took. [Second,] they stayed true to their message and made sure to communicate the most knowable truth at any point in time. [Third,] they communicated directly with the stakeholders involved, external and internal, and created a unity of purpose. [Fourth,] leaders intertwined the communications strategy with the business strategy; they were almost intimately interconnected. [Fifth,] leaders removed themselves from the center of upheaval by not taking a crisis personally, dispassionately bringing in the context, creating the plans, and executing them. [Finally,] they did not try to distract or deflect."

Caroline Stockmann, Chief Executive, Association of Corporate Treasurers

"I've found that fear is one of the primary reasons leaders are less transparent or prone to giving false information during a crisis. They are afraid of giving bad news. They are afraid of repercussions. They are afraid of being seen in a bad light. They are afraid of conflict.

"I think it's down to fear and awkwardness with people thinking, 'Oh, what do I do if they ask me questions?' Well, just say it like it is. When I have to brief my team during a crisis, I tell them that I will be transparent and that if things are not going well, they will know about them from me. And we've tried to keep that up throughout COVID-19 so that people don't get surprised; they feel included."

Kola Adesina, Group Managing Director, Sahara Power Group

"The best leaders are storytellers. I have learned that leaders are more credible and trusted storytellers when they are vulnerable enough to tell their own stories. Through telling my story, my people know me, my [past] challenges, successes, and failures.

"So, when I incorporate relevant parts of my personal stories into crisis communication, it leads to a stronger level of engagement and a boost to the trust quotient. The trust quotient is very rare; it's one of the areas of deficiency globally regarding leadership."

Ann Cairns, Executive Vice Chair, Mastercard Inc.

"Get to the facts fast! By facts, I mean as much of an unbiased view as possible. Make sure your communication never, ever misleads anyone about circumstances, intentionally or unintentionally. You have to have the unbridled truth. People understand that mistakes happen and may pardon accidents and errors, but are more unforgiving of willful deception.

"One of the most important communication rules is that 70% to 90% of communication is nonverbal. So, keep in mind that your people are always watching you and your body language speaks volumes. Think ahead about how you show up, and don't leave that [up to] impulsiveness."

Connecting to Caring Systems

Ann Cairns, Executive Vice Chair, Mastercard Inc.

"I think the support you receive from loved ones, friends, and colleagues when going through a difficult patch is indispensable. But as potentially valuable as it is, the benefit you gain from those relationships depends on how open you are to them. You need to take the time to invest in them and listen to them; you will learn a lot about yourself through their eyes."

Dr. Johannes Boroh, Airline Pilot (Captain, B737 Fleet), Singapore Airlines, and Course Director of BSc in Aviation Operations, Kingston University, London

"I have found that having people who support you and are on your side during a crisis goes a long way in equipping you to succeed. However, regardless of whether they are family members, colleagues, friends, etc., the key is to know how to leverage them: know what you want from them and ask for the help you need."

Thomas Kolditz, Brigadier General (retired), author of *In Extremis Leadership*, and former head of the Department of Behavioral Sciences and Leadership at the US Military Academy, West Point

"I learned this the hard way as a lieutenant colonel: committed leaders can sometimes play Superman and, unfortunately, work themselves into incompetence. They will not get [enough] sleep. They will not take care of themselves. And they'll keep doing that until they're making dumb decisions. So, it's important for leaders to allow people around them to force the issue."

Kola Adesina, Group Managing Director, Sahara Power Group

"Having the support of family and friends is extremely important for leaders. When facing challenging times, you need somebody to tell you: 'Please calm down'... 'Please check your [blood pressure]'... 'Please be careful'... 'I wish you well'... 'Don't worry; all will be well'... 'I am here for you'... and 'You mean the world to me'... because we are human. That balance is a critical requirement for leadership success.

"When I hear those positive affirmations, I tend to excel more. Such genuine support reminds you that you are not alone. But when you wrongfully assume you are a superhero in one of the Marvel [comic books] or movies, you will feel lonely as a leader."

David Curmi, Executive Chairman, Air Malta PLC

"It is one thing to have a wide network of industry contacts, colleagues, friends, and family, and it is another to connect and communicate with these people deliberately. That is when the leader can feel the true value of that network. Virtual meeting technology has been really helpful to me and made keeping in touch less burdensome, so I advise leaders to take advantage of it. A social network is useless without the leader actively investing in it.

"I think close friends and family networks can keep you going during challenging times and instill confidence in you. When you're being supported and encouraged by others, it's a huge plus in life. No matter how much personal motivation you might have, the extra boost you get from outsiders significantly affects you."

AFTERWORD

*Education's purpose is to replace an empty mind
with an open one.*

– **Malcolm Forbes**, publisher

My Foray into Crisis Leadership

I was on vacation in the summer of 2014 when I received an update from the postgraduate administration office of the Alliance Manchester School of Business (AMBS), University of Manchester, about my earlier interest in pursuing a doctorate program, specifically a Doctor of Business Administration (DBA) degree, in the field of leadership. I was told, "Your proposed area of research, leadership, is too broad. You need to narrow it down to an area of interest with a specific gap in existing knowledge." It took me a week to come up with an acceptable answer that formed the core of my research proposal: crisis leadership became my research interest, and I explored the crisis management impact of decision-makers' views of the future—primarily optimism since most human beings are optimistic and organizations are built around optimism—on crisis management.

In the introduction section of this book, I discussed my three justifications for choosing this area of study, based on my practitioner's point of view. At that time, I was an Executive Vice President at an

S&P 100 company wearing two hats—I had a general management role, including P&L responsibilities for almost 50 countries, and led a global business unit I established across over 200 countries and territories. In this and previous leadership positions, I had experienced intense first-hand crises and had been in a front-row seat as I witnessed several leaders handle adversities. Also, at that time, I already had fourteen years of leadership speaking experience under my belt and knew how organizations avoid that topic. Lastly, I struggled to find relevant publications when preparing to speak on the subject.

Three Evidence-Based Justifications for Crisis Leadership

In addition to my practitioner's view, I discovered several other justifications for delving into crisis leadership from a plethora of existing studies after honing my researcher's view through the AMBS DBA's rigorous training program. Here are three such research-based justifications that drove me to study crisis leadership.

First, crisis leadership is not a specialization of leadership. Instead, it sits at the core of what defines authentic leadership because that's what is needed to successfully respond to and lead the organization out of a predicament. Just as a captain is most required when a ship or aircraft is facing a storm, so is an authentic leader indispensable when an individual, family, team, group, division, organization, or country is staring down the barrel. In other words, the quality of one's leadership is transparent and becomes easily discernible during a crisis. Nothing exposes leadership quality like a crisis. Therefore, reflect on and find meaning in your crisis response to accelerate your leadership development.

Second, personality is central to leadership but is subject to change under severe stress. The differences in individual personalities are the chief driver of the highly subjective nature of leadership. There is not one way to lead because personalities vary. Thus, a well-developed leadership book or training program does not seek to transform you into a replica of some leaders, no matter how successful they are, but strives to help you discover and nurture your principles-based leadership paradigm. To further complicate matters, an individual's personality changes, mostly unconsciously, when under enormous pressure and stress, which typifies a crisis. This decades-old and work-based research on stress-induced personality change stunned me. However, it explained why I had seen many leaders with a long history of success in making informed decisions suddenly fumble a major crisis response with a series of ill-advised decisions incompatible with what made them successful before the crises.

The leaders' power to override creates the likelihood that a crisis-triggered fearful personality could cause a decision-maker to overrule a valid, fact-based, and technically-sound solution in favor of a problematic alternative that allays their fears. I couldn't tell you how often I have witnessed similar leadership failures in practice.

Third, the nascent and ongoing Fourth Industrial Revolution (4IR) is exerting new crisis challenges for organizations. The digital technology-based and interconnectivity-driven 4IR is changing the scale, speed, and severity of crises. On the change in scale, what used to be a local crisis secluded in the corner of an organization can quickly morph into a city, state, industry, national or worldwide crisis, thanks to social media and other technologies.

On the 4IR's breakneck speed of information flow, leaders no longer have the luxury of time to respond to crises, and most now do so on the fly. The change in scale and speed combine to up the ante on the severity of crises. No wonder a communications expert observed that crises have not suddenly increased in frequency, but our knowledge of them, powered by digitally connected technologies of the 4IR, has grown exponentially. Unfortunately, this increased exposure negatively affects individuals and leaders at every level of the organization.

The Final Word

Quite different from Malcolm Forbes' quote at the beginning of this section that suggests education fills an empty mind, my observation is that leadership education involves transforming a seasoned mind into an adaptable one. That is because no one has a blank mind regarding leadership since the subject has been modeled to us from childhood by several leadership authorities. In short, we all come to leadership with both beneficial but mostly detrimental baggage from past experiences.

Thus, one of your biggest takeaways from leadership books like this is clarity and commitment to what you'd start, stop, and continue doing. Leadership programs fail when leaders who pass through them do not change their behavior. I designed this book's structure, content, and exercises to allow you to apply the start-stop-continue retrospective. One of the best ways to kick old habits is to kick-start new ones—to achieve a change of behavior, substitution is often more effective than discontinuation.

Best wishes on your journey through adversity to becoming a better version of yourself.

ACKNOWLEDGEMENTS

In June 2019, I stumbled on a Word document that contained my analysis of various universities' doctorate programs, and I had narrowed my choices to three schools. The system-generated "date modified" of the document showed 2009. So, for over five years, I had put off applying for a doctorate program because of my extensive work schedule that included fifteen-hour workdays and over ninety (mostly long haul) flights a year. However, by 2014, I was convinced that waiting for my workload to lighten up meant missing out on the academic exposure and rigor I would need later in my career. So, I bit the bullet, and I am glad I did. Many colleagues and friends, too numerous to name, positively contributed to this study by encouraging me along the way (even though many of them thought I was crazy to take on such a demanding project); thank you!

I am indebted to Dr. Audra Diers-Lawson. From the Skype interview I had with Audra as part of my application process for the program in the summer of 2014, she provided phenomenal support to me throughout the thesis development, from conceptualization to execution. Thank you for making this experience rewarding. Thanks to Prof. Emma Banister and Dr. Helen Bruce, my co-supervisors, for your counsel, direction, and support. I deeply appreciate your encouragement, especially in the home stretch.

I am grateful for the unwavering support of my wife and son, Ola and David. Thank you for your selflessness and understanding while I did a demanding job and pursued this study. You endured long hours of listening to my passionate explanations of my research findings, and you contributed some useful ideas.

I am grateful to the total of forty-two executives who not only gave me access, but freely shared exceptional insights from their crisis leadership experiences. Despite the evidence showing that leaders generally shy away from discussing crisis events with academics, especially poorly managed crises, you spoke with sincerity and authenticity as you shared your learnings, failures, successes, and advice. Thirty-five of you cannot be named because we agreed to keep you anonymous. The seven participants who can be identified are Ann Cairns (Executive Vice Chair, Mastercard Inc.), Caroline Stockmann (Chief Executive, Association of Corporate Treasurers), Christine Elliott (Chief Corporate Affairs Officer, Moody's Corp.), David Curmi (Executive Chairman, Air Malta PLC), Dr. Johannes Boroh (Airline Pilot, Captain, B737 Fleet, Singapore Airlines, and Course Director of BSc in Aviation Operations, Kingston University, London), Kola Adesina (Group Managing Director, Sahara Power Group), and Dr. Thomas Kolditz (Brigadier General, US Army (ret), Professor Emeritus at the US Military Academy, West Point, and author, *In Extremis Leadership: Leading as if Your Life Depended on It*). You are the backbone of this study and book.

I am profoundly appreciative of a distributed team that supported me in the book's production, editing, and marketing: Erica Reed, Kate Victory Hannisian, Richard Sine, and Travis Cody.

Last but not least, I am grateful to Marshall Goldsmith for his generosity demonstrated in the writing of the foreword to this book. To Kate Clark and Frank Wagner, thank you.

Endnotes

1   Jackson, D., & Moloney, K. (2019). 'Uneasy lies the head that wears a crown.' A qualitative study of ethical PR practice in the United Kingdom. *Public Relations Inquiry, 8*(1), 87-101.

2   Pauley, J. (n.d.). *Philip Burguieres: 'Faces of Depression - Philip Burguieres.'* PBS. https://www.pbs.org/wgbh/takeonestep/depression/faces-philip.html

3   Ghaemi, N. (2012). *A first-rate madness: Uncovering the links between leadership and mental illness.* Penguin.

4   Miller, D.C. (2016, May 20). *Note to CEOs: don't let depression get in the way of your success.* Industry Week. www.industryweek.com/leadership/article/21973072/note-to-ceos-dont-let-depression-get-in-the-way-of-your-success

5   The World Bank (n.d.) *Small and medium enterprises (SMEs) finance.* https://www.worldbank.org/en/topic/smefinance

6   Freeman, M. A., Staudenmaier, P. J., Zisser, M. R., & Andresen, L. A. (2019). The prevalence and co-occurrence of psychiatric conditions among entrepreneurs and their families. *Small Business Economics, 53*(2), 323-342.

7   Walton, A.G. (2015, January 26). *Why the super-successful get depressed?* Forbes. https://www.forbes.com/sites/alicegwalton/2015/01/26/why-the-super-successful-get-depressed/?sh=341bef463850

8   Schwartz, M. (2022, April 1). *5 ways to protect your mental health.* Entrepreneur. https://www.entrepreneur.com/article/421719#:~:text=A%20study%20out%20of%20UC,11%25%20reported%20having%20bipolar%20disorder.

9   Dollmann, J., Jonsson, J. O., Mood, C., & Rudolphi, F. (2021). Ethnic gaps in Swedish upper secondary school completion: Is 'immigrant optimism' the problem?

10   Pascual-Leone, A., Cattaneo, G., Macià, D., Solana, J., Tormos, J. M., & Bartrés-Faz, D. (2021). Beware of optimism bias in the context of the COVID-19 pandemic. *Annals of Neurology, 89*(3), 423.

11   Banaji, M. R., & Greenwald, A. G. (2013). *Blindspot: Hidden biases of good people*. Bantam.

12   Gigerenzer, G., & Garcia-Retamero, R. (2017). Cassandra's regret: The psychology of not wanting to know. *Psychological review*, *124*(2), 179.

13   Brown, E. (1981, September 27). *Writing is third career for Morrison*. The Cincinnati Enquirer. https://www.newspapers.com/clip/21863475/tonimorrison/

14   Barnard, J. W. (2008). Narcissism, over-optimism, fear, anger, and depression: The interior lives of corporate leaders. *U. Cin. L. Rev.*, *77*, 405.

15   Collins, J. C. (2009). *How the mighty fall: And why some companies never give in*. Random House.

16   Stone, J. R. (2006). *The Routledge book of world proverbs*. Routledge.

17   Oxford dictionary: late Middle English (denoting the turning point of a disease): medical Latin, from Greek *krisis* 'decision', from *krinein* 'decide'. The general sense 'decisive point' dates from the early 17th century.

18   Oxford University Press. (2005). Crisis. In *The New Oxford American Dictionary*. New York, N.Y.

19   Schwartz, D. B., Shimabukuro, K., Meyers, K., Gautschi, H., Bernardi, F., Spelic, S., ... & Carlson, B. (2020, May). Educators Reflect on the COVID-19 Crisis. In The National Teaching & Learning Forum (Vol. 29, No. 4, p. 3). Wiley-Blackwell.

20   Bennis, W. G., & Thomas, R. J. (2020). Crucibles of leadership. *Harvard business review*, *80*.

21   Aven, T. (2014). *Risk, surprises and black swans: fundamental ideas and concepts in risk assessment and risk management*. Routledge.

22   Avishai, B. (2020). *The Pandemic Isn't A Black Swan But A Portent Of A More Fragile Global System*. The New Yorker

23   Hinchcliffe, P. (1977). *Doctor Who, Fourth Doctor, 'The Face of Evil', Season 14 Episode 4* [Television series]. BBC1

24   Tseng, C. P., & Chan, Y. J. (2015). Overview of Ebola virus disease in 2014. *Journal of the Chinese Medical Association*, *78*(1), 51-55.

25   Gates. B. (2015, March). The next outbreak? We're not ready [Video]. TED Conferences. https://www.ted.com/talks/bill_gates_the_next_outbreak_we_re_not_ready?language=dz

26   Cameron, E. E., Nuzzo, J. B., Bell, J. A., Nalabandian, M., O'Brien, J., League, A., & Warmbrod, L. (2019). Global Health security index. *Nuclear Threat Initiative*.

27   ICM. (2015). *ICM annual crisis report*. Retrieved from Denver, CO, USA

28   Sreenivasan, N. S., & Narayana, V. (2008). *Continual improvement process*. Pearson Power.

29   Andersen, H. C. (1837). Fairy Tales Told for Children. First Collection. Third Booklet.

30   Taleb, N. N. (2020, May 16). *Identify stocks that will see a boom because of virus: Nassim Nicholas Taleb*. The Economic Times. https://economictimes. indiatimes.com/markets/expert-view/identify-robust-stocks-that-will-boom-due-to-virus-nassim-nicholas-taleb/articleshow/75756955.cms?from=mdr

31   Diers-Lawson, A., & Collins, L. (2022). Taking off the rose-colored glasses: the influence of crises on employee relationship management. *Employee Relations: The International Journal*.

32   Berg, J. (2018). *Danske Bank's management and governance in relation to the AML case at the Estonian branch*. Danske Bank. https://danskebank.com/-/media/danske-bank-com/pdf/investor-relations/fsa-statements/fsa-decision-re-danske-bank-3-may-2018.pdf?rev=47d2a3f36ea54a27a4a06315617e48e3 &hash=6FF0797DF9CCBCD211BD1D0578406123

33   *Danske Bank*. (2018, September). Archived from the original on 2018-07-11. Retrieved 2018-10-14. https://danskebank.com/about-us/corporate-gover-nance/investigations-on-money-laundering

34   Beck, A. T. (1964). Thinking and depression: II. Theory and therapy. *Archives of general psychiatry, 10*(6), 561-571.

35   Assigana, E., Chang, E., Cho, S., Kotecha, V., Liu, B., Turner, H., . . . Stevens, S. M. (2014). *TF-CBT triangle of life: a game to help with cognitive behavioral therapy*. Paper presented at the Proceedings of the first ACM SIGCHI annual symposium on Computer-human interaction in play.

36   Nichols, M. P., & Schwartz, R. C. (2001). *The essentials of family therapy*. Boston, MA, USA: Allyn and Bacon.

37   Graham, B., Dodd, D. L. F., & Cottle, S. (1934). *Security analysis* (Vol. 452). New York: McGraw-Hill.

38   APA Dictionary. (n.d.) *Pessimism*. https://dictionary.apa.org/pessimism.

39   Heath, R. L. (1998). *Dealing with the complete crisis—the crisis management shell structure*. Safety Science, 30(1-2), 139-150.

40   Chaves, J. F., & Brown, J. M. (1987). *Spontaneous cognitive strategies for the control of clinical pain and stress*. Journal of behavioral medicine, 10(3), 263-276

41   Carver, C. S., & Scheier, M. F. (2014). *Dispositional optimism.* Trends in Cognitive Sciences, 18(6), 293-299. doi:10.1016/j.tics.2014.02.003

42   Scheier, M. F., & Carver, C. S. (1992). Effects of optimism on psychological and physical well-being: Theoretical overview and empirical update. *Cognitive therapy and research, 16*(2), 201-228.

43   Jansen, L. A. (2011). *Two concepts of therapeutic optimism.* Journal of medical ethics, 37(9), 563-566.

44   Korman, A. K. (2012). Self-enhancement and self-protection: Toward a theory of work motivation Work motivation in the context of a globalizing economy (pp. 127-136): Psychology Press.

45   Scheier, M. F., Carver, C. S., & Bridges, M. W. (1994). *Distinguishing optimism from neuroticism (and trait anxiety, self-mastery, and self-esteem): a reevaluation of the Life Orientation Test.* Journal of Personality and Social Psychology, 67(6), 1063.

46   Gillham, J.E., Shatté, A.J., Reivich, K.J. and Seligman, M.E. (2001). *Optimism, pessimism, and explanatory style.* In E. C. Chang (Ed.), *Optimism and pessimism: Implications for theory, research, and practice* (Vol. 53, pp. 53-75). Washington D.C.: American Psychological Association.

47   Semmel, A., Abramson, L.Y., Seligman, M.E.P. and Von Baeyer, C. (1978). *A scale for measuring attributional style.* Manuscript in preparation, University of Pennsylvania.

48   Sharot, T., Korn, C. W., & Dolan, R. J. (2011). How unrealistic optimism is maintained in the face of reality. *Nature neuroscience, 14*(11), 1475-1479.

49   Gassen, J., Nowak, T. J., Henderson, A. D., Weaver, S. P., Baker, E. J., & Muehlenbein, M. P. (2021). Unrealistic optimism and risk for COVID-19 disease. *Frontiers in psychology, 12*, 647461.

50   Schnusenberg, O. (2020). Overconfidence in salary expectations after graduation. *Journal of Education for Business, 95*(8), 513-518.

51   Frame, M. C., & Reichin, S. (2019). Emotion and sport performance: Stress, anxiety, arousal, and choking. In *APA handbook of sport and exercise psychology, volume 1: Sport psychology, Vol. 1* (pp. 219-243). American Psychological Association.

52   Radcliffe, J. (2018). Psychological issues during assessment of performance. In *Performance Assessment in Strength and Conditioning* (pp. 13-22). Routledge.

53 Arent, S.M. and Landers, D.M., (2003) Arousal, anxiety, and performance: A reexamination of the inverted-U hypothesis. *Research quarterly for exercise and sport, 74*(4), pp.436-444.

54 UNM (2021), *American Psychosis - Chris Hedges on the US empire of narcissism and psychopathy.* 12 December. https://www.youtube.com/watch?v=-fIxPv2Dn_P0&ab_channel=UNM

55 The U.S. Securities and Exchange Commission (2001), *Dow Jones Industrial Average* SEC.gov https://www.sec.gov/Archives/edgar/data/357298/000035729801500016/dowjones.html

56 Glassman, J., & Hassett, K. (1999). *Dow 36,000: The New Strategy for Profiting from the Coming Rise in the Market.* Crown Business

57 Morris, S. (1996). *Speculative investor behavior and learning.* The Quarterly Journal of Economics, 111(4), 1111-1133.

58 Otto, A. R., Fleming, S. M., & Glimcher, P. W. (2016). *Unexpected but incidental positive outcomes predict real-world gambling.* Psychological Science, 27(3), 299-311.

59 Coleman, M. (2021, March 28). SPIVA: 2021 Mid-Year Active vs. Passive Scorecard. *Index Fund Advisors.* https://www.ifa.com/articles/despite_brief_reprieve_2018_spiva_report_reveals_active_funds_fail_dent_indexing_lead_-_works/

60 Arrington, C. (1985). *Sly's Silent Son* People https://people.com/archive/cover-story-slys-silent-son-vol-23-no-22/

61 Porter, E.H. (1913). *Pollyanna* Colonial Press, Boston

62 Matlin, M. W., and Stang, D. J. (1978) *The pollyanna principle: Selectivity in language, memory, and thought* Cambridge: Schenkman.

63 Boucher, J., & Osgood, C. E. (1969). *The Pollyanna hypothesis.* Journal of verbal learning and verbal behavior, 8(1), 1-8.

64 Sharot, T., & Garrett, N. (2016). Forming beliefs: Why valence matters. *Trends in cognitive sciences, 20*(1), 25-33.

65 Loeb, M. (2022) *Global M&A market defies gravity in 2021 second half* McKinsey & Company

66 Weber, Y., Oberg, C., & Tarba, S. (2014). The M&A paradox: Factors of success and failure in mergers and acquisitions. In *Comprehensive Guide to Mergers & Acquisitions: Managing the Critical Success Factors Across Every Stage of the M&A Process*, 3-11.

67 Kenny, G. (2020). *Don't Make This Common M&A Mistake* Harvard Business Review https://hbr.org/2020/03/dont-make-this-common-ma-mistake

68   Parashar, F. (2017). The psychology of optimism and pessimism: theories and research findings. *Preuzeto, 16,* 2017.

69   Maddux, C. D. (1989). The harmful effects of excessive optimism in educational computing. *Educational Technology, 29*(7), 23-29.

70   Niiniluoto, Ilkka. 2004. *Critical scientific realism.* Oxford: Oxford University Press.

71   American Psychological Association (n.d.). *Realism.* APA Dictionary of Psychology. Retrieved from https://dictionary.apa.org/realism

72   Haselton, M. G., & Nettle, D. (2006). The paranoid optimist: an integrative evolutionary model of cognitive biases. *Personality and Social Psychology Review,* no. 1, pp 47–66

73   Koetsier, J. (2021) *IBM's Weather Company Has A Path To Billions In New Revenue, Thanks To The Rise Of The Subscription Economy.* Retrieved from https://www.forbes.com/sites/johnkoetsier/2021/04/08/ibms-weather-company-has-a-path-to-billions-in-new-revenue-thanks-to-the-rise-of-the-subscription-economy/?sh=1d0fafda7828.

74   De Meza, D., & Dawson, C. (2021). Neither an optimist nor a pessimist be: mistaken expectations lower well-being. *Personality and Social Psychology Bulletin, 47*(4), 540-550.

75   Bouchard, L. C., Carver, C. S., Mens, M. G., & Scheier, M. F. (2017). Optimism, health, and well-being *Positive Psychology* (pp. 112-130): Routledge.

76   Gillham, J. E., Shatté, A. J., Reivich, K. J., & Seligman, M. E. P. (2001). *Optimism, pessimism, and explanatory style.* In E. C. Chang (Ed.), Optimism and pessimism: Implications for theory, research, and practice (Vol. 53, pp. 53-75). Washington D.C.: American Psychological Association.

77   Kubzansky, L. D., Kubzansky, P. E., & Maselko, J. (2004). Optimism and pessimism in the context of health: bipolar opposites or separate constructs? *Personality and social psychology bulletin, 30*(8), 943-956.

78   Dember, W. N., Martin, S. H., Hummer, M. K., Howe, S. R., & Melton, R. S. (1989). The measurement of optimism and pessimism. *Current Psychology, 8*(2), 102-119.

79   Herzberg, P. Y., Glaesmer, H., & Hoyer, J. (2006). Separating optimism and pessimism: A robust psychometric analysis of the Revised Life Orientation Test (LOT-R). *Psychological assessment, 18*(4), 433.

80   Festinger, L. (1962). Cognitive dissonance. *Scientific American,* 207(4), 93-106.

81   Ploger, G. W., Dunaway, J., Fournier, P., & Soroka, S. (2021). The psycho-physiological correlates of cognitive dissonance. *Politics and the Life Sciences, 40*(2), 202-212.

82   Peterson, C., & Seligman, M. E. (1984). Causal explanations as a risk factor for depression: theory and evidence. *Psychological review, 91*(3), 347.

83   Seligman, M. E. (2006). *Learned optimism: How to change your mind and your life.* New York, USA: Vintage Books.

84   Scheier, M. F., Carver, C. S., & Bridges, M. W. (2001). Optimism, pessimism, and psychological well-being. *Optimism and pessimism: Implications for theory, research, and practice, 1,* 189-216.

85   Beck, J. S. (1995) *Cognitive therapy: basics and beyond.* New York: Guilford Press.

86   Beck, A. T., Rush, A. J., Shaw, B. F., & Emery, G. (1979) *Cognitive therapy of depression.* New York: Guilford Press.

87   Golin, S., Terrell, F., Weitz, J., & Drost, P. L. (1979). The illusion of control among depressed patients. *Journal of abnormal psychology, 88*(4), 454.

88   Matlin, M., & Stang, D. (1978). Pollyanna principle. *Psychology Today, 11*(10), 56.

89   O'Sullivan, O. P. (2015). The Neural Basis of Always Looking on the Bright Side. *Dialogues in Philosophy, Mental & Neuro Sciences, 8*(1)

90   Taylor, S. E., & Brown, J. D. (1994). Positive illusions and well-being revisited: separating fact from fiction. *Psychological Bulletin, 116*(1), 21-27

91   Johnson, D. D., & Fowler, J. H. (2011). The evolution of overconfidence. *Nature, 477*(7364), 317-320.

92   Ho, P. H., Huang, C. W., Lin, C. Y., & Yen, J. F. (2016). CEO overconfidence and financial crisis: Evidence from bank lending and leverage. *Journal of Financial Economics, 120*(1), 194-209.

93   Lewinsohn, P. M., Mischel, W., Chaplin, W., & Barton, R. (1980). Social competence and depression: the role of illusory self-perceptions. *Journal of abnormal psychology, 89*(2), 203.

94   Roth, G., & Dicke, U. (2005). Evolution of the brain and intelligence. *Trends in cognitive sciences, 9*(5), 250-257.

95   Nieuwenhuys, R. (1994). The neocortex. *Anatomy and embryology, 190*(4), 307-337.

96   Robinson, D. J. (2022). Abstract Algebra. In *Abstract Algebra.* de Gruyter.

97   Bowen, J. P. (1995). A brief history of algebra and computing: An eclectic oxonian view. *IMA Bulletin, 31*(1/2), 6-9.

98   Hager, W. W. (2022). *Applied numerical linear algebra* (Vol. 87). SIAM.

99   NASA. (2020, March 5). *The Mars 2020 Rover Has a Name!* [Press release]. Retrieved from https://mars.nasa.gov/mars2020/participate/name-the-rover/

100 NASA. (2021, November 18). *Twin Of NASA's Perseverance Mars Rover Begins Terrain Tests* [Press release]. Retrieved from https://www.nasa.gov/feature/jpl/twin-of-nasa-s-perseverance-mars-rover-begins-terrain-tests

101 Irvine, W. B. (2008). *A guide to the good life: The ancient art of Stoic joy.* Oxford University Press.

102 Pigliucci, M., & Lopez, G. (2019). *A Handbook for New Stoics: How to Thrive in a World Out of Your Control—52 Week-by-Week Lessons.* The Experiment.

103 Vissing, Y., & Burke, M. (1984). Visualization techniques for health care workers. *Journal of Psychosocial Nursing and Mental Health Services, 22*(1), 29-32.

104 Ming-Dao, D., & Deng, M. D. (1996). *Everyday Tao: Living with balance and harmony.* HarperCollins.

105 Peterson, C. (2000). The future of optimism. *American psychologist, 55*(1), 44.

106 Braathen, V. M. L., & Sørensen, M. W. (2017). *Unconscious bias against introverts in the recruitment and selection process* (Master's thesis, BI Norwegian Business School).

107 Lebin, L. G., Riddle, M., Chang, S., & Soeprono, T. (2019). Continuing the quiet revolution: developing introverted leaders in academic psychiatry. *Academic Psychiatry, 43*(5), 516-520.

108 Eysenck, H. (2018). *Dimensions of personality.* Routledge.

109 Conklin, E. S. (1927). The determination of normal extravert-introvert interest differences. *The Pedagogical Seminary and Journal of Genetic Psychology, 34*(1), 28-37.

110 Cohen, D., & Schmidt, J. P. (1979). Ambiversion: characteristics of midrange responders on the Introversion-Extraversion continuum. *Journal of personality assessment, 43*(5), 514-516.

111 Grant, A. M. (2013). Rethinking the extraverted sales ideal: The ambivert advantage. *Psychological science, 24*(6), 1024-1030.

112 Cuomo, C. (2020, March 25). Dr. Anthony Fauci on how he manages his optimism during a pandemic. *CNN/Cuomo Primetime.* http://www.cnn.com/TRANSCRIPTS/2003/25/CPT.01.html

113 Bosveld, E. (2021). Positive vibes only. *Sandberg Instituut.*

114 Boulicault, M., & Richardson, S. (2020). Analyzing COVID-19 sex difference claims. *Apa Newsletter on Feminism and Philosophy*, *20*(1).

115 Collinson, D. (2012). Prozac leadership and the limits of positive thinking. *Leadership*, *8*(2), 87-107.

116 Goodman, W. (2022). Toxic Positivity: keeping it real in a world obsessed with being happy. *TarcherPerigee: New York.*

117 Princing, M. (2021). What you need to know about toxic positivity. *Right as Rain by UW Medicine.* https://rightasrain.uwmedicine.org/mind/well-being/toxic-positivity

118 Kovoor-Misra, S., Clair, J. A., & Bettenhausen, K. L. (2001). Clarifying the Attributes of Organizational Crises. *Technological Forecasting and Social Change, 67*(1), 77-91. doi:https://doi.org/10.1016/S0040-1625(99)00081-5

119 Toft, B., & Reynolds, S. (2016). *Learning from Disasters.* United Kingdom: Palgrave Macmillan.

120 Carver, C. S., & Scheier, M. F. (2001a). *On the self-regulation of behavior*: Cambridge University Press.

121 Collins, J. (2016). *Good to great: Why some companies make the leap and others don't.* HarperBusiness.

122 Nietzsche, F.W. (1968). *Twilight of the idols.* Penguin.

123 Frankl, V. E. (1992). *Man's search for meaning: An introduction to logotherapy.* Beacon Press.

124 Li, P. J., Wong, Y. J., & McDermott, R. C. (2021). Examining Nietsche's Epigram: Having a Why Helps Your Bear Almost Any How?. *Journal of Humanistic Psychology*, 00221678211041828.

125 Längle, A., & Sykes, B. M. (2006). Viktor Frankl—Advocate for humanity: on his 100th birthday. *Journal of humanistic psychology*, *46*(1), 36-47.

126 Castelfranchi, C., & Falcone, R. (1997). *From task delegation to role delegation.* Paper presented at the Congress of the Italian Association for Artificial Intelligence.

127 Braubach, L., Pokahr, A., Moldt, D., & Lamersdorf, W. (2004). *Goal representation for BDI agent systems.* Paper presented at the International Workshop on Programming Multi-Agent Systems.

128 Geers, A. L., Wellman, J. A., & Lassiter, G. D. (2009). Dispositional optimism and engagement: the moderating influence of goal prioritization. *Journal of Personality and Social Psychology, 96*(4), 913.

129 Mckeown, M. (2019). *The strategy book.* Pearson UK.

130 West. M. & Schaeffer, C. (2022, January 26) *American Greed - Boeing's deadly design*. [Television Broadcast]. CNBC.

131 Stoddart, M., Siu, B. (2019, October 18). Boeing pilots messaged about 737 Max issues years before 2 crashes killed 346. *ABC News*. https://abcn. ws/32FI1nu

132 Bhattacharya, S., & Nisha, Y. (2020). A Case Study on Boeing's 737 MAX Crisis on Account of Leadership Failure. *International Journal of Research in Engineering, Science and Management, 3*(9), 116-118.

133 The Boeing Company. (n.d.). *Our values*. Boeing. https://www.boeing.com/ principles/values.page.

134 Isidore, C. (2020, November 17). Boeing's 737 Max debacle could be the most expensive corporate blunder ever. *CNN*. https://www.cnn.com/2020/11/17/business/boeing-737-max-grounding-cost/index. html

135 Gates, D. (2020, November 18). Boeing 737 MAX can return to the skies, FAA says. *The Seattle Times*. https://www.seattletimes.com/business/boeing-aero-space/boeing-737-max-can-return-to-the-skies-says-faa/?utm_source=e-mail&utm_medium=email&utm_campaign=article_inset_1.1

136 Scheier, M. F., & Carver, C. S. (1985). Optimism, coping, and health: assessment and implications of generalized outcome expectancies. *Health psychology, 4*(3), 219-247.

137 Zhang, Y., Fishbach, A., & Dhar, R. (2007). When thinking beats doing: The role of optimistic expectations in goal-based choice. *Journal of Consumer Research, 34*(4), 567-578.

138 Lieberman, H. R., Bathalon, G. P., Falco, C. M., Morgan, C. A., Niro, P. J., & Tharion, W. J. (2005). The fog of war: decrements in cognitive performance and mood associated with combat-like stress. *Aviation, Space, and Environmental Medicine, 76*(7), C7-C14.

139 Carver, C. S., & Scheier, M. F. (2014). Dispositional optimism. *Trends in Cognitive Sciences, 18*(6), 293-299. doi:10.1016/j.tics.2014.02.003

140 Segerstrom, S. C., & Nes, L. S. (2006). When goals conflict but people prosper: The case of dispositional optimism. *Journal of Research in Personality, 40*(5), 675-693.

141 The Nobel Prize. (2022, February). *Thank you for saving my life*. [Post]. LinkedIn. https://www.linkedin.com/posts/nobelprize_worldcancerday-activ-ity-6895421697676128256-MQKJ?utm_source=linkedin_share&utm_medi-um=member_desktop_web.

142 Duckworth, A. (2016). *Grit: The power of passion and perseverance* (Vol. 234). New York, NY: Scribner.

143 Duckworth, A. L., & Quinn, P. D. (2009). Development and validation of the Short Grit Scale (GRIT–S). *Journal of personality assessment, 91*(2), 166-174.

144 Council of Graduate Schools. (2008). Ph. D. completion and attrition: Analysis of baseline demographic data from the Ph. D. completion project.

145 Paez, D., Liu, J. H., Techio, E., Slawuta, P., Zlobina, A., & Cabecinhas, R. (2008). "Remembering" World War II and willingness to fight: Sociocultural factors in the social representation of historical warfare across 22 societies. *Journal of Cross-Cultural Psychology, 39*(4), 373-380.

146 Atran, S., Sheikh, H., & Gómez, Á. (2014). For cause and comrade: Devoted actors and willingness to fight. *Cliodynamics, 5*(1).

147 Inglehart, R. F., Puranen, B., & Welzel, C. (2015). Declining willingness to fight for one's country: The individual-level basis of the long peace. *Journal of Peace Research, 52*(4), 418-434.

148 Starr, B. (2015, May 24). Carter: Iraqis showed 'no will to fight' in Ramadi. *CNN.* https://www.cnn.com/2015/05/24/politics/ashton-carter-isis-ramadi/index.html -

149 Dimoka, A. (2010). What does the brain tell us about trust and distrust? Evidence from a functional neuroimaging study. *Mis Quarterly*, 373-396.

150 Harrison, N. A., Gray, M. A., Gianaros, P. J., & Critchley, H. D. (2010). The embodiment of emotional feelings in the brain. *Journal of Neuroscience, 30*(38), 12878-12884.

151 Jung, C.G. (1954) Psychological aspects of the mother archetype. In *Four archetypes: mother, rebirth, spirit, trickster* (pp. 7-44)

152 Jung, C. G. (2014). *Aion: Researches into the Phenomenology of the Self.* Routledge

153 Ashkanasy, N. M., & Dasborough, M. T. (2003). Emotional awareness and emotional intelligence in leadership teaching. *Journal of education for business, 79*(1), 18-22.

154 Lane, R. D., & Schwartz, G. E. (1987). Levels of emotional awareness: a cognitive-developmental theory and its application to psychopathology. *The American journal of psychiatry*.

155 Lane, R. D. (2000). Levels of emotional awareness: Neurological, psychological, and social perspectives.

156 Grace, S. C., Mejia, J. M., Inhofe Rapert, M., & Thyroff, A. (2021). Emotional awareness in time of disruption: The impact of tolerance for ambiguity, worry, perceived stress, helpful communication, and past experience on student satisfaction. *Marketing Education Review*, *31*(3), 226-240.

157 Shayganfar, M., Rich, C., Sidner, C., & Hylák, B. (2019, September). " It Was Not Your Fault"–Emotional Awareness Improves Collaborative Robots. In *2019 IEEE International Conference on Humanized Computing and Communication (HCC)* (pp. 7-15). IEEE.

158 Keating, C. F. (2018). About face! Facial status cues and perceptions of charismatic leadership. In *The facial displays of leaders* (pp. 145-170). Palgrave Macmillan, Cham.

159 Dixon, N. F. (1976). Decisions and Disaster. *The RUSI Journal*, *121*(2), 50-53.

160 Brown, J. A. (1954). Leaders and leadership.

161 Furtner, M. R., & Rauthmann, J. F. (2010). Relations between self-leadership and scores on the Big Five. *Psychological Reports*, *107*(2), 339-353.

162 Kaplan, R. E., & Kaiser, R. B. (2003). Developing versatile leadership. *MIT Sloan Management Review*, *44*(4), 19-26.

163 Rao, M. S. (2013). Soft leadership: a new direction to leadership. *Industrial and Commercial Training*.

164 Dangmei, J., & Singh, A. (2017). How aesthetic leadership style might relate to employee morale at workplace? An analytical study. *Asia Pacific Journal of Research, 1*.

165 Zimmerman, B. J. (2000). Attaining self-regulation: A social cognitive perspective. In *Handbook of self-regulation* (pp. 13-39). Academic press.

166 Boekaerts, M., Zeidner, M., & Pintrich, P. R. (Eds.). (1999). *Handbook of self-regulation*. Elsevier.

167 Wiebe, D. J., & Korbel, C. (2003). Defensive denial, affect, and the self-regulation of health threats. *The self-regulation of health and illness behaviour*, 184-203.

168 Sosik, J. J., Potosky, D., & Jung, D. I. (2002). Adaptive self-regulation: Meeting others' expectations of leadership and performance. *The Journal of Social Psychology*, *142*(2), 211-232.

169 Peterson, R. S., & Behfar, K. J. (2004). Leadership as group regulation. In *The psychology of leadership* (pp. 157-178). Psychology Press.

170 Legge, J. (1885). The book of rites.

171 Hamburger, M. (1959). Aristotle and Confucius: A comparison. *Journal of the History of Ideas*, *20*(2), 236-249.

172 Ekman, P. (2004). Emotions revealed. *Bmj*, *328*(Suppl S5).

173 Plutchik, R. (1991). *The emotions*. University Press of America.

174 A wheel of human emotions. (n.d.) https://www.phoenixperform.com/single-post/a-wheel-of-human-emotions

175 Welch, J. (2003). The best teams are emotionally literate. *Industrial and Commercial Training*.

176 Sifneos, P. E. (1988). Alexithymia and its relationship to hemispheric specialization, affect, and creativity. *Psychiatric Clinics of North America*.

177 Salminen, J. K., Saarijärvi, S., Äärelä, E., Toikka, T., & Kauhanen, J. (1999). Prevalence of alexithymia and its association with sociodemographic variables in the general population of Finland. *Journal of psychosomatic research*, *46*(1), 75-82.

178 Routley, N. (2021, April 8). A visual guide to human emotion. Visual Capitalist. Retrieved https://www.visualcapitalist.com/a-visual-guide-to-human-emotion/

179 Hogan, J., Hogan, R., & Kaiser, R. B. (2009). Hogan Assessment Systems.

180 Hogan, R. (2007). *The Hogan guide: Interpretation and use of Hogan inventories*. Tulsa, OK: Hogan Assessment Systems.

181 Hogan, R. (2020). How to build Hogan Assessment Systems. *Consulting Psychology Journal: Practice and Research*, *72*(1), 50.

182 Mansi, A. (2007). Executive coaching and psychometrics: A case study evaluating the use of the Hogan Personality Inventory (HPI) and the Hogan Development Survey (HDS) in senior management coaching. *The Coaching Psychologist*, *3*(2), 53-58.

183 Nesbit, Paul L. "The role of self-reflection, emotional management of feedback, and self-regulation processes in self-directed leadership development." *Human Resource Development Review* 11.2 (2012): 203-226.

184 Branson, C. M. (2007). Improving leadership by nurturing moral consciousness through structured self-reflection. *Journal of Educational Administration*.

185 David, S. (2016). *Emotional agility: Get unstuck, embrace change, and thrive in work and life*. Penguin.

186 Oatley, K., Keltner, D., & Jenkins, J. M. (2006). *Understanding emotions*. Blackwell publishing.

187 Kwon, K., Liu, Y. H., & Johnson, L. P. (2014). Group regulation and social-emotional interactions observed in computer supported collaborative learning: Comparison between good vs. poor collaborators. *Computers & Education*, *78*, 185-200.

188 Saab, N. (2012). Team regulation, regulation of social activities or co-regula-
tion: Different labels for effective regulation of learning in CSCL. *Metacogni-
tion and Learning, 7*(1), 1-6.

189 Treviño, L. K., & Brown, M. E. (2005). The role of leaders in influencing
unethical behavior in the workplace. *Managing organizational deviance, 69,*
87.

190 Latu, I. M., Mast, M. S., Lammers, J., & Bombari, D. (2013). Successful
female leaders empower women's behavior in leadership tasks. *Journal of
Experimental Social Psychology, 49*(3), 444-448.

191 Klann, G. (2011). *Building Your Team's Morale, Pride, and Spirit* (Vol. 109).
John Wiley & Sons.

192 Altman, W. (2010). High morale and working wonders. *Engineering & Technology, 5*(3), 70-71.

193 Weakliem, D. L., & Frenkel, S. J. (2006). Morale and workplace performance.
Work and occupations, 33(3), 335-361.

194 Bowles, D., & Cooper, C. (2009). *Employee morale: Driving performance in
challenging times*. Springer.

195 Bütje, K. J., & Hodzic, H. (2017). Groupthink in Boardrooms: Harmonious
or Hazardous. *The Impact of Groupthink on Board Directors in the Strategic
Decision Making Process.*

196 Mead, E. (2019, April 8) *What are Negative Emotions and How to Control
Them?* Positive Psychology. https://positivepsychology.com/negative-emo-
tions/

197 Schwarz, N., & Clore, G. L. (1996). Feelings and phenomenal experiences. In
E. T. Higgins & A. Kruglanski (Eds.), *Social psychology: Handbook of basic
principles* (pp. 433-465). New York, NY: Guilford.

198 Bless, H., Clore, G. L., Schwarz, N., Golisano, V., Rabe, C., & Wölk, M.
(1996). Mood and the use of scripts: Does a happy mood really lead to mind-
lessness?. *Journal of personality and social psychology, 71*(4), 665.

199 Forgas, J. P. (2014). Four Ways Sadness May be Good for You. *Greater Good
Science Center, June, 4.*

200 Zein, M. E., Wyart, V., & Grezes, J. (2015, December 29). Anxiety dissociates
the adaptive functions of sensory and motor response enhancements to social
threats. Retrieved from https://elifesciences.org/articles/10274

201 Biswas-Diener, R. & Kashdan, T. (2014). *The upside of your dark side: Why
being your whole self—not just your "good" self—drives success and fulfillment*. New York, NY: Avery Publishing.

202 Nezlek, J. B., & Kuppens, P. (2008). Regulating positive and negative emotions in daily life. *Journal of personality*, *76*(3), 561-580.

203 Schwarz, N., Bless, H., & Bohner, G. (1991). Mood and persuasion: Affective states influence the processing of persuasive communications. In *Advances in experimental social psychology* (Vol. 24, pp. 161-199). Academic Press.

204 van de Ven, N., Zeelenberg, M., & Pieters, R. (2011). Why envy outperforms admiration. *Personality and social psychology bulletin*, *37*(6), 784-795.

205 Greer, S., & Morris, T. (1975). Psychological attributes of women who develop breast cancer: A controlled study. *Journal of Psychosomatic Research*, *19*(2), 147-153.

206 Penedo, F. J., Molton, I., Dahn, J. R., Shen, B. J., Kinsinger, D., Traeger, L., ... & Antoni, M. (2006). A randomized clinical trial of group-based cognitive-behavioral stress management in localized prostate cancer: development of stress management skills improves quality of life and benefit finding. *Annals of Behavioral Medicine*, *31*(3), 261-270.

207 Thomas, S. P., Groer, M., Davis, M., Droppleman, P., Mozingo, J., & Pierce, M. (2000). Anger and cancer: an analysis of the linkages. *Cancer Nursing*, *23*(5), 344-349.

208 Elliott, R., Bohart, A. C., Watson, J. C., & Greenberg, L. S. (2011). Empathy. *Psychotherapy*, *48*(1), 43.

209 Ruiz-Fernández, M. D., Ramos-Pichardo, J. D., Ibáñez-Masero, O., Carmona-Rega, M. I., Sánchez-Ruiz, M. J., & Ortega-Galán, Á. M. (2021). Professional quality of life, self-compassion, resilience, and empathy in healthcare professionals during COVID-19 crisis in Spain. *Research in Nursing & Health*, *44*(4), 620-632.

210 Canales-Lavigne, M. (2022, May 2). *Survey suggests fewer Canadians feel empathetic amid ongoing COVID-19 pandemic*. Global News. https://globalnews.ca/news/8803870/canadian-mental-health-association-survey-empathy-sask/ -

211 Whitaker, R. (Director). (2012). *When Ali came to Ireland* [Film]. True Films.

212 Haggbloom, S. J., Warnick, R., Warnick, J. E., Jones, V. K., Yarbrough, G. L., Russell, T. M., ... & Monte, E. (2002). The 100 most eminent psychologists of the 20th century. *Review of General Psychology*, *6*(2), 139-152.

213 Bandura, A. (1977). Self-efficacy: toward a unifying theory of behavioral change. *Psychological review, 84*(2), 191.

214 Useem, M., Cook, J. R., & Sutton, L. (2005). Developing leaders for decision making under stress: Wildland firefighters in the South Canyon Fire and its aftermath. *Academy of Management Learning & Education, 4*(4), 461-485.

215 Bekkers, F. (1977). Threatened leadership and intergroup conflicts. *Journal of Peace Research, 14*(3), 223-237.

216 Rahman, W. A. W. A. (2012). *A study to determine the impact of empathy on leadership effectiveness among business leaders in the United States and Malaysia* (Doctoral dissertation, Lawrence Technological University).

217 Burch, G. F. (2013). *Interactive empathy and leader effectiveness: An evaluation of how sensing emotion and responding with empathy influence corporate leader effectiveness.* Virginia Commonwealth University.

218 Bakar, A. Y. A., Ishak, N. M., & Abidin, M. H. Z. (2014). The relationship between domains of empathy and leadership skills among gifted and talented students. *Procedia-Social and Behavioral Sciences, 116*, 765-768.

219 Thurman, R. L. (2012). *One More Step the 638 Best Quotes for the Runner: Motivation for the Next Step!* Indiana: iUniverse.

220 Dewar, Keller & Malhotra (March 15, 2022) *CEO Excellence: The Six Mindsets That Distinguish the Best Leaders from the Rest*

221 Peale, N. V. (2003). *Enthusiasm makes the difference.* Simon and Schuster.

222 Bandura, A. (1977). Self-efficacy: toward a unifying theory of behavioral change. *Psychological review, 84*(2), 191.

223 Muretta Jr, R. J. (2005). *Exploring the four sources of self-efficacy* (Doctoral dissertation, ProQuest Information & Learning).

224 Bandura, A., Freeman, W. H., & Lightsey, R. (1999). Self-efficacy: The exercise of control.

225 Burton, R. E. (1995). *Self-remembering.* Weiser Books.

226 *Bits & Pieces*, September 19, 1991, p. 9.

227 da Silva, C. F., & Hare, T. A. (2020). Humans are primarily model-based learners in the two-stage task. *BioRxiv*, 682922.

228 Roberts, D. (2010). Vicarious learning: A review of the literature. *Nurse Education in practice, 10*(1), 13-16.

229 Mayes, J. T. (2015). Still to learn from vicarious learning. *E-Learning and Digital Media, 12*(3-4), 361-371.

230 Chan, C. K., & Lovibond, P. F. (1996). Expectancy bias in trait anxiety. *Journal of abnormal psychology, 105*(4), 637.

231 Wilson, E. J., MacLeod, C., Mathews, A., & Rutherford, E. M. (2006). The causal role of interpretive bias in anxiety reactivity. *Journal of abnormal psychology*, *115*(1), 103.

232 Cabeleira, C. M., Steinman, S. A., Burgess, M. M., Bucks, R. S., MacLeod, C., Melo, W., & Teachman, B. A. (2014). Expectancy bias in anxious samples. *Emotion (Washington, D.C.)*, *14*(3), 588–601. https://doi.org/10.1037/a0035899

233 Shell, H. R. (2021). The skin of a living thought: Art, science, and STS in practice. In *Routledge Handbook of Art, Science, and Technology Studies* (pp. 81-90). Routledge.

234 Alberini, C. M. (2010, September). Long-term memories: The good, the bad, and the ugly. In *Cerebrum: the Dana forum on brain science* (Vol. 2010). Dana Foundation.

235 Cacioppo, J. T., Cacioppo, S., & Gollan, J. K. (2014). The negativity bias: Conceptualization, quantification, and individual differences. *Behavioral and Brain Sciences*, *37*(3), 309.

236 Federico, C. M., Johnston, C. D., & Lavine, H. G. (2014). Context, engagement, and the (multiple) functions of negativity bias. *Behavioral and Brain Sciences*, *37*(3), 311.

237 Isaacowitz, D. M. (2005). The gaze of the optimist. *Personality and social psychology bulletin*, *31*(3), 407-415.

238 Tight, M. (2022). Positivity bias in higher education research. *Higher Education Quarterly*.

239 Aithal, M., & Tan, C. (2021). On positivity bias in negative reviews. *arXiv preprint arXiv:2106.12056*.

240 Sharot, T. (2011). *The optimism bias: A tour of the irrationally positive brain.* Pantheon/Random House.

241 Joët, G., Usher, E. L., & Bressoux, P. (2011). Sources of self-efficacy: An investigation of elementary school students in France. *Journal of educational psychology*, *103*(3), 649.

242 Freeman, J., & Peisah, C. (2022). Imposter syndrome in doctors beyond training: a narrative review. *Australasian Psychiatry*, *30*(1), 49-54.

243 Mager, R. F. (1992). No self-efficacy, no performance. *Training*.

244 Ackerman*, R. H., & Maslin-Ostrowski, P. (2004). The wounded leader and emotional learning in the schoolhouse. *School Leadership & Management*, *24*(3), 311-328.

245 Bandura, Albert. "Self-efficacy conception of anxiety." *Anxiety research* 1, no. 2 (1988): 77-98.

246 Ptaszynski, M., Dybala, P., Shi, W., Rzepka, R., & Araki, K. (2008). Disentangling emotions from the Web. *Internet in the service of affect analysis. KEAS, 8*, 51-56.

247 Kolesch, D., & Knoblauch, H. (2019). Audience emotions. In *Affective Societies* (pp. 252-264). Routledge.

248 Andrade, E. B., & Ariely, D. (2009). The enduring impact of transient emotions on decision making. *Organizational behavior and human decision processes, 109*(1), 1-8.

249 Alsharif, A. H., Salleh, N. Z. M., & Baharun, R. (2021). To better understand the role of emotional processes in decision-making. *International Journal of Academic Research in Economics and Management Sciences, 10*(2), 49-67.

250 Kim, J., Kwon, J. H., Kim, J., Kim, E. J., Kim, H. E., Kyeong, S., & Kim, J. J. (2021). The effects of positive or negative self-talk on the alteration of brain functional connectivity by performing cognitive tasks. *Scientific reports, 11*(1), 1-11.

251 Tetenbaum, T., & Laurence, H. (2011). Leading in the chaos of the 21st century. *Journal of Leadership Studies, 4*(4), 41-49.

252 Arnold, M., & Rigotti, T. (2021). Leaders as role models: Effects of leader job crafting on team and employee job crafting.

253 Gautrey, C. (2014). *Influential leadership: A leader's guide to getting things done*. Kogan Page Publishers.

254 Elms, A. K., Gill, H., & Gonzalez-Morales, M. G. (2022). Confidence Is Key: Collective Efficacy, Team Processes, and Team Effectiveness. *Small Group Research*, 10464964221104218.

255 Bandura, A. (2000). Exercise of human agency through collective efficacy. *Current directions in psychological science, 9*(3), 75-78.

256 Moisio, R., Capelli, S., & Sabadie, W. (2021). Managing the aftermath: Scapegoating as crisis communication strategy. *Journal of Consumer Behaviour, 20*(1), 89-100.

257 Gao, H., Knight, J. G., Zhang, H., Mather, D., & Tan, L. P. (2012). Consumer scapegoating during a systemic product-harm crisis. *Journal of Marketing Management, 28*(11-12), 1270-1290.

258 Wright, F. (2022). Making Good of Crisis: Temporalities of Care in UK Mental Health Services. *Medical Anthropology, 41*(3), 315-328.

259 Nutt, P. C. (1999). Surprising but true: Half the decisions in organizations fail. *Academy of Management Perspectives, 13*(4), 75-90.

260 Strouse, J. (2014). *Morgan: American Financier*. Random House Trade Paperbacks.

261 Al-Dabbagh, Z. S. (2020). The role of decision-maker in crisis management: A qualitative study using grounded theory (COVID-19 pandemic crisis as a model). *Journal of Public Affairs, 20*(4), e2186.

262 Cornell, D. G., & Sheras, P. L. (1998). Common errors in school crisis response: Learning from our mistakes. *Psychology in the Schools, 35*(3), 297-307.

263 Grebe, S. K. (2013). Things can get worse: How mismanagement of a crisis response strategy can cause a secondary or double crisis: the example of the AWB corporate scandal. *Corporate Communications: An International Journal.*

264 Sagir, C. (2022). British government failed to provide quick and effective support for afghans as Taliban took over, report finds. *Guardian (Sydney)*, (1998), 11.

265 Robert, B., & Lajtha, C. (2002). A new approach to crisis management. *Journal of contingencies and crisis management, 10*(4), 181-191.

266 Dzeng, E. (2014, February 26) *How Academia and Publishing are Destroying Scientific Innovation: A Conversation with Sydney Brenner*. Elizabeth Dzeng, MD, PhD, MPH. https://elizabethdzeng.com/2014/02/26/how-academia-and-publishing-are-destroying-scientific-innovation-a-conversation-with-sydney-brenner/

267 Kotter, J. P. (2008). *A sense of urgency*. Harvard Business Press.

268 Nutt, P. C. (1993). The identification of solution ideas during organizational decision making. *Management Science, 39*(9), 1071-1085.

269 Heath, C., Sibony, O., Webb, A. (2013). Making great decisions. McKinsey Quarterly. https://www.mckinsey.com/business-functions/strategy-and-corporate-finance/our-insights/making-great-decisions

270 Farshbafnadi, M., Agah, E., & Rezaei, N. (2021). The second brain: The connection between gut microbiota composition and multiple sclerosis. *Journal of Neuroimmunology, 360*, 577700.

271 Mayer, E. A. (2011). Gut feelings: the emerging biology of gut–brain communication. *Nature Reviews Neuroscience, 12*(8), 453-466.

272 The Gut-Brain Connection: How it Works and The Role of Nutrition. (n.d.). Retrieved from https://www.healthline.com/nutrition/gut-brain-connection

273 Samples, B. (1976). *The metaphoric mind: A celebration of creative consciousness.* Addison Wesley Publishing Company.

274 Klein, G. A. (2004). *The power of intuition: How to use your gut feelings to make better decisions at work.* Currency.

275 Blinder, A. S., & Morgan, J. (2000). Are two heads better than one?: An experimental analysis of group vs. individual decisionmaking.

276 Sutter, M. (2005). Are four heads better than two? An experimental beauty-contest game with teams of different size. *Economics letters, 88*(1), 41-46.

277 Blinder, A. S., & Morgan, J. (2005). Are two heads better than one? Monetary policy by committee. *Journal of Money, Credit and Banking,* 789-811.

278 Boynton, A. C., Gales, L. M., & Blackburn, R. S. (1993). Managerial search activity: The impact of perceived role uncertainty and role threat. *Journal of Management, 19*(4), 725-747. doi:http://dx.doi.org/10.1016/0149-2063(93)90025-I

279 Cooper, C. L., & Marshall, J. (2013). Occupational sources of stress: A review of the literature relating to coronary heart disease and mental ill health. In C. L. Cooper (Ed.), *From stress to wellbeing volume 1: The theory and research on occupational stress and wellbeing* (pp. 3-23). London: Palgrave Macmillan UK.

280 Carver, C. S., Scheier, M. F., & Segerstrom, S. C. (2010). Optimism. *Clinical Psychology Review, 30*(7), 879-889. doi:10.1016/j.cpr.2010.01.006

281 Sagar, S. S., & Jowett, S. (2015). Fear of failure and self-control in the context of coach-athlete relationship quality. *International Journal of Coaching Science, 9*(2).

282 Ramírez-Maestre, C., Esteve, R., López-Martínez, A. E., Serrano-Ibáñez, E. R., Ruiz-Párraga, G. T., & Peters, M. (2019). Goal adjustment and well-being: The role of optimism in patients with chronic pain. *Annals of Behavioral Medicine, 53*(7), 597-607.

283 Carver, C. S., & Scheier, M. F. (2018). Generalized optimism.

284 Hogan, J., & Feeney, S. (2012). Crisis and policy change: The role of the political entrepreneur. *Risk, Hazards & Crisis in Public Policy, 3*(2), 1-24.

285 Saterbak, A., & Wettergreen, M. (2021). Step 4: Brainstorm Solution Options. In *Introduction to Engineering Design* (pp. 61-81). Springer, Cham.

286 Vegt, N., Visch, V., Vermeeren, A., de Ridder, H., & Hayde, Z. (2019). Balancing Game Rules for Improving Creative Output of Group Brainstorms. *International Journal of Design, 13*(1).

287 Curhan, J. R., Labuzova, T., & Mehta, A. (2021). Cooperative Criticism: When Criticism Enhances Creativity in Brainstorming and Negotiation. *Organization Science*, *32*(5), 1256-1272.

288 Anderson, C., Sharps, D. L., Soto, C. J., & John, O. P. (2020). People with disagreeable personalities (selfish, combative, and manipulative) do not have an advantage in pursuing power at work. *Proceedings of the National Academy of Sciences*, *117*(37), 22780-22786.

289 Six, F., & Sorge, A. (2008). Creating a high-trust organization: An exploration into organizational policies that stimulate interpersonal trust building. *Journal of Management Studies*, *45*(5), 857-884.

290 Norton, M. I. (2009): Breakthrough Ideas for 2009. The IKEA effect: When labor leads to love, *Harvard Business Review*, 87, 30.

291 Norton, M. I., Mochon, D., & Ariely, D. (2012). The IKEA effect: When labor leads to love. *Journal of consumer psychology*, *22*(3), 453-460.

292 Hart, A. (2018, November 6). How Viagra was discovered by accident [Audio podcast episode]. In *BBC Discovery – The Genius of Accidents*. https://www.bbc.co.uk/programmes/p06qxjcb

293 FDA Approves Viagra. (1998, March 27). In *History*. A&E Television Networks. Retrieved from https://www.history.com/this-day-in-history/fda-approves-viagra

294 Jay, E. (2010, January 20). Viagra and other drugs discovered by accident. *BBC News*. Retrieved from http://news.bbc.co.uk/2/hi/health/8466118.stm

295 Loudon, I. (2000). *The tragedy of childbed fever*. OUP Oxford.

296 Kadar, N., Romero, R., & Papp, Z. (2018). Ignaz Semmelweis: the "Savior of Mothers": On the 200th anniversary of his birth. *American Journal of Obstetrics & Gynecology*, *219*(6), 519-522.

297 Kadar, N. (2019). Rediscovering Ignaz Philipp Semmelweis (1818– 1865). *American journal of obstetrics and gynecology*, *220*(1), 26-39.

298 Schreiner, S. (2020). Ignaz Semmelweis: a victim of harassment?. *Wiener Medizinische Wochenschrift*, *170*(11), 293-302.

299 O'donnell, K. F. (2021). Wisdom from Ignaz Semmelweis. *Nursing2021*, *51*(10), 69-70.

300 Dunn, P. M. (2005). Ignac Semmelweis (1818–1865) of Budapest and the prevention of puerperal fever. *Archives of Disease in Childhood-Fetal and Neonatal Edition*, *90*(4), F345-FF348.

301 Cavaillon, J. M., & Chrétien, F. (2019). From septicemia to sepsis 3.0–from Ignaz Semmelweis to Louis Pasteur. *Microbes and Infection*, *21*(5-6), 213-221.

302   Semmelweis, I., & Semmelweis, I. F. (1983). *The etiology, concept, and pro-phylaxis of childbed fever* (No. 2). Univ of Wisconsin Press.

303   Tandon, R. (2020). COVID-19 and mental health: preserving humanity, main-taining sanity, and promoting health. *Asian journal of psychiatry, 51*, 102256.

304   Carson, E. A., & Toodayan, N. (2018). Ignaz Philipp Semmelweis (1818–1865): herald of hygienic medicine. *Medical Journal of Australia, 209*(11), 480-482.

305   Semmelweis, I., & Semmelweis, I. F. (1983). *The etiology, concept, and pro-phylaxis of childbed fever* (No. 2). Univ of Wisconsin Press.

306   Mouta, C., & Meneses, R. (2021). The impact of CEO characteristics on or-ganizational culture and on the silo effect. *Revista Brasileira de Gestão de Negócios, 23*, 207-225.

307   Tett, G. (2015). *The silo effect: The peril of expertise and the promise of break-ing down barriers*. Simon and Schuster.

308   Ziglar, Z. (1997). *Great Quotes from Zig Ziglar: 250 Inspiring Quotes from the Master Motivator and Friends*. Gramercy Books.

309   McChrystal, G. S., Collins, T., Silverman, D., & Fussell, C. (2015). *Team of teams: New rules of engagement for a complex world*. Penguin.

310   Singer, J. B. (2008). Five Ws and an H: Digital challenges in newspaper news-rooms and boardrooms. *The International Journal on Media Management, 10*(3), 122-129.

311   Weber, M. (1987). Decision making with incomplete information. *European journal of operational research, 28*(1), 44-57.

312   Cabrerizo, F. J., Al-Hmouz, R., Morfeq, A., Martínez, M. Á., Pedrycz, W., & Herrera-Viedma, E. (2020). Estimating incomplete information in group de-cision making: A framework of granular computing. *Applied Soft Computing, 86*, 105930.

313   McKee, S. (Writer), & Davidson, A. (Director). (2005, November 6). Some-thing to talk about [Television series episode]. In Rhimes, S. (Creator). *Grey's anatomy*. ABC.

314   The cost of bad communication is skyrocketing – what CMOs need to know. Grammarly Business. (2022, February 24). https://www.grammarly.com/busi-ness/learn/communication-cost-infographic/

315   Porter, M. E., & Nohria, N. (2018). How CEOs manage time. *Harvard Busi-ness Review, 96*(4), 42-51.

316　Coleridge, S.T. (1834). The rime of the ancient mariner. Poetry Foundation. Retrieved https://www.poetryfoundation.org/poems/43997/the-rime-of-the-ancient-mariner-text-of-1834

317　Cuncic. A. (2021, June 25). The spotlight effect and social anxiety. Not everyone is staring at you. *VeryWellMind*. Retrieved https://www.verywellmind.com/what-is-the-spotlight-effect-3024470

318　Roy, R., Sharma, P., Chan, R. Y., & Potdar, V. (2021). Exploring the role of spotlight effect in pay-what-you-want (PWYW) pricing—An anchoring and adjustment perspective. *Psychology & Marketing, 38*(5), 866-880.

319　Zhao, X., & Epley, N. (2021). Kind words do not become tired words: Undervaluing the positive impact of frequent compliments. *Self and Identity, 20*(1), 25-46.

320　Boothby, E. J., & Bohns, V. K. (2021). Why a simple act of kindness is not as simple as it seems: Underestimating the positive impact of our compliments on others. *Personality and Social Psychology Bulletin, 47*(5), 826-840.

321　Burleson, B. R., Daly, J., & Wiemann, J. (1994). Comforting messages: Features, functions, and outcomes. *Strategic interpersonal communication*, 135-161.

322　Ruesch, J., Bateson, G., Pinsker, E. C., & Combs, G. (2017). *Communication: The social matrix of psychiatry.* Routledge.

323　Behrens, T. E., Woolrich, M. W., Walton, M. E., & Rushworth, M. F. (2007). Learning the value of information in an uncertain world. *Nature neuroscience, 10*(9), 1214-1221.

324　Solomon, L. (2016, March 9). Two-thirds of managers are uncomfortable communicating with employees. Harvard Business Review. Retrieved https://hbr.org/2016/03/two-thirds-of-managers-are-uncomfortable-communicating-with-employees

325　Brown, A. D., Colville, I., & Pye, A. (2015). Making sense of sensemaking in organization studies. *Organization studies, 36*(2), 265-277.

326　Alvesson, M., & Jonsson, A. (2022). Organizational dischronization: On meaning and meaninglessness, sensemaking and nonsensemaking. *Journal of Management Studies, 59*(3), 724-754.

327　Chace, S., Lynerd, B. T., & DeSantis, A. (2021). "A distant mirror": Sensemaking in the era of Trump. *Leadership, 17*(2), 212-229.

328　Tourish, D., & Robson, P. (2006). Sensemaking and the distortion of critical upward communication in organizations. *Journal of Management Studies, 43*(4), 711-730.

329 Brown, F. W., & Reilly, M. D. (2009). The Myers-Briggs type indicator and transformational leadership. *Journal of Management Development, 28*(10), 916-932.

330 Petric, D. (2022). The Introvert-Ambivert-Extrovert Spectrum. *Open Journal of Medical Psychology, 11*(3), 103-111.

331 Plonien, C. (2015). Using personality indicators to enhance nurse leader communication. *AORN Journal, 102*(1), 74-80.

332 Petric, D. (2019). Introvert, extrovert and ambivert. *The Knot Theory of Mind.*

333 Järvinen, B. (2020). Introverts in the Business Field: Study of introverts in a line of business where being an extrovert is considered the norm.

334 Agashe, R., & Dhar, S. (2020) Impact of Experience, Commissioning Type and Branch on Learned Optimism: A Study of Armed Force Officers in India. *Impact of research on society: evolving perspectives.*

335 McGinnis, K. (2017). Building Communications' Influence During Corporate Transformation *Mastering Business for Strategic Communicators: Insights and Advice from the C-suite of Leading Brands* (pp. 177-183): Emerald Publishing Limited.

336 Millar, D. P., & Heath, R. L. (Eds.). (2003). *Responding to crisis: A rhetorical approach to crisis communication.* Routledge.

337 Wunderley, L. J., Reddy, W. B., & Dember, W. N. (1998). Optimism and Pessimism in Business Leaders 1. *Journal of Applied Social Psychology, 28*(9), 751-760.

338 Mazarr, M. J. (1998). The pessimism syndrome. *Washington Quarterly, 21*(3), 93-108.

339 Bundy, J., Pfarrer, M. D., Short, C. E., & Coombs, W. T. (2017). Crises and crisis management: Integration, interpretation, and research development. *Journal of management, 43*(6), 1661-1692.

340 Chang, E. C., & Farrehi, A. S. (2001). Optimism/pessimism and information-processing styles: can their influences be distinguished in predicting psychological adjustment?. *Personality and individual differences, 31*(4), 555-562.

341 Maruf, R. (2021, December 6). Better.com CEO fires 900 employees over Zoom. *CNN.* https://www.cnn.com/2021/12/05/business/better-ceo-fires-employees/index.html

342 Azevedo, M., Ramaswamy, A. (2021, November 30). Better.com gets $750M cash infusion in new agreement with its SPAC backers. *TechCrunch.* https://tcrn.ch/3d3wFAG

343 Dean, G. (2021, December 9). Former Better.com staff describe their shock and disbelief after being abruptly fired on Zoom. *Insider*. https://www.businessinsider.com/better-bettercom-staff-zoom-mass-firing-layoff-vishal-garg-reactions-2021-12

344 Hanson, M., Beckman, S. (2021, December 7). 'It's such an emotional catastrophe' | Charlotte woman among Better.com employees fired over Zoom. *WCNC Charlotte*. https://www.wcnc.com/article/news/local/charlotte-woman-laid-off-bettercom-zoom/275-11da4d5e-8c77-454e-a4ba-185fb71f289a

345 Graziosi, G. (2021, December 7). Better.com flooded with negative reviews after 900 employees laid off via Zoom. *Independent*. https://www.independent.co.uk/news/world/americas/better-negative-reviews-zoom-sacking-b1971472.html

346 Aratani, L. (2021, December 10). Better.com CEO to take time off after firing hundreds of employees over Zoom. *The Guardian*. https://www.theguardian.com/us-news/2021/dec/10/bettercom-ceo-vishal-garg-time-off-firing-employees-zoom?CMP=share_btn_link

347 Vishal Garg-run Better.com to 'lay off' 4,000 people this week: Report (2022, March 8). Business Standard. https://www.business-standard.com/article/international/vishal-garg-run-better-com-to-lay-off-4-000-people-this-week-report-122030800259_1.html

348 Bhowmik, S. (2022, June 8). Former executive alleges Better.com, CEO misled investors to ensure SPAC deal. *Reuters*. https://www.reuters.com/markets/deals/former-executive-alleges-bettercom-ceo-misled-investors-ensure-spac-deal-2022-06-08/

349 Lunenburg, F. C. (2010). Communication: The process, barriers, and improving effectiveness. *Schooling*, *1*(1), 1-10.

350 Taylor, B.D., Gross, J. (2021, December 8). The Better.com C.E.O. says he's 'deeply sorry' for firing workers over Zoom. *New York Times*. https://www.nytimes.com/2021/12/08/business/better-zoom-layoffs-vishal-garg.html?smid=em-share

351 Lee, N., & Kim, Y. (2018). A conceptual framework for effective communication in construction management: Information processing and visual communication. In *Construction Research Congress 2018* (pp. 531-541).

352 Henderson, L. S. (2004). Encoding and decoding communication competencies in project management–an exploratory study. *International Journal of Project Management*, *22*(6), 469-476.

353 Guinote, A. (2017). How power affects people: Activating, wanting and goal seeking. *Annual review of psychology*, 68, 353-381.

354 van Ham, P. (2010). *Social power in international politics*. Routledge.

355 Smith, P. K., Jostmann, N. B., Galinsky, A. D., & Van Dijk, W. W. (2008). Lacking power impairs executive functions. *Psychological Science, 19*(5), 441-447.

356 van Kleef, G. A., Oveis, C., van Der Löwe, I., LuoKogan, A., Goetz, J., & Keltner, D. (2008). Power, distress, and compassion: Turning a blind eye to the suffering of others. *Psychological science, 19*(12), 1315-1322.

357 Hogeveen, J., Inzlicht, M., & Obhi, S. S. (2014). Power changes how the brain responds to others. *Journal of Experimental Psychology: General, 143*(2), 755.

358 Elliott, R., Bohart, A. C., Watson, J. C., & Greenberg, L. S. (2011). Empathy. *Psychotherapy, 48*(1), 43.

359 Guinote, A. (2007). Power and goal pursuit. *Personality and Social Psychology Bulletin, 33*(8), 1076-1087.

360 Decker, P., Mitchell, J. (2016, December 15). Tunnel Vision – Its Drawbacks and How to Stay Clear of it. *Manage Magazine*. https://managemagazine.com/article-bank/self-handicapping-leadership/tunnel-vision-its-drawbacks-and-how-to-stay-clear-of-it/

361 Davis, M. H. (2006). *Empathy. In Handbook of the sociology of emotions* (pp. 443-466). Springer, Boston, MA.

362 Wunderley, L. J., Reddy, W. B., & Dember, W. N. (1998). Optimism and Pessimism in Business Leaders 1. Journal of Applied Social Psychology, 28(9), 751-760.

363 Schweitzer, A. (1998). *Out of my life and thought: An autobiography.* JHU Press.

364 Hinckley, G.B. (1969, November 4). *The loneliness of leadership.* [Speech audio recording]. BYU Speeches. https://speeches.byu.edu/talks/gordon-b-hinckley/loneliness-leadership/

365 Shackleton, E. (2014). *South: The last Antarctic expedition of Shackleton and the Endurance.* Bloomsbury Publishing.

366 Shakespeare, W. (2016). *King Henry IV Part 2: Third Series.* Bloomsbury Publishing.

367 Merriam-Webster. (n.d.). Lone wolf. In *Merriam-Webster.com dictionary.* Retrieved July 10, 2021, from https://www.merriam-webster.com/dictionary/lone%20wolf

368 Where does the term "lone wolf" come from? (2020, November 3). *Wolf Education & Research Center*. https://www.wolfcenter.org/where-does-the-term-lone-wolf-come-from/ - :~:text=These%20%E2%80%9Clone%20wolves-%E2%80%9D%20are%20actually,wolf%20population%20into%20new%20areas.

369 Yang, I., & Li, M. (2017). Can absent leadership be positive in team conflicts? An examination of leaders' avoidance behavior in China. *International Journal of Conflict Management*.

370 Blomberg, S., & Rosander, M. (2021). When do poor health increase the risk of subsequent workplace bullying? The dangers of low or absent leadership support. *European Journal of Work and Organizational Psychology*, 1-11.

371 Hoffend, P., & Ban, S. W. (2019). Evaluating the Effectiveness and Effects of Fear-based Leadership.

372 Guo, L., Decoster, S., Babalola, M. T., De Schutter, L., Garba, O. A., & Riisla, K. (2018). Authoritarian leadership and employee creativity: The moderating role of psychological capital and the mediating role of fear and defensive silence. *Journal of Business Research, 92*, 219-230.

373 Lazarus, R. S., & Folkman, S. (1984). *Stress, appraisal, and coping*. Springer publishing company.

374 Qi, F. S., & Ramayah, T. (2022). Defensive Silence, Defensive Voice, Knowledge Hiding, and Counterproductive Work Behavior Through the Lens of Stimulus-Organism-Response. *Frontiers in Psychology, 13*.

375 Najiya, F., & Thomas, S. (2021). Self-esteem, empathy and introversion among adolescent readers. *The International Journal of Indian Psychology* DOI: 10.25215/0901.059

376 Gillet, J., Cartwright, E., & Van Vugt, M. (2011). Selfish or servant leadership? Evolutionary predictions on leadership personalities in coordination games. *Personality and Individual Differences, 51*(3), 231-236.

377 e Cunha, M. P., Clegg, S. R., Rego, A., & Berti, M. (2021). *Paradoxes of power and leadership*. Routledge.

378 Kaletta, J., & Reuther, K. (2021, November). Dark Triad Versus Light Triad: A Comparison and Analysis in the Context of Agile Leadership. In *ECMLG 2021 17th European Conference on Management, Leadership and Governance* (p. 241). Academic Conferences limited.

379 Brissette, I., Scheier, M. F., & Carver, C. S. (2002). The role of optimism in social network development, coping, and psychological adjustment during a life transition. *Journal of Personality and Social Psychology, 82*(1), 102.

380 Karademas, E. C. (2006). Self-efficacy, social support and well-being: The mediating role of optimism. *Personality and Individual Differences, 40*, 1281–1290. https://doi.org/10.1016/j.paid.2005.10.019

381 Andersson, M. A. (2012). Dispositional optimism and the emergence of social network diversity. *The Sociological Quarterly, 53*(1), 92-115.

382 Vickers, K. S., & Vogeltanz, N. D. (2000). Dispositional optimism as a predictor of depressive symptoms over time. *Personality and Individual Differences, 28*(2), 259-272.

383 Soong, J. (2021, July 8). 6 Common Depression Traps to Avoid. *WebMD.* https://www.webmd.com/depression/features/depression-traps-and-pitfalls

384 Matthews, T., Danese, A., Wertz, J., Odgers, C. L., Ambler, A., Moffitt, T. E., & Arseneault, L. (2016). Social isolation, loneliness and depression in young adulthood: a behavioural genetic analysis. *Social psychiatry and psychiatric epidemiology, 51*(3), 339-348.

385 Luo, F., Guo, L., Thapa, A., & Yu, B. (2021). Social isolation and depression onset among middle-aged and older adults in China: Moderating effects of education and gender differences. *Journal of affective disorders, 283*, 71-76.

386 Segerstrom, S. C. (2007). Optimism and resources: Effects on each other and on health over 10 years. *Journal of Research in Personality, 41*(4), 772-786.

387 Hmieleski, K. M., & Baron, R. A. (2009). Entrepreneurs' optimism and new venture performance: A social cognitive perspective. *Academy of Management Journal, 52*(3), 473-488.

388 Carter, D. R., DeChurch, L. A., Braun, M. T., & Contractor, N. S. (2015). Social network approaches to leadership: An integrative conceptual review. *Journal of Applied Psychology, 100*(3), 597.

389 Waldinger, R. (2015, December 23). What makes a good life? Lessons from the longest study on happiness [Video]. *TED Conferences.* https://www.ted.com/talks/robert_waldinger_what_makes_a_good_life_lessons_from_the_longest_study_on_happiness

390 Solan, M. (2017, October 5). The Secret to Happiness? Here's Some Advice from the Longest-Running Study on Happiness. *Harvard Health Blog.* https://www.health.harvard.edu/blog/the-secret-to-happiness-heres-some-advice-from-the-longest-running-study-on-happiness-2017100512543

391 Newman, R. S., & Goldin, L. (1990). Children's reluctance to seek help with schoolwork. *Journal of educational psychology, 82*(1), 92.

392 Radez, J., Reardon, T., Creswell, C., Lawrence, P. J., Evdoka-Burton, G., & Waite, P. (2021). Why do children and adolescents (not) seek and access

professional help for their mental health problems? A systematic review of quantitative and qualitative studies. *European child & adolescent psychiatry, 30*(2), 183-211.

393 Konnikova, Maria, (2016). Why Are Babies So Dumb If Humans Are So Smart? *The New Yorker.* https://www.newyorker.com/science/maria-konnikova/why-are-babies-so-dumb-if-humans-are-so-smart

394 Samuelson, S., Willén, C., & Bratt, E. L. (2015). New kid on the block? Community nurses' experiences of caring for sick children at home. *Journal of Clinical Nursing, 24*(17-18), 2448-2457.

395 Brody, A. C., & Simmons, L. A. (2007). Family resiliency during childhood cancer: The father's perspective. *Journal of Pediatric Oncology Nursing, 24*(3), 152-165.

396 Kämmerer, A. (2019, August 9). The Scientific Underpinnings and Impacts of Shame. *Scientific American.* https://www.scientificamerican.com/article/the-scientific-underpinnings-and-impacts-of-shame/

397 Scannell, C. (2021). By helping others we help ourselves: insights from peer support workers in substance use recovery. *Advances in Mental Health,* 1-10.

398 Roberts, G., Raihani, N., Bshary, R., Manrique, H. M., Farina, A., Samu, F., & Barclay, P. (2021). The benefits of being seen to help others: indirect reciprocity and reputation-based partner choice. *Philosophical Transactions of the Royal Society B, 376*(1838), 20200290.

399 Scannell, C. (2021). By helping others we help ourselves: insights from peer support workers in substance use recovery. *Advances in Mental Health,* 1-10.

400 Spitzmuller, M., Park, G., Van Dyne, L., Wagner, D. T., & Maerz, A. (2021). When do you benefit? Differential boundary conditions facilitate positive affect and buffer negative affect after helping others. *European Journal of Work and Organizational Psychology, 30*(4), 482-494.

401 Milinski, M., Semmann, D., & Krambeck, H. (2002). Donors to charity gain in both indirect reciprocity and political reputation. *Proceedings of the Royal Society of London. Series B: Biological Sciences, 269*(1494), 881-883.

402 Rose, C. M. (1995). Trust in the Mirror of Betrayal. *BUL Rev., 75,* 531.

403 Holton, R. (1994). Deciding to trust, coming to believe. *Australasian journal of philosophy, 72*(1), 63-76.

404 Orloff, J. (2017). *The empath's survival guide: Life strategies for sensitive people.* Sounds True.

405 AAA Foundation for Traffic Safety (2012, May 8). *Teen Driver Risk in Relation to Age and Number of Passengers.* [Press release]. Retrieved from https://

aaafoundation.org/wp-content/uploads/2012/05/Teen-Driver-Risk-with-Passengers-Fact-Sheet.pdf

406 Putnam, R. D. (2020). "Bowling Alone: America's Declining Social Capital": Journal of Democracy (1995). In *The City Reader* (pp. 142-150). Routledge.

407 Nemanick, R. (2007, June 10). Building the social capital of leaders. *The Leadership Effect.* https://leadership-effect.com/articles/building-the-social-capital-of-leaders/

408 Lin, N. (2017). Building a network theory of social capital. *Social capital,* 3-28.

409 Steinfield, C., DiMicco, J. M., Ellison, N. B., & Lampe, C. (2009). *Bowling online: social networking and social capital within the organization.* Paper presented at the Proceedings of the fourth international conference on Communities and technologies.

410 Balkundi, P., & Kilduff, M. (2006). The ties that lead: A social network approach to leadership. *The Leadership Quarterly, 17*(4), 419-439

ABOUT THE AUTHOR

Dr. Daniel Monehin, DBA, is a leadership keynote speaker and adjunct professor who uniquely combines his real-life multinational executive experience with a rigorous foundation in academic research. He was most recently a global leader in digital technology, with over 30 years' experience across multiple industries, including S&P 100 and Fortune 500 companies.

Daniel earned his Doctor of Business Administration (DBA) degree from the University of Manchester, U.K. His 5-year doctorate research in organizational leadership focused on leadership in turbulent times. He received a Master of Business Administration (MBA) degree from Queen's University, Canada. He is a U.S. Certified Public Accountant (CPA) and a Fellow of the Chartered Professional Accountants of Canada (FCPA, FCMA).

He holds certifications in the Marshall Goldsmith Stakeholder Centered Coaching® and the Hogan Assessments®, a global science-based personality assessment with a high level of predictive validity.

He is a Member of the Board of Directors at American Express Bank of Canada and Chair of the Board's Conduct Review Committee. He resides in Toronto, Canada, and travels globally for speaking engagements.

Seventy9°
WEST

Printed in Great Britain
by Amazon

10989172R00188